SECOND CHANCE

A Broken Marriage Restored

by

David and Sarah Van Wade

LOGOS INTERNATIONAL
Plainfield, New Jersey

We wish to thank Leonard LeSourd and his wife Catherine Marshall for their patient and careful guidance and encouragement through the shaping of this manuscript to its final form.

Our story is true, but in the telling of it we have changed some names and dates and places. We think that the important point is not *who* the story happened to, but *that* it happened, and can happen again.

Chapter 1

DAVID   *Miami, Florida*

The little room was dirty, with grease-stained walls, and the lumpy mattress smelled sour. In the muggy heat I had stripped to my shorts, but perspiration rolled off my body in streams. I sipped carefully from my last bottle of Scotch. Fifteen cents was all I had left, and I wondered where the next drink would come from.

I hated the miserable little room and the circumstances that had brought me there. The noises were driving me crazy. A steady stream of curse words in Spanish came through the thin plywood wall from the next apartment. The slow screeching of a rusty awning outside the door grated on my nerves, but the croaking frogs were worse. They stayed in the old, cracked swimming pool where stagnant water and trash gathered in the deep end.

The croaking built to a mind-splitting crescendo, and filled with sudden fury, I reached for the loaded .32 automatic pistol on my table. Steadying myself, I stepped outside on the cracked blue and white tiles of the pool deck. The full moon shone in the slimy green water where the frogs perched on rotting pieces of wood and the rusty skeleton of a baby buggy. With a jerk I lifted the gun and the explosion of bullets shattered the night. Dead silence followed and there was no sign of the frogs.

The stench from the pool hung in the sticky hot air, blending with the heavy smell of magnolia blossoms. Sudden stomach pains made me double over as I staggered back to my bed. I longed for sleep, but the croaking of the frogs had begun again.

Something like a sob forced its way past my clenched teeth. As a boy in a small Missouri town, frog-hunting on hot summer nights had been a wonderful adventure. My room was in the attic of our white frame house near the creek, and the sound of big frogs calling in the night had accompanied my boyhood dreams of an exciting future. As a top student in my class I would go to the university in the big city, and after that, the wide open world beckoned. I had been so confident of success.

Perspiration ran in salt streams down my face, and I passed my tongue over my cracked lips. I was dying of thirst, but forced myself to leave the near-empty bottle alone a while longer. The croaking of the frogs hammered in my head.

I had gone to the university and graduated with honors. Then followed a promising business career, a house in the suburbs, a wife, and four beautiful children. In a flash I saw their faces before me; Leif, now thirteen, with his mother's brown eyes and dimples; John, at eleven, looked like myself as a boy, sturdy and given to daydreaming about great adventures; Andrew, now ten, blue-eyed and blond like his Norwegian grandfather; and Christine, shy, but already a blond beauty at nine, with wistful, hazel eyes.

I tossed on the creaking bed. How could it *all* have been lost? I was trapped in this hellhole. Sarah and the children had a life of their own. My career was gone. And those damn frogs were laughing at me. . . .

I struggled to my feet and grabbed the pistol once more. A desperate desire to kill every one of those cursed creatures burned within me. The moon was still between the tall palm trees, and the eyes of the frogs, unblinking, stared at me. The shots rang wildly, raising small fountains of stinking water where the frogs had been.

With a feeling of triumph I returned to my room. Drinking deeply from the bottle, I lay back to close my eyes when into my aching mind came the sound of the frogs again—croaking, mocking, teasing.

SARAH   *Sunrise Beach, Florida*

Why did the nightmare keep recurring? Icy fingers of fear still held me, and I moved closer to Christine's sleeping form. In the moonlight her long, blond hair lay tousled on the pillow. She was clutching the stuffed Snoopy dog David had given her for Christmas. I had dreamed again that David came back to move in with me and the children, and I had been unable to prevent it. In his old, cocky way he had grinned, "I'm going to give you another chance, Sarah. Don't make a mess of it again."

Through the open window I could hear the sound of the surf pounding on the lonely stretch of sandy beach below our house. I had brought the children to Florida over a year ago hoping to build a new life, and wanting to be near the sea again. The gray-green Atlantic Ocean moving endlessly with the wind and current from the northeast helped me to imagine the white-crested waves thundering against the rocky coast of Norway thousands of miles away. Somehow I felt closer to my homeland with the salt spray in my face and the water lapping at my feet.

Usually the surf lulled me to sleep, but now the sharp, thudding sound held an ominous threat. David had followed us to Florida just as the wounds of our past were beginning to heal. His presence was like a dark shadow hovering over us, bringing back the pain and guilt of the last thirteen years. Here in Florida I had found new hope, a career as a writer-editor, and new relationships in a friendly, warm church. I had begun to experience a sense of forgiveness, of peace, and promise for a new life ahead, perhaps even a new marriage.

David's bi-weekly visits with the children, his gaunt, pale face and dark, hostile eyes upset us all. And now my recurring dreams. O God—would it never end?

Chapter 2

Hermosa Beach, California

We met in California. A mutual friend had taken me to Sarah's apartment where we sat on the floor talking till past midnight, sipping wine from old jelly glasses, discussing politics, books, and religion. I had not done anything like that since my early college days, but with Sarah it was a way of life. Her brown eyes shone with sincerity and enthusiasm, and her expressive hands drew figures in the air while she talked. She smoked one slim British cigarette after the other while her six-month-old baby son slept through it all on a blanket by her side.

She was different from any girl I had ever dated, and I was fascinated from the start. Perhaps it was her European background. She had come from Norway two years earlier to study sociology. Before that, she had worked as a journalist on the staff of a large daily newspaper in Oslo. A now defunct marriage and a baby had altered her immediate plans, but she still talked earnestly about doing something meaningful to make the world a better place for "the suffering and poverty-ridden masses."

Her world and her ideas could not have been more different from mine. I was proud to be an ex-Marine and a college graduate. I had come from a small town in Missouri where my family for several generations had been prosperous merchants. At times I had thought of a career in the academic world as a college professor, but more basic was the desire to succeed in a material way, to prove that hard work, ability, and perseverance could take me to whatever goal I chose.

I had tried marriage just after getting out of the Marine Corps. In the service the "sweetheart letters" from a hometown girl had meant a great deal, but our thoroughly unpleasant union lasted only a couple of months, and exploded my romantic notions of love. If I thought of marriage for the future at all, it was in terms of a practical arrangement between two mature people.

Sarah's idealism and my materialism seemed almost contradictory, yet I found myself in a surprising predicament: Wherever I went, the memory of Sarah's expressive face and her voice with the slight, lilting accent burned in my mind. I returned almost daily to her small beach-front apartment. Even her careless housekeeping failed to deter me. She had other virtues: an eye for poetry and beauty, compassion for people, and a genuine interest in me.

Within two months from the evening we met I proposed, Sarah accepted, and we slipped across the border to Tijuana, Mexico, to be married. We returned to take Sarah's and Leif's few belongings to the large, two-story house in Hermosa Beach I shared with a bachelor friend. Duke Massey was a tall, handsome Tennessean who held a job as an office manager, while dividing the rest of his time between roles in Little Theatre plays and pretty girls. Moving Sarah and the baby into our bachelor pad seemed a practical arrangement since we were approaching marriage with caution. If things did not work out, we agreed to part with a minimum of fuss.

SARAH

Hermosa Beach, California

I really did not want to marry again so soon, but David was different from the men I had known, the writers, artists, and dreamers. He talked about books and ideas, but knew how to clean spark plugs, fix a leaky faucet, or a broken lamp. I had failed in the past, and being alone with little Leif was more frightening than I cared to think about. David would provide the solid core I needed in my life.

There were drawbacks to living in his old bachelor quarters, but the house had a beautiful view of the ocean and a small fenced-in garden where Leif could stay for hours in his playpen content to watch the bright butterflies among the red geraniums. Duke was gone most of the week, but loved to bounce Leif on his knees when he was home. I liked Duke, even if he added to the chaos of our household.

As a housekeeper I was a total failure. I despaired over the piles of dirty dishes, wet diapers, and cluttered rooms, and managed to spend entire days working frantically without making a dent in the mess. David could not understand my helplessness. "Why don't you start in one corner and work your way through?" He looked exasperated. "Housework is really quite simple if you organize your efforts."

My incompetence with the simplest household task stemmed, no doubt, from my childhood when I was allowed to shirk all chores while mother taught a succession of maids how to be efficient housekeepers. The lessons never passed to me, and I grew up assuming that I would have a newspaper career and leave the more mundane tasks of homemaking to someone else. The assumption had been unrealistic, and I was suffering agonies over it now.

Panic usually struck at mealtime. My limited menu consisted of soup heated from a can, greasy spaghetti, hot dogs with baked beans, or hamburgers fried crisp on the outside. The second week we were married David bought me a cookbook, but that only heightened my sense of failure.

Weekends were disasters, with long drinking parties. One Sunday I woke up to sunlight streaming in our window and the happy sounds of the ice cream wagon and children laughing. Then a car door slammed, bringing a quiver of apprehension to my stomach.

"Breakfast time!" It was Duke. He had left with friends, as usual without his keys, while the party was still going strong. In dismay I looked at David who was snoring slightly with an aroma of stale beer like a halo around the bed. Leif didn't stir in his crib.

I ran downstairs in my robe, pushing the hair out of my face, and groaned at the sight of the living room. Empty beer cans, glasses, and overflowing ashtrays crowded every surface and spilled onto the floor. Duke wore a dripping wet swimsuit with a colorful towel draped across his shoulders. His black hair was plastered in wet ringlets to his forehead, and his blue eyes were red-rimmed from too much beer and too little sleep. Two strangers were with him and each waved a six-pack of beer.

"Where's breakfast?" Duke strode through the dining room into the kitchen. Stacks of dirty dishes, caked with egg and bacon grease, were everywhere.

"So you've been lazy this morning, shame on you." He frowned, and I smiled uncertainly. It was difficult to tell when he was joking.

"Don't worry, honey," Duke's long arm gave me a reassuring squeeze. "I never spoil a good drunk with solid food. . . ."

David came downstairs looking sleepy, and his friends greeted him with a shout, "We brought you a cold one. . . ."

"How about bacon and eggs for everybody?" David looked at me, and I shook my head.

"The refrigerator is empty. Someone must have raided it after we went to bed."

"No problem," David shrugged. "We'll run down to the store." He took the cold beer Duke had opened for him and kissed me lightly on the cheek. "See you later, honey. . . ."

The four of them piled into Duke's convertible and took off with a roar. I knew I would not see them for a while. They usually stopped at a bar—to give me time to straighten up the house—and returned later with a new crowd from the beach. I sighed and went back upstairs. Leif was crying for his breakfast and morning bath.

In moments like this I longed for the time when David and I would have a home of our own away from the stream of bachelor friends.

In time we would both get over the scars from our first marriages. We would dare to be close to each other. I hoped we would soon have other children. When Leif was born I had felt a oneness with life, a happiness beyond anything I had imagined. Holding that tiny, squealing bundle, knowing that the miracle had taken place in me, I felt for the first time that my life had a purpose. As a wife and mother I hoped to find identity and fulfillment.

DAVID   *Columbia, Missouri*

Sarah was not adjusting as quickly to her role as wife and homemaker as I had hoped. I returned to graduate school at the University of Missouri, thinking she would pitch in with greater enthusiasm for our future. Our economy was tight, on a student loan and a part-time job. Our "home" was two dark and damp basement rooms. Consequently, Sarah's depression worsened. I often came home to find her in bed in the middle of the day, overwhelmed by her simple duties of housekeeping and grocery shopping. Even allowing for her limited vocabulary in English, I found her helplessness exaggerated.

She snapped out of her inertia when a Norwegian newspaper offered her a writing assignment. Amazed, I watched her transformation from whimpering, inadequate housewife to self-confident, efficient journalist. Why couldn't she use some of that zeal in keeping our apartment clean and getting a decent meal on our table?

"I want you to be wife and mother first—journalist second," I tried not to sound annoyed.

"I promise I'll try harder." Her eyes met mine only briefly, then looked away. I wanted to believe her, but could see no change in her attitude at home. When the writing assignment was over, the old defeatist attitude returned.

SARAH   *Columbia, Missouri*

Why was it so hard to do what David wanted me to do? No matter how hard I tried our little apartment was a mess. I had met David's mother, a super-efficient housekeeper and excellent cook, who had time left over for involvement in numerous community affairs. I would never be able to live up to her.

To top it off, David seemed to dislike my ability as a writer. The writing assignment took me on a week's trip away from home, and I was ashamed to admit to David I felt a little like a fish back in water. Only one incident marred my happiness. A reporter from New York bought my lunch one day and casually remarked, "You know, I've never yet met a woman who was able to combine a successful newspaper career with a happy marriage. It takes a full-time commitment to be a top reporter, and you can't be married both to a typewriter and a man."

"Maybe I'll be the first one to make it," I tried to smile confidently, but his words etched themselves on my mind. If necessary, I would put the typewriter aside for a while. My marriage *had* to succeed.

David   *Vestfjord, Norway*

The second semester at the university was over when Sarah announced that she was pregnant. Our relationship was less than satisfactory. Hoping to improve the communications between us, I looked for an opportunity to go to Europe. Perhaps a visit home would give Sarah a better perspective. I also wanted to spend at least one semester at a European university.

A loan and an opportunity to travel by Norwegian freighter made the trip possible, but I soon discovered that Sarah was even more of a stranger to me in her own environment.

The language barrier now loomed larger between us. I found myself isolated from my surroundings, while she was obviously delighted to be with her family and old friends. We arrived in Norway in early April, and I found the lingering darkness of the bleak, northern winter depressing.

We stayed with Sarah's widowed mother in her large house. Leif was cared for by a maid and his doting grandmother. In contrast to this life style, the dark little basement rooms we had lived in back at the University of Missouri seemed doubly dismal. I could suddenly understand Sarah's feelings of isolation and frustration. It was unrealistic to expect her to go through more of the same. Better to leave her in Norway than to continue a marginal marriage in what for her was an alien country.

With that idea in the back of my mind, I enrolled for a semester at the university in Munich, Germany, leaving Sarah in Norway. But between study periods I discovered, to my dismay, that I was lonely. The thought of being permanently separated from Sarah was unbearable. The fascination I had felt when we first met was as strong as ever.

When her letters told that her mother had become seriously ill, I was glad for an impelling reason to return to Norway.

SARAH   *Vestfjord, Norway*

Mother was dying. Her pale face looked helpless on the hospital pillow, her dark eyes veiled by an empty gaze, her toneless voice repeating over and over, "Your father is gone—I am so lonely."

Helpless anger surged through me. Mother did not want to live. Since father's death she had slipped slowly away from contact with her surroundings. I felt resentment mingling with grief. She was only fifty. I needed her. Why did she desert me now?

On my last visit, as I walked into the hospital room, her eyes sought mine, and for a moment, I thought the veil between us had lifted. She was like a small child wanting to be comforted. I felt the tugging inside, the desire to take her in my arms, begging her to live. Then I steeled myself. Mother had never liked a display of emotions. If she wanted to die—why should I try to change it?

My face a cold mask, I turned and walked away. David was waiting outside and put his arm around me. I felt the baby kicking in my stomach. Life was waiting for me, and I would not look back.

That night mother died. I did not cry. Something had clamped shut inside me, like a hard shell protecting a wound. The door to the past had closed. I wanted to remove myself from all painful reminders. Suddenly I was anxious to return to the United States. I belonged with David.

Summer turned to fall, and our baby would soon arrive. While waiting, I helped Aunt Eldrid in the kitchen, making jams and jellies from the berries in our garden. As the pantry shelves filled with jars, I experienced a wonderful sense of accomplishment. David had been right when he said I would be happier once I learned to be more effective in the kitchen.

The birth of the new baby brought back the intense feeling of fulfillment I had sensed when Leif was born. We named him John, and following family tradition, he was christened in the old stone cathedral in town.

Mother's house was sold, and we said elaborate farewells to my relatives. I felt as if I was burning bridges behind me, and was anxious to get settled in a home of our own as soon as possible.

DAVID   *Green River, Missouri*

Reluctantly I gave up the idea of going back to the university to finish my graduate studies. With two small children we needed to establish a home.

My father offered the prospect of a full partnership in the family business in Green River. Ours was the only lumberyard in the county, and enough new industry was moving into the area to promise a good future. Swallowing my dislike of the small, rural community, I accepted.

We bought a 100-acre farm outside town and built a comfortable house. The setting was picturesque, but within a year I regretted our decision to settle in my home town. Dad, still in his early sixties, and in full strength of manhood, postponed the full partnership arrangement. I suspected it would be years before he would relinquish the controls of the business. Now I felt bitter disappointment, and much of the challenge was gone from my job.

Sarah was making an effort to be a good housekeeper, but our relationship was strained. Our third son, Andrew, arrived when we had lived in Green River for a year. Sarah was worn out with the continuous diapering and feeding of babies, and the house was filled with chronic noise and confusion. I found it impossible to rest. Meals were never on time, and Sarah was tense and argumentative. Driven from the house, I spent my evenings in the radio shack I had built nearby, or in the taverns in town. A few drinks seemed to ease the tension and trapped feeling.

The winter months always depressed me, and the hour of dusk came early. Dad showed no signs of giving me more authority in the business, and I toyed with the idea of packing my family and leaving the community. Before my plans were concrete, Sarah announced the coming of a fourth baby. Exhausted physically and emotionally, we quarreled bitterly and consistently. I felt neither of us was to blame; we were both trapped by unfortunate circumstances.

My drinking increased, and one hot and humid morning in late August I awoke with a painful ringing noise in my ears which drowned out the normal sounds of birds singing in the trees outside our open window. The noise increased during the day. Drinking brought partial relief that evening, but the ringing returned with greater intensity later.

An ear specialist in Kansas City could find no physical cause for my suffering, but suggested that excessive drinking or smoking and emotional strain could be contributing factors. As long as we remained in Green River, I could see no hope for relief.

SARAH   *Green River, Missouri*

At first, I loved Green River. The quiet streets were lined with tall trees, and the old houses looked so friendly with their wide porches and swings. No one remained strangers for long, and I felt at home.

An ancient oak spread its branches protectively over our roof. Our view was of forest-clad hills and blue ridges disappearing into the horizon. Here we could be happy—if only I could learn to organize my daily housekeeping.

I studied women's magazines and books on homemaking and family life. Carefully following instructions, I sewed and canned and baked, painted and re-covered furniture. Still I felt frustrated. My daily chores mounted with three little ones to care for, and it seemed I was forever behind my schedule. When would I ever master the household? Have meals on time? Order instead of chaos? Peace instead of the constant clamor of little children?

Only time could take care of it. In time my exhaustion would ease, and David's tension and impatience would be gone. Now a perpetual frown forged a line between his eyebrows, and his brown eyes had a dark, troubled look. We seldom talked without arguing, and I felt the cold distance separating us. Yet somehow I was confident that in time things would improve. The magic word we both used often to console ourselves was *time*. In time things would change. With its passing we would mature, the children would grow past the demanding stage, and we would all arrive at the state of happiness we now lacked.

Occasionally we attended the Presbyterian church in Green River, since that was where David's name was on the membership roll. He had joined as a twelve-year-old when religion, to him, was a serious matter. The minister was a shy young Yale Divinity School graduate who peered at the congregation through thick glasses, and spoke of God in abstract terms.

Once we were having coffee on the church lawn after the Sunday service when Reverend Stoller approached us. He cleared his throat nervously. "Why don't you join the church, Sarah?"

"I can't," I smiled politely. "I can't profess belief in Jesus Christ as the Son of God and make a liar of myself."

A shadow of a smile crossed Mark Stoller's sensitive face. "It's just a formality. I doubt if many people really believe it."

"I'm sorry," I said. "I just can't make myself say those words."

Often, late at night, with the children in bed and David gone to town, I stepped outside on the lawn and leaned against the gnarled trunk of the old oak tree next to our house. It was as if I hoped to draw strength from those deep roots. There was an aching inside me, a hollow place, that having a husband and children and a home did not fill.

"I don't feel *real*," I whispered, but there was no answer in the white mist shimmering over the valley in the moonlight.

When I discovered my fourth pregnancy, things became rapidly worse. For the first time I worried about David's drinking. The vacant look in his eyes and face when he had drunk to excess, frightened me. He had always appeared so strong, capable of handling any situation, but now something was terribly wrong. I cried alone at night and knew with frightening clarity that this would not simply pass away with time.

David often disappeared for days and my fears mounted to panic. Once the Presbyterian minister came on an evening visit and found me crying at the foot of the old oak tree. He looked shocked and embarrassed at the sight of my swollen face. "Is there anything I can do to help?" he asked.

"You are a minister—don't you know what to do?" I looked up at him with something like hope stirring inside.

He avoided my eyes. "I'm only human. But if you need to talk, I'll be glad to listen."

The futility washed over me. The baby kicked against my ribs, and I leaned my forehead against the rough bark of the tree.

"O God," I groaned. "Why do we suffer like this?" I did not expect an answer and Mark Stoller remained silent. The moon shone over the valley, but I felt as if a menacing power lurked in the beauty of the warm summer night, waiting to destroy us. I knew that to survive we *had* to leave Green River.

DAVID   *Crescent Beach, California*

The day our baby daughter was born, two friends from California arrived in Green River. Jack and Lydia Morris had been in the carefree crowd that regularly descended on our beach house for weekend parties. Jack and I had spent long hours over steins of beer discussing the destiny of man. Often he had echoed my own sentiment, "Man is the ultimate thrust of life itself, creating his own destiny!"

That seemed ages ago, and Jack's sandy colored hair was thinning on top. He had left college to become a longshoreman, but his deep-set gray eyes burned with the same fervor. "Come back to California, Dave. That's where you belong. Don't bury yourself in this hole when there is a whole world waiting outside."

His words tore a veil from my mind. There was still a future beyond Green River. Silence had fallen on the room. We were sitting by the fireplace, Jack and I with our beers; Sarah was nursing five-day-old Christine. The three boys had climbed up on Aunt Lydia's generous lap. Now she looked over the heads of the children. "Do come back to California, Sarah. We miss you."

Sarah's face paled, then she flushed with color. "But we have a large family."

"So did the pioneers who came to California in covered wagons." Lydia's laughter pealed, and the boys on her lap squealed with delight.

"Let's go see the Indians, dad!" John's eyes were round with excitement.

I laughed back at him. "Maybe that's a good idea, son." Exhilaration flooded me at the thought. The obstacles that had once seemed overwhelming now appeared less formidable. We could sell our property and have ample funds for a new start in California.

Once the decision was made I wondered why we had waited so long. Our business and personal affairs were soon taken care of. When Christine was three months old, we packed everything and headed west—to a new beginning.

We settled in Crescent Beach, just south of Los Angeles and not far from Jack and Lydia. A few others from the old gang were still around. Duke Massey, now a confirmed bachelor, was doing bit parts on television and hoped for a movie career.

Mel Goodson, whom I had first met in the Marine Corps, was enrolled at UCLA working towards his doctorate in political science. Quiet when sober, with dark hair graying prematurely, and a bushy mustache giving his features a certain broodiness, Mel could be eloquent when he chose to, and he had a fine sense of humor. He was married with two children, but the marriage was strained.

Cliff Barnhouse, a skinny blond fellow who had kept the parties going with jokes and an unusual capacity for drinking, had acquired a wife and four children. Struggling under heavy financial burdens, he had enrolled as a trainee with a Los Angeles stock brokerage house and persuaded me to join him. "There's a great future in the stock market," his blue eyes were eagerly hopeful. "You'll be a success. I know it."

The job was a letdown. "Churning" old ladies' accounts was not my idea of a meaningful challenge. Cliff disagreed with me. "You're too naive and too much of an idealist," he argued over a martini lunch. "Accept the job for what it is, a way to make a living."

Cliff looked less than a picture of success himself. His suit was frayed and his fingernails were dirty. His aging Chrysler had broken down again, and he had spent most of the morning tinkering with the engine. I shook my head, "Sorry, friend. I believe in American business, but I want a chance to prove that hard work and integrity are still the best way to succeed."

In less than two weeks I was hired as a salesman for one of the leading building products manufacturers in the nation. I had handled their product line in the lumberyard and knew it to be one of the best. I felt confident as I started my rounds to dealers and contractors all over Southern California.

Four months later I was promoted to assistant sales manager, the fastest rise in company history. My hard work and honest dealings with customers were paying off. Success looked certain. The only problem was Sarah's defeatist attitude. Her moods were unpredictable and her housekeeping sloppy. How could I devote all my time and energy to the job when I had to worry about her management of the simplest household details?

SARAH   *Crescent Beach, California*

David was full of enthusiasm over his business career, but somehow I felt left out. He and I were poles apart. We had a nice house, but I had lost the zest for housekeeping. Back in Green River my bread baking and pickle making, sewing and restoring furniture had not produced the happiness I sought. Now I felt like giving up. Just coping with four wild pre-schoolers took all my energy and time.

One day I wandered aimlessly between tall book racks in the city library when a title caught my eye: *The Feminine Mystique*, by Betty Friedan. Suddenly curious, I took the book home. Reading it was like being awakened from a nightmare to discover that reality is a beautiful sunlit morning. My depression, my frustration, and my "trapped" feeling were perfectly understandable. My concept of womanhood had simply been too narrow. I needed to find fulfillment as a total, creative person.

Eagerly I enrolled in evening college, taking courses in psychology and philosophy; I also joined several community organizations. My new freedom was exhilarating, and the vague sense of guilt I felt when the children complained about staying with a babysitter was probably just a hangover from my old, narrow attitude.

David was pleased with the "new" me. With a life of my own, I no longer clamored for his attention. He encouraged me to take a step further and find a job. The old fear of failure, still lurking inside, made me realize that the job was necessary if I was ever to overcome my sense of inferiority as a woman, and find my identity as a creative, productive member of society. I still felt hollow inside. The job would give me a new purpose in living.

We found a Norwegian housekeeper who cheerfully put our house in better order than it had ever been, while I started my new job as editor of a weekly trade paper. The challenge was exciting, but coming home, I felt a pang of envy. The spotless house was filled with the aroma of an excellent dinner cooking, while Kari, the housekeeper, was playing happily with my contented children. Somehow her expertise was a pointed reminder of my own failure.

"What's your secret?" The question finally popped out of me one afternoon when I found her folding my linen in neat stacks in the closet. When I did the job, sheets and towels always looked as if they had been crammed in place.

Kari's green eyes sparkled over her upturned, freckled nose. She was a pretty girl in her early twenties, and I often wondered how she could be so content caring for someone else's house and children. "I enjoy it!" She spoke in the melodic accent of western Norway. "God put me here, and I thank Him for it."

I shuddered involuntarily at her words and turned without answering. I had observed Kari's well-thumbed Bible on the shelf next to my cookbooks, and had deliberately avoided the subject of religion. Now I was secretly grateful that her English vocabulary was too limited to make her a dangerous influence on the children.

David and I had discussed the children's need for some religious training, and agreed that they should go to a Sunday school where they would learn about the Judeo-Christian traditions of our culture, but we did not want them exposed to the naive emotional-ism of Kari's brand of Christianity. As soon as her language improved, she would have to leave our household.

In spite of my busy schedule, I still fought a vague sense of emptiness inside. It was as if I was playing an elaborate game both at work and at home. I had not "found" myself in my new career, and it hurt to live in a marriage where communication was almost nonexistent. David seemed satisfied, and often stressed the idea that marriage was only a convenient partnership between two independent people.

Looking around us, I had to agree that most of our friends were worse off. Mel and Mary Goodson lived in a state of chronic domestic warfare, arguing openly in front of us. Jack and Lydia Morris were separated. Jack was drinking more and taking pills. When we last heard, he had signed on a ship as a crewman for a six-month tour. Cliff and Alice Barnhouse seemed to co-exist fairly peacefully, but their struggle for solvency and Alice's total preoccu-pation with the children made their lives look pretty bleak.

In contrast we seemed to have reached a compromise, function-ing fairly well in our separate roles within the marriage framework. David called it a realistic approach. "If we don't expect anything of each other, we won't be disappointed," he often said.

At his request, I took the children to Sunday school in a small Methodist chapel down the street. The pastor taught an art class on Wednesday evenings instead of holding a prayer meeting, and his unorthodox sermons rang with enthusiasm.

"The real secret of Christianity is creativity," he said, as he pounded the pulpit with his paint-stained hand. "Negative thinking binds us in failure . . . but we are made for abundant living . . . with a tremendous capacity to love and create."

A surge of hope shot like a ray of light into my world of gray resignation. In Pastor Houston's study I poured out my woes, "David and I are poles apart. How can we have the creative relationship you talk about?"

Roy Houston's blue eyes probed mine deeply. "I understand your problem, Sarah. My wife doesn't share my enthusiasm for living. Our marriage is in a deadlock as well."

The disappointment I felt was like a blow. "If *you* can't live what you preach, how can anyone else hope to?"

Pastor Houston's large frame had slumped a little, and his hands played with the bristle of a paint brush on his desk. "The vision of abundant life is so clear," his voice faltered, then his eyes met mine again. "Perhaps with another woman it can become reality."

My cheeks were hot as I fled from the study, trembling inside. Was the search for deeper meaning in life and in relationships just a cruel hoax? Was there no answer to the yearning inside me? Sudden panic tightened my throat, "I can't stand it if there's nothing more to life and marriage than this." I nearly stumbled up the walk to our house. How much longer could I go on like this?

DAVID   *Crescent Beach, California*

Our lives were running smoothly now, and I was pleased. Seldom did Sarah rock the boat with her emotional outbursts, and she was functioning more like the poised and efficient wife of a rising young executive.

After a year and a half with the company, Bob Koenig, vice president of sales for the western division, called me to his office. A short, graying man in his fifties, his hawk-like nose and quick brown eyes gave him an appearance of youthful decisiveness. He greeted me with a handshake and a warm smile. "Congratulations on a top job, Dave." He motioned for me to sit down and fixed us both a highball from the wet bar concealed in the mahogany cabinet by his desk.

He came right to the point. "How would you like to be the new district sales manager for Arizona? We need young blood over there, and you have good ideas."

I felt a quick surge of pride. I had worked long hard hours to produce the results Bob referred to, but I had not expected to be rewarded this soon. "I would like that opportunity, sir," I smiled broadly and sipped my drink. "When do I start?"

At home I broke the news to Sarah after the children were in bed. We drank champagne by the fireplace, and I lifted my glass in a toast: "To a new chapter in our lives, honey."

Her brown eyes shone in the candlelight, and I put my arms

around her. "Let's do more things together in Arizona," I whispered in her ear. "These past eighteen months have been hard, but now the biggest hurdle is over. We're on our way."

The triumph was heady. I felt like a man in perfect charge of the future. I knew where I was going and how to get there. My formula for success was working.

SARAH   *Crescent Beach, California*

For the first time in our marriage I felt the promise of a new closeness. In Arizona our lives would finally come into focus and be real. The expectation made me giddy as a young girl spinning beautiful daydreams.

Lydia Morris invited us to dinner the Sunday before we left. We had not seen them for a year. Their house was filled with sunlight and the smell of freshly baked apple pie. Lydia wiped her hands on her apron and hugged each of us warmly.

"It's so *good* to see you!" There were sudden tears in her eyes, and I wondered why she was so emotional about our leaving.

At the table Jack bowed his head, "Dear God, thank You for this food and for bringing our friends to share it. In Jesus' name, Amen."

There was an awkward silence. Only the children attacked their plates of fried chicken and mashed potatoes with gravy. Jack grinned at the expression of incredulity on David's face. "That prayer was for real, old friend. . . . You remember last year our marriage failed, and we were pretty miserable. Since then we've discovered that God can pick up the broken pieces and make us whole."

Lydia's eyes were brimming. "Oh Sarah, I'm so happy. I never knew that God cared, and that Jesus is real."

I wanted to get up and leave. How could Lydia be so naive? Lydia who had been my good friend for years. She had been honest and open in her search for a real meaning in life. Now she had deliberately closed herself off from all that and settled for pat answers.

David cleared his throat and seemed to have regained his composure. "We're happy that you two are back together," his face looked grim. "But don't try to impose your ideas on us!"

Jack laughed, and the tension in the room suddenly eased. "Fair enough," he said, as he punched David lightly in the shoulder. "We just want you to know we've found something that is very real to us."

We left as soon as we could without hurting their feelings. In the car David lit two cigarettes and handed me one. "I'm sorry Jack and Lydia went to such extremes." He touched my hand with his. "I'm glad we know better. There is more to life than the box they've climbed into."

I felt a heaviness inside. We had lost two of our best friends.

Chapter 3

Paradise Valley, Arizona

At thirty-four I was the youngest district manager in the company, and was confident that I would make an impressive increase in sales for the Arizona district. I knew the formula for success: know-how, hard work, and integrity. The outcome was certain.

The men caught my enthusiasm and increased their efforts. I personally visited every lumberyard and sales outlet in the state. In six months our sales shot up to exceed what the district had done in the five years of its existence. The men and I got sizeable bonuses, and the president of the company sent word of approval.

We bought a house with a pool on an acre in Paradise Valley, winter haven for wealthy northerners. We had a maid, and Sarah was free to pursue her own interests. At last, the life style we had been seeking was taking shape. Sitting at the poolside, I enjoyed surveying our little domain: an attractive and prosperous looking house and garden, my family healthy and tanned. The all-American dream come true.

Leif, at eight, was bright and outgoing, active in Cub Scouts and sports. John, at seven, looked like my childhood pictures. Strong and muscular for his age, he was sensitive and more interested in animals and nature studies than in people. Five-year-old Andrew was a strong-willed perfectionist—I recognized myself in his determined stick-to-itiveness. Fascinated by trucks, he was always taking apart and reassembling his growing fleet of models. Christine, at four, was sweet and affectionate, and a little shy. A pretty little girl who liked to climb on my lap whenever I sat down.

During our first few weeks in Arizona we spent much time together; I enjoyed showing Sarah and the kids around their new home state. But then business demanded more and more of my time. At the office trouble was brewing. My assistant had hoped to get the manager's job when my predecessor left. Envious of my management, he now deliberately tried to undermine my authority. He succeeded with some of the men, and the sales force split into two camps competing against and obstructing each other's efforts.

I had found it easy to iron out difficulties over a few drinks in the past. Now the formula didn't work. The conflict sharpened as our two groups mustered after work in separate bars verbally tearing each other to pieces. It was petty and short-sighted, and disastrous for the morale, but I was helpless to stop it.

Kirk Pickens, my most loyal supporter, was an Arkansas farmboy who wore rumpled suits and colorful ties in open defiance of my request for more conservative attire for the men, but I couldn't argue with his topnotch sales performance, the highest in our office. Kirk had a seemingly unlimited capacity for beer, and often spoke his mind about what he called my "hard stand" against the disloyal members of the staff. "Your biggest problem is trying to force everybody into a preconceived mold. Why don't you listen to a guy and accept him for what he is? It takes more than one kind of good man to make a good team."

Kirk's disarming laughter took the edge off his words, and I sensed that he was at least partially correct. I had always been prone to form advance opinions about people and situatio is, and became impatient and frustrated when things didn't follow the expected pattern.

Company politics provided an even more disheartening blow. As district manager I had expected to have considerable authority in decision making. Now I learned that I was a pawn in a greater game of company politics and intrigue.

As a salesman for the company in Southern California, I often heard rumors from customers that certain accounts and contractors were receiving cash rebates "under the table." I mentioned it to Bob Koenig, certain that only our "second-rate" competitors would stoop to such unethical and illegal tactics.

"You know better than that, Dave," Bob's open smile and hearty laughter confirmed my thinking. "Contractors and dealers always gossip. Don't take them seriously. . . ."

Now I remembered his reassuring words with a sick feeling in my stomach. One morning exactly two weeks after I had taken over the job, a blue envelope marked "confidential" appeared in my office mail. It contained a cashier's check for $1630.00 made out to one of my top ten customers. Attached was a note from Bob Koenig: "Dave, this check represents Don Keller's rebate for products bought during January and February. Hand it to him personally and thank him for the business."

I reached for the phone and dialed Bob's private number, a direct line that didn't go through the switchboard.

"Bob, I just got Don Keller's check," I said. "You told me we didn't give that kind of kickback."

Bob's voice was patient, "Dave, maybe you should go into a monastery. Are you really that naive? When you were a salesman— even an assistant district manager—you couldn't be told how things operate on the executive level. Now you are an executive—so shut up and do what you're told!"

I felt sick inside, but my response was smooth, "Thanks Bob, I'll call Don for a luncheon appointment right away!"

The clean air of pure motives I had hoped to find at the top of the pyramid of American business wasn't there. Instead the stench of pollution tore at my nostrils. But for the moment, at least, I did not voice my objections. I refused to admit that my dream was a fantasy. I was just beginning to go places—it *had* to be all right.

I threw myself into the work with stubborn determination as if my sincere efforts would make up for any failings in the system, but at night I had trouble going to sleep. I sat in the living room with lights out, sipping several nightcaps, listening to my favorite Hank Williams records while the brilliant Arizona stars were reflected in the swimming pool. There was a tight ball at the pit of my stomach and a persistent voice in the back of my mind, "Life isn't the neat little package you thought it was. It's bigger . . . you're losing control . . ."

"Damnit!" I spoke out loud in the dark room. "There's nothing I can't handle if I work at it. Just watch me!"

Bob Koenig announced a weekend sales meeting in Palm Springs, and I called the two warring factions of my team together. "Let's forget petty differences," I tried to sound confident. "We can beat all previous records if we pull together. Let's make a start this weekend." I thought I sensed approval among the men.

In Palm Springs the vice president announced that my assistant had been promoted to manager of another district. I was tremendously relieved. The event called for a round of celebrations and inadvertently I had one drink too many. Vaguely I remembered getting up on a chair to make a speech and singing with the band!

The next morning I apologized to Bob who laughed understandingly. "Don't worry about it, Dave. It can happen to anyone." He cleared his throat and looked straight at me. "Drinking is part of our game, but don't let it go too far too often. It is bad for the image."

I was proud of my reputation as a hard drinker who seldom appeared affected by alcohol. I knew it was a matter of self-discipline, and I regretted the unfortunate incident. To be on the safe side, I decided to lay off all drinking for a while, at least till the assistant manager was gone from our office.

Four days later I was at my desk looking through the morning mail when I discovered my predecessor's salary sheet in a stack of papers. Its presence was obviously an oversight by the regional office. I glanced at the figures and froze. The man had been with the company for twenty years, but his salary was still not much more than mine. The disappointment sank in slowly. I was trying to adjust to the fact that my work wasn't as honorable as I once dreamed, but I still thought that at least there would be ample financial compensation for my moral compromise. Wrong again! What was I struggling for?

These thoughts were going through my mind as I stepped outside into the bright, March sunlight just as Kirk drove up from a customer call. He wore a satisfied grin and no tie.

"How about lunch and a game of pool?"

"Why not?" I tried to shrug off my depression. "I think I'll follow your advice and not work myself to death."

"Now you're talking sense," Kirk slapped my back.

I bought the first round of beer, and Kirk looked relieved. "Man, I was afraid you were going to stay dry for a while."

I shrugged, "There's no reason to be a fanatic. I just won't make another slip-up."

Just before suppertime I remembered to call Sarah. "Put the kids to bed early and fix something special for us," I said. "Let's relax and go for a swim later under the stars. . . ."

Sarah's voice was eager, "That's wonderful, David."

But somehow I lost track of the time, and we broke up the pool game after midnight. The lights were off at home, but I was sure Sarah was awake.

She stirred when I turned on the light. "Let's get it over with," I was edgy. "Why don't you yell at me now instead of dragging it out all night—I've had a hard day and need my rest."

"You promised to quit drinking." Sarah's eyes were dark with reproach.

"That wasn't a promise," I said stiffly. "I made a decision, and I'm man enough to make a new decision anytime I please."

"I'm sick of your empty promises!" Sarah's voice cracked, and I steeled myself for her well-worn tirade.

"You promise to come home. You promise to spend more time with us—but we never see you."

I felt anger and frustration. "I don't want your complaint. If you were a little more understanding you'd see more of me, but you're selfish, moody, and demanding. I can't succeed with a wife like you draining the marrow out of me."

"You're the selfish one," Sarah's voice rose to a scream. She had angry red spots in her cheeks and her brown eyes were flashing. "I'm sick of your talk about success, success, success. I need a husband and our kids need a father, not a success machine!"

In the sudden silence I heard sobs coming from the doorway. Eight-year-old John was barefoot with a hole in his pajama knee. His face was streaked with tears and his large, brown eyes stared solemnly from his mother to me.

"Why do you always fight? Why can't you love each other?"

"Honey, it's O.K. Go back to bed," Sarah tried lamely, but John ignored her. "I get a stomach ache every time you argue. If you don't stop it I'll run away," he announced gravely and turned without another word to leave. We heard the door to his bedroom squeak on its hinges, but he didn't close it completely.

"Look what we do to the children," Sarah whispered angrily.

"Not *we*," I hissed back. "You are the one who always demands from me more than I can give."

In the silence the tension was a hard edge between us.

Sarah's moods were getting worse. I often wished she would find a hobby or interest to take the pressure off me. I encouraged her to go to church; the social contacts there would be good for business, but she came home more depressed than before. Her up and down periods nearly drove me crazy. With mounting pressure at work as well, I didn't think I could take it much longer.

SARAH   *Paradise Valley, California*

The first couple of months in Arizona David kept his word and spent more time with me and with the children. We took weekend trips around our new state and spent evenings together at home reading, playing games, or swimming under the stars. I caught a glimpse of a more relaxed David. Perhaps that was why I was doubly disappointed when the business began to keep him away from home more and more. I developed tension headaches and intense stomach pains, in spite of daily dosages of aspirin.

Outwardly we were lacking in nothing yet I had never been so miserable in all my life. A meaningful relationship with David had been my last hope for happiness. Now it crumbled as our communication dwindled to brief surface conversation when David occasionally appeared at a meal with the rest of us. We argued whenever I tried to reach out for his understanding. He complained of pressure at work—and I sympathized with him—but I was sick and tired of always being the first to get cut off when something else came up. Of his priorities, I was the last on the list.

Searching for something to relieve my lonely and empty feeling, I went the round of the major denominational churches, but it seemed as if every one of them was in the middle of an ambitious building program and only looked for new members who could contribute. I decided against them all, until on one of my black days a letter came from an old girl friend who wrote: "I'm terribly depressed . . . Have you ever wondered if God really exists?"

The thought gripped me. If God really existed it might make a difference. Suddenly eager I went back to the last church I had visited and asked to borrow books from the pastor's library. With an armload I retreated to the little study at home.

Within a month I had plowed through a considerable number of books by a long list of famous theologians from Tillich to Bonhoeffer. I even tried some of the church fathers and reformers: Augustine, Calvin, and Luther. Their arguments and ideas made my head spin but I was no closer to my goal. I had learned something about what those men thought of God, but *I* hadn't found conclusive evidence of His existence; *who* He was, *what* He was, and *how* He could be found—*if* He existed at all.

My despair was growing, and at times I felt as if I was moving closer to the edge of a black chasm waiting to swallow me up. It was as if my mind was slipping away, hurtling towards a magnetic darkness, and it required a real effort to pull myself back. In moments I longed to let go, to escape. Would I find a deeper reality in insanity? To attempt it was enticing.

At night I looked up at the brilliant desert stars. Was God really a presence in our universe? My heart was pounding furiously as I thought of it. Could He hear me? With cheeks suddenly burning I whispered, "If You're real, please let me know, God." I felt silly and, of course, there was no answer. . . . Only the warmth of the desert night around me like a cloak. . . .

I walked back into my study and stared at the book-lined shelves. A Bible was stuck away in the corner, a Sunday school gift for Leif. I had always considered the book a collection of fables and myths of no historic value, hardly a place to look for reality. Yet this was the book all the theologians had used in their research. Could there be something in it that I had missed?

Gingerly I held it in my hand, blew the dust from the top, and started to read from the beginning. There was the story of God forming the universe—the idea now struck me as less fantastic than the theory of evolution where it all began with an accidental collision of molecules. The first human beings in rebellion against God and then separated from Him made a striking illustration of mankind alienated from itself and its maker.

What I had read so far made more sense than I had hoped for. Moses was a fascinating character, and I followed him into the desert where the voice spoke to him from a burning bush.

"Who do I say you are?" Moses asked. "What is your name?" I stared at the next words with intense concentration. "Tell them that I AM sent you!" I shivered and felt goosebumps. If God was the original I AM who created each of us in His image, a relationship with Him was necessary in order to find my own identity. No wonder I had always felt like an empty shell!

My heart was pounding. God was real! I knew it by negative proof—I had identified His absence within me. Was this the clue I had been looking for? Something told me it was. A clue to God's identity—and to my own.

Eagerly I read on, but felt curiously let down. Nothing else made much sense. The butchering of the Passover lamb in Egypt and the blood painted on the doorpost to avoid the angel of death sounded abhorrent. So that was where Christians got the morbid idea of Jesus as the Sacrificial Lamb of God.

Flipping the pages to the New Testament I felt on more familiar ground. It had been required reading in the public school in Norway. I knew the parables, the miracles, and Jesus' command that we forgive and love one another. My disappointment grew. Had I not tried repeatedly to love and to forgive—and failed? Jesus' statement "I am the Way" only left me frustrated. *How* was He the Way? When I came to the passages on the Crucifixion, I closed the book. The Bible wasn't speaking to me after all. If God was the great I AM, I didn't know where to find Him. My quest had led to a dead end.

Our Christmas was bigger and more expensive than ever. David read the traditional Christmas story. The fireplace and the candles were lit. The children sat on the floor at David's feet, their eyes reflecting the lights from the tree. What a beautiful scene, I thought with sudden bitterness.

"For unto you is born this day in the city of David a Savior . . . peace on earth . . . good will toward men."[1] David's voice was deep and resonant.

I wanted to cry, but there were no tears behind my burning lids. Each year Christmas came with a letdown. Each year I hoped for something, that the words of the commercials and the Christmas cards would come true: "May you have the peace and joy of Christmas. . . ."

What a terrible hoax, each year a little worse. I didn't want to live through another one.

In the middle of Christmas week, our doorbell rang. David was home for a change, reading his evening paper in silence. I had just put the children to bed and dreaded the empty hours stretched out ahead of me.

Outside stood a young state senator we had met at a pre-Christmas party. He lived nearby, and we had invited him to drop by sometime, the kind of polite invitation people seldom take you up on.

"I was on my way home and saw your lights," John Conlan smiled. "I hope it isn't inconvenient."

"Of course not!" David extended his hand. "Come in, have a drink with us."

The senator declined the drink, but accepted a glass of ice water and lowered his lanky frame into a chair. There was something different about him. I had noticed it when we met briefly the first time. He was handsome in a clean-cut way and his eyes held an unusually clear look. In a flash I realized "He actually looks *happy!*" The thought left me with a feeling of near envy.

"So how do you like Arizona?"

"We love it. It's a beautiful state."

"It reminds me of Israel," Conlan smiled. "Especially at Christmas. I went there once to see the birthplace of Christ."

David did not conceal his curiosity, "Surely, senator, you don't connect December 25th with the birth of a historical Jesus Christ?"

John Conlan chuckled. "Christ was probably born in the spring, but I find it significant that we celebrate His birth *some* time during the year."

"Why is that?" David looked directly at our visitor, and the atmosphere in the room seemed suddenly charged. Conlan's eyes were smiling but he spoke with certainty, "Because I am convinced that His birth was the most important event in the history of our world."

The statement hung between us, and I caught my breath sharply. The conversation had taken an unexpected turn.

David shook his head in amazement, "I find it incredible that a man of your background and intellect holds such a view."

John Conlan shrugged. "There are many with far greater knowledge of history, science, and politics who have reached the same conclusion. They are convinced, as I am, that the situation in our world and in our nation can best be understood in light of God's revelation to us in the Bible."

David's smile was a little forced. "I appreciate your candid statement, senator, but I find Christianity too confining. For example, I enjoy a few drinks. As a Christian I would have to give that up."

Conlan threw back his head and laughed. "Christianity isn't a set of rules and regulations, although some people make it appear that way. You don't become a Christian by not drinking or smoking . . . but if you do become a Christian, you may discover that alcohol and tobacco no longer hold the same attraction for you."

David looked thoughtful and sipped his drink in silence while John Conlan turned to me. "What do *you* think about Christianity?"

My cheeks burned. "I have only lately become convinced there is a God and I've been reading the Bible, but the Crucifixion of Christ doesn't make sense. I'm sorry."

The senator looked at me intently, and I felt his clear gaze penetrate the confused jumble of thoughts and feelings inside. He reached into his brief case and brought out a large, well-worn Bible. Flipping through the pages he said, "See if *this* makes sense. . . ." There was a tightening in my chest as I listened to his steady voice. " . . . that ye, being rooted and grounded in love, may be able to comprehend with all saints what is the breadth, and length, and depth, and height; and to know the love of Christ, which passeth knowledge, that ye might be filled with all the fulness of God." [2]

With a rush of emotion I realized that I yearned for those words to be true. Slowly I nodded, and Senator Conlan closed his book with a smile. "There's a tremendous reality in those words and, if you want it, I know you'll find it." He stood up and held out his hand to David. "It's been good getting to know you folks better. How about coming with me to church sometime?"

"We're not much for going to church," David smiled politely.

"You can't judge the validity of Christianity without exposing yourself to the real thing. I believe you would find our church interesting. There are many young people there of your age and interests, and the case for Christianity is presented without compromise or excuse." Conlan spoke with the smooth ease of a seasoned politician.

"Maybe some day. . . ." David was hesitant, and Conlan said immediately, "Great, how about this Sunday?" To my surprise, David grinned, "Why not? Thank you."

"I'll be by to pick you up at 9:45."

When the door closed behind our visitor David shook his head unbelievingly, "Who would have figured that fellow for a religious fanatic? He has a fine voting record in the Senate and I always considered him a capable and promising young politician." [3]

I was still in a half daze. We had never permitted anyone to read to us from a Bible in our own home before. Some insistent soul savers had tried and had been shown to the door. I had pitied them as naive and narrow minded; but the young lawyer and state senator who had talked so matter-of-factly about God and Jesus Christ didn't quite fit the picture.

Conlan's church was just around the corner from our house, but I had never been there. The name, Scottsdale Bible Church, sounded too fundamental for our taste. That Sunday morning I was slightly uncomfortable at the sight of so many people carrying Bibles, but the atmosphere in the large, crowded room was unmistakably friendly and cheerful. I had never seen so many happy faces in a crowd before.

John Conlan had told us that a large percentage of the congregation were professional people, many from the university at Tempe. I wondered what attracted them. Christianity could not have that much to offer anyone.

The pastor was Dr. Jim Borror, a short and slender young man with a boyish face and a contagious grin. I immediately liked his direct, no-nonsense way of speaking about Christianity not as a philosophy but a practical way of life.

"It's all here," he held his Bible high. "How to run your business, how to be a wife or a husband or a parent, how to be a good friend, or get along with your enemies." He leaned eagerly over the pulpit. "If I didn't think this book was valid I'd throw it away and go look for some other answer. To me the proof is that it works. But don't take my word for it," he continued, "or judge by the experience of others. Christianity is one thing you can't find out about second-hand."

It sounded as if the knowledge of God was easily available to anyone who wanted it. With rising expectation I waited for the explanation of *how* to reach it. Instead I felt disappointed as the pastor ended his sermon with a pat invitation to accept Jesus Christ as savior.

On our way out Conlan introduced us to the pastor.

"I'm glad you came," Dr. Borror said. "If you have any questions, drop by my study. If I don't know the answer, we can look for it together."

"I liked the first part of your sermon," I said. "But I don't think Jesus is the way to God. You are limiting our great Creator."

There was a glimmer of interest in the pastor's eyes. "Thank you for the comment," he smiled. "I wish you would take time someday to tell me what alternative you think works better."

At home, David exploded. "I'll never set foot in that place again! I got enough of that nonsense in the Baptist church back home! The biggest hypocrites I ever met were Bible-carrying, Scripture-quoting, holier-than-thou Christians." Sadly I agreed with him. There was not much use in looking for answers in a place like that. Still, those people had seemed so rational and well-informed—and happy.

The children had overheard our conversation and Leif spoke up, "I want to go back." He looked determined. "That's the nicest Sunday school we ever went to."

John's brown eyes showed disgust, "You never let us stay long enough in a Sunday school to get any friends. Why don't you let us walk to this church and you can stay home?"

David poured himself a cup of coffee and opened the Sunday edition of the newspaper. "We'll see," he said absent-mindedly.

John Conlan called Thursday afternoon. "How about church Sunday?"

"David won't be able to," I felt flustered. "And the heavy emphasis on Jesus isn't for me."

"You haven't heard enough to back off yet," John insisted. "How long did you study other religions before you rejected them?"

He had put me on the spot. I ought to stay with it long enough to understand the main ideas. Then I could honestly say that I had tried.

The children came along enthusiastically while David stayed

home. I enrolled in an adult discussion group following the worship service and found that I was the only non-believing participant. It was a little like visiting another planet. The thirty-odd members of the class spoke about their daily struggles in grappling with life's problems, but they all were convinced that valid solutions could be found in a personal relationship with Jesus Christ. Listening, I sometimes wondered if they—or I—were completely mad. It was as if they saw and experienced an invisible dimension that I knew nothing about.

In contrast, my own despair and doubt became more unbearable with each visit to the church. After six weeks I could not restrain myself anymore but burst out in class, "You talk about how hard it is to live *in* the faith, how do you think *I* feel—without any faith at all!" I felt hysterical, and the girl beside me quickly reached out to touch my hand.

"Hang in there," she said. "The Bible says, 'Seek and you will find.' Before long it will make sense to you."

Her words only made my frustration worse.

"I'm like a kid with my nose pressed against the candy store window," I complained to Jim Borror. "You are all inside and you say I can step through the door anytime I want to, but I'm not even sure there is a door!"

"So what do you think faith is?" Jim looked at me with patience, and I wondered how much longer he would put up with my questioning.

"I would feel it if I had it, wouldn't I?"

"Not necessarily." Jim ran his fingers through his short dark hair. "Faith is initiated by will, not feeling. Even some Christians are confused on that point. They *feel* close to God one day and far from Him the next, and measure their faith by feeling. Real faith is based on facts.

"For instance," Jim continued, "the scientist uses faith in his search for new truth. He accumulates the available evidence to support his theory, then takes a step of faith into the unknown. He may be reasonably certain of the outcome, but he can't have proof until *after* the step is taken.

"You must approach God the same way. Collect all the evidence you can find on this side of the door, then decide to step through, on faith. There is an element of uncertainty, but it isn't a blind, mystical thing."

This was an approach to faith I had never considered. I had been waiting for some kind of mystical revelation—perhaps a voice in the night—something that would suddenly convince me of God's presence and the truth of His Word.

Jim Borror was looking directly at me, and I squirmed a little under his steady, clear gaze. The same clear look that had once attracted me to John Conlan.

"If you want to know God personally," Jim went on, "you will have to move by an act of your own will from observer of Christianity to participant. Someday that decision will seem important to you. That moment comes to all of us sometime in our life."

I wasn't convinced that Christianity was worth committing myself to. It would mean a surrender of my will to God's, and I preferred the freedom to make my own choices. To accept what the Bible had to say about God and Jesus Christ seemed like intellectual suicide.

The next morning, after David and the children had left, I sat down with a second cup of coffee and another cigarette. My eyes followed the profile of Camelback Mountain when, without any warning, my mouth went dry and I shivered with an ominous sense of urgency. Thoughts whirled in my head. Yesterday Christianity had been something I could take or leave alone, Jesus Christ had seemed like a good man who taught good rules for living. Now the awesome possibility gripped me: *What if it is true? What if Jesus is who He said He was?*

The question burned in my mind. I was suddenly desperately involved. I *had* to choose whether I believed or not, and the choice seemed to involve life or death.

For three weeks my agony grew. I was drawn to church, but every meeting was torture. Pastor Borror seemed to speak directly to me:

"No one is neutral in his relationship to God. You are either out there separated from Him, or you are united to Him. If you know in your heart you are off the mark, you must look to Jesus and decide for yourself if He was history's most flagrant liar, or the Son of God who can save you from the dead-end street you are in, and become your new way of life."

At the close of each service, while the congregation stood to sing and the pastor gave the usual challenge to accept Jesus at His word, I clung to the chair in front of me with whitening knuckles. What if God wasn't even there? That possibility seemed suddenly more frightening than if He was there and waiting for me.

I dared not postpone the choice any longer. I would choose God whether He was there or not. To do otherwise meant to cut off any possibility of life in relationship with Him.

It was a Wednesday night and although we had a famous guest speaker I didn't hear a word of the service. Ahead loomed the rendezvous with destiny I had set for myself.

When the invitation to trust Jesus finally came, I wanted to sink through the floor. Doubts battered my aching head: "Don't make a public spectacle of yourself. Do it at home, then no one will know if it turns out to be a flop. Don't be a hypocrite. You can't commit yourself to something you aren't sure of. Wait till next week—or maybe next month."

The people were singing and the words filtered into my consciousness:

> Just as I am, though tossed about,
> With many a *conflict*, many a *doubt.*
> *Fightings* and *fears* within, without,
> O Lamb of God, *I come, I come!* [4]

Blindly I groped my way forward and fell to my knees by the platform.

"O God, I have so many doubts, but I'm here. I surrender to you and accept Jesus for what He says He is. I want Him to be in charge of my life from now on. . . . Amen."

My knees hurt against the hard floor. I could *feel* no evidence that anyone had heard my prayer. But the butterflies were gone from my stomach and the whirling thoughts in my head were stilled. I felt calm, like after a storm.

"I've chosen," I thought. "I'll stick by it whatever happens next."

Pastor Borror came up to me and said, "If you have a minute I'd like to talk to you in my office."

We stepped into the little cubicle and Jim looked intently at me across his desk.

"Did you act on an impulse, or was it premeditated?"

I told him about the struggle of the last three weeks and he relaxed in his chair.

"Good! Now what do you think?"

"I don't feel a thing!" I smiled and suddenly realized that my feelings didn't matter. "I won't go back on it. I'll operate on faith based on the facts I already know. I'll take the Bible's word for it, like you've preached. The rest is up to God." I felt calmly businesslike, as if I was talking about a lifetime contract I had just signed.

"I'm glad it wasn't emotional," Jim smiled. "Emotions can be deceptive. Now you're on solid ground." He touched the Bible on his desk. "Everything in here written 'to believers' now applies to you. You've stepped inside the door," he grinned and I thought I saw a hint of moisture in his direct, blue eyes. "This is just the beginning, you know. . . ."

I walked home under the stars and didn't feel lonely. There was a new quietness inside.

In the study I picked up the J. B. Phillips translation of the New Testament John Conlan had given me. I opened it at random and read out loud, "The letter to the Christians in Rome. . . ." I smiled and added, ". . . and Paradise Valley, Arizona," continuing till I came to a line that suddenly stood out, as if in bold letters: "Don't let the world around you squeeze you into its own mold, but let God re-mold your minds from within, so that you may prove in practice that the plan of God for you is good, meets all his demands and moves towards the goal of true maturity . . ." [5]

I was sick and tired of squeezing myself into molds that didn't quite fit. I leaned back in my chair and felt a tremendous sense of relief.

The front door slammed, and David walked through the living room. Suddenly I wanted to share with him what had happened. If he would only make the same decision to trust God, our marriage and our lives would be transformed. I was sure of it.

He stood in the doorway, and I struggled to find the right words.

"I decided to believe in Jesus Christ tonight," I said. "It's hard to explain, but I feel like I've been floating all my life, and now I've got a solid point to stand on. Why don't you try it? Nobody can make it without God."

From the look in his eyes I could tell he didn't know what I meant. We were staring at each other across a bottomless chasm. I felt a sudden chill.

Yesterday we had been unable to communicate, but we had been on the same side of that chasm. Now I couldn't go back.

"O God," I thought. "We can never really be together until we're both on Your side." The thought was frightening.

Chapter 4

DAVID   *Paradise Valley, Arizona*

The building industry suffered a nationwide slump, and I was under pressure to make deals with customers and competitors in order to keep up our sales. I became increasingly uncomfortable at the glaring discrepancy between my ideas of honest business and the double standards I was now required to operate under. Still I clung to my belief that I could reach my own goals by hard work and integrity. On that basic conviction hung my sense of dignity as a man.

The situation on the homefront was deteriorating as well. Sarah was falling deeper into the religious trap and was almost impossible to live with. Her constant refrain was, "You ought to read the Bible!" She waved the book at me and was obviously unaware that she sounded like the religious fanatics we had both avoided for so long. In spite of fervent talk about God's love, she was too busy with her church activities to fix meals on time or clean the house. I frequently woke up with a headache in the morning, but instead of bringing me coffee and aspirin, she lectured me on my need for Jesus.

At the office Kirk listened to my woes and clucked his tongue knowingly. "Women always expect too much from a man. When they don't get it, they turn to religion. Some of them never get over it."

Clearly Sarah had fallen for the same error. She had always demanded more from our relationship than could realistically be expected. My only hope for our marriage now was that her religious fixation would blow over like the other fads she had periodically embraced in the past.

As a temporary measure, in order to avoid our many painful arguments, I asked Sarah to move out of the bedroom so that I could have some privacy at home. I had expected a fuss and was relieved when she moved in with Andrew and Christine without argument. But true to her old nature, she ignored my plea for privacy.

"We can't live like this," she stubbornly insisted. "The children ask why I don't sleep with you, and why you refuse to talk to me. It's putting us all under tension." The only alternative remaining was for me to move out.

Motel-life provided an immediate sense of relief, although the loneliness held a threat of its own. I didn't like to be alone with the uncomfortable thoughts that haunted me so often. Restlessness kept me from reading, my old favorite pastime, and I no longer had the desire to spend my evenings working overtime promoting the affairs of the company.

One evening in the motel bar I struck up a conversation with an attractive young philosophy student from the University of Arizona. Linda was witty and bright, and we soon discovered that our tastes in books and ideas were similar.

"My wife has become a Christian," I told her and she looked immediately sympathetic.

"How sad! Christianity is such a fake. I can understand why you cannot communicate with her anymore." Linda's attitude was encouraging, and I observed the soft sweep of her long brown hair and her bright, sincere eyes with a new interest. In some ways she reminded me of the enthusiastic young Sarah of ten years ago. She was a refreshing experience, proof that life still offered unspoiled beauty and promise. Too long I had buried myself in hard work while home had become a gray drudgery of small talk, endless crisis, whining children, and a nagging wife. It had caused me to feel older than my thirty-five years. It was time to break out of that rut.

I called Sarah and asked her to contact an attorney. "You get the divorce; charge me with desertion. You and the children will be well taken care of. I'm sure we can settle this as mature adults."

"Can't we meet and talk about it?" Sarah's voice shook. "What about the children? We can't just give up like this."

"We've never been able to talk," I was impatient. "The children are bright and healthy. They will do fine. I'll spend as much time with them as they need."

Having made the decision I felt much better, but a week later I received summons to appear in Conciliation Court. Sarah had taken action on her own.

Seething with displeasure I called her. "Why couldn't you just do as I said?"

"I wanted us to try everything." She sounded more sure of herself, and I felt like slapping her in the face.

"I had hoped we could be mature about this. Now you insist on putting our dirty laundry out in front of a stranger."

"That's exactly what I want. Maybe if it all comes out we can do something about it." Her voice was high-pitched and nervous.

I slammed down the receiver and stalked angrily outside. I had always detested talking about my personal affairs. They were nobody else's business.

The interview with the court-appointed counselor came out better than I had thought. The man was in his fifties, with a quiet smile. He encouraged us to state our position, and waited calmly till we each had had our say. Sarah was a little hysterical in claiming that she found it unbearable to live with me as long as I refused to communicate with her. I stated that I no longer felt any desire to share my life with her, but that I would be willing to live in the same house, provided she left me alone, if that solution was better for the children.

The counselor looked at us both in silence for a while before speaking. "Unless you two want to make a sincere effort to communicate with each other, you should not live together." He allowed that thought to sink in, then continued, "I seldom recommend divorce, but the solution you suggest would be considerably more damaging to the emotional health of your children and yourselves." He smiled as if to soften the impact of his words. "In your case I would say—you either make up or break up. A compromise would eventually do untold harm to every family member."

"That settles it, I'm glad to hear it from an outsider," I lit a cigarette and inhaled calmly. "Since I have no intentions of ever making up, I take it that you recommend a breakup?"

The counselor stood to indicate that our time was up.

"If you feel as you say, I certainly do."

I shook his hand and left without looking in Sarah's direction. Now that she had heard the recommendation from a professional marriage counselor, she could no longer raise an objection to our divorce.

When the news got out, Bob Koenig called from Los Angeles. "I'm sorry to hear it, Dave. Is there anything I can do?"

"Thanks, Bob, but it can't be helped."

"Are you sure?" Bob sounded anxious. "The company doesn't like divorces, especially in management."

"You mean because my marriage is falling apart I'm no longer capable of doing my job?" I felt smoldering anger.

"Of course not," Bob was apologetic. "But some people feel that tension at home impairs a man's work efforts."

"Are you complaining about my performance?" I had a strong urge to tell Bob I was quitting anyway.

"Don't take it personally, Dave. I know you're a good man, and I hope you and Sarah get back together soon."

I hung up and stared out the window at the cars and people on the street below. Everything was turning sour. Those marvelous dreams and ideas I had once held back at the university were certainly taking a beating in real life situations. The urge to tell Bob I was through was still strong, but what would I try next? With a sense of mounting despondency I decided to do nothing. It was an unusual feeling for me, not to care anymore.

One Saturday afternoon I took the children to a movie and out for hamburgers. They were demonstratively happy to see me.

John told me about catching three scorpions in a glass jar and his plan to collect poisonous snakes. "You know I'm too old for rabbits and hamsters—I like dangerous stuff!" His eager face was losing some of its little boy roundness and his brown hair stood straight up from the crown of his head in defiance of the comb.

Leif was excited about horses. The girl next door was letting him ride in return for help with the chores. His dimples were showing, "When can I have a horse of my own, daddy?"

"I don't want us to have a horse!" Andrew's blue eyes were riveted on mine. "I just want you to come home. When are you coming home, daddy?" Four solemn faces were turned to me, and I tried to sound reassuring. "I'm afraid it's impossible right now—but we can still have fun together, can't we?" Christine pushed away her ice cream soda. Her moist lips were quivering.

"I love you so much, daddy, and I love mommy too. Why can't I love you both in the same house?"

I had no immediate answer and forced a smile. "Hurry up and finish your meal. Then I'll take you to a toy store and you can pick a gift for five dollars each!"

The awkward moment was gone. Later I dropped the children at the gate and watched them run up the driveway waving their new toys. Sarah was watering the garden, and I felt her eyes burning me as I drove off quickly.

At work I sometimes felt an unreality about what I was doing. A deepening depression hung over me every waking moment. Drinking only heightened the anger I felt—alternately against my job, against Sarah, against the world. Nothing was going the way I had expected it.

I started to neglect customers and did not call on new accounts. It was the only outward way I knew to demonstrate rebellion against my involuntary lame-duck position in the company. When Bob Koenig flew from Los Angeles unannounced to see me, I knew that things had deteriorated enough to cause concern on a higher level.

Bob arrived late in the afternoon and asked me to have dinner with him. I avoided his direct gaze and lied, "Sorry, Bob, I have a previous engagement."

"Fine. Then how about breakfast in the morning?"

"Sorry, that won't be possible either."

"I'll see you in the office after breakfast then?"

I knew what he was after. He wanted me to tell him about my personal problems. But I had no desire to unburden myself to Bob or anyone else or to try any well-meaning advice. My refusal to cooperate would mean the end of my job, but this was strangely enough what I wanted—an escape from the deadlock I was in, without having to make the move myself.

In the morning Bob went with me to call on customers. He picked the accounts, and by peculiar coincidence they happened to be new accounts I had neglected to call on. Bob was visibly disappointed over my indifference.

"Let's talk over lunch," he suggested, but again I excused myself and said I had another appointment.

"What about dinner then?" Bob was about to lose his patience.

"It just isn't convenient. . . ."

"Then take me to the airport right now!" His face was suddenly grim. We drove in silence and while waiting for the plane Bob said, "I suppose you know what you're doing?"

"Yes, I do."

"I want to help you," there was still a hint of our old camaraderie in his voice. "I know you have problems. Perhaps a change, a transfer back to Los Angeles."

I shook my head and kept my face a mask. "I appreciate it, but no, thanks. I'm doing what I want to do."

He held out his hand. "I can't tell you how sorry I am, Dave. You've been a good man for the company. Too bad it has to end like this."

I watched him walk towards the plane, slightly stooped in the shoulders, looking suddenly tired and old. He had worked for the company for more than thirty years.

"For what?" I thought. "Thirty years of a man's life belonging to the company. On call twenty-four hours a day. Moving his family from one end of the United States to the other at the company's bidding. Compromising his values. For what?"

I turned and walked away, feeling oddly relieved. It would be only a matter of time before I was notified of my "resignation." There would be no more backbiting, vicious competition, or juggling of facts. No double standards and shady deals.

For the next few days I put in a token appearance at the office, waiting for the ax to fall. Then Bob sent his assistant, Steve, to notify me that I was relieved of my duties, effective immediately. Steve was an eager young man in his twenties, obviously ambitious. He tried to sound regretful, "You need to take some time off, Dave. Have a rest and get back on your feet."

I wanted to laugh at him. There was nothing wrong with me. I was only glad to be out of the meaningless rat race I had discovered big company management to be.

As an immediate consequence to my layoff, I could no longer

afford a divorce. Instead I would sell our house and use the capital to start again somewhere else, I hoped in California.

I called Sarah. "This is not an effort to reconciliate, just a temporary arrangement," I made my voice brisk and businesslike. "We'll continue to sleep in separate rooms, of course, but you will have another chance to prove your good will towards me."

SARAH   *Paradise Valley, Arizona*

In the beginning I watched David expectantly every day, waiting for him to discover that God was real, and to decide to trust Him, just as I had done. I was sure that would solve all our problems. I tried to share some of the marvelous discoveries I made in the Bible, but that only made him furious. Our arguments grew more intense, but I was not as upset as I used to be. David and I were no longer fighting it out on our own. God was alive and involved with us personally. Sooner or later everything would work out.

I read the Bible several hours daily. It was exciting. All those promises! I had not dared to ask anything specific of God yet, although I read that if I asked for something I knew to be God's will, I could be sure He would answer.[1] I was almost afraid to. What if nothing happened? On the other hand, unless I asked I would never know how it worked.

One evening about two weeks after I had made my monumental decision to trust God, I was alone in the study. The children were in bed and David gone. I had just read in my New Testament that the body of a Christian is the temple of the living God, and therefore belongs to God. No one should deliberately do anything to harm or destroy that "temple."[2]

I felt the heavy pounding of my heart. What about my smoking? Instinctively I knew the answer. Tobacco was harmful to my health! For ten years I had been literally a slave of the cigarettes. Repeatedly I had tried to quit, but had given up after suffering agonies of tension and craving. Mustering my will power I had managed to stay away from cigarettes since that Wednesday evening in church, but the urge was nagging me constantly.

My mouth had gone dry and I clasped my hands around the book. "I don't think You want me to pollute my body with the poison of tobacco," my voice shook. "I'll continue to stay away from cigarettes, but I ask You to take away the urge. Please God!" Talking out loud made me feel awkward, but somehow I was sure He was listening.

It was three days before I thought about it again. I watched David light up a cigarette and suddenly realized that I had not wanted one since the prayer. In fact the smell of smoke was making me a little nauseous. As the awareness sank in, I felt faint. I had been willing to believe God's word without any signs; now something had actually happened inside me, and I hadn't even noticed when it took place! It was a little frightening. Like turning on electricity for the very first time and *seeing* it shine.

That evening my hands shook as I opened the pages of the book again. Dr. Borror had talked about tasting the pudding—what would I stumble over next? For years I had suffered from nightmares and uncontrollable fears. As a rule I woke up at least half a dozen times during the night, thinking I heard a noise. Terror held me paralyzed while I imagined a killer coming towards me in the dark. The baseball bat I kept within reach was of no use, since I could not move a finger or utter a sound.

My new faith had not helped. I tried repeating to myself the words I had read, "Fear not, for I am with you. . . ." The passages were scattered throughout the book. But the ominous threat of darkness soon overcame my feeble thoughts. I did not *want* to be afraid. I was willing to believe God's word in the book, so why did the *feeling* of fear overwhelm me?

I turned the page and the words suddenly burned into my conscience, ". . . God is love . . . Love contains no fear—indeed fully-developed love expels every particle of fear, for fear always contains some of the torture of feeling guilty!" [3]

A sudden shiver ran through me. Was I feeling guilt? I had confessed to God that I was a sinner and I knew that He had forgiven me. Was not that a basic tenet of my new faith? Then could I still *feel* guilt? Could the guilt that produced my fears be hidden in my unconscious?

"O God!" The words poured out of me. "If I've repressed old memories and guilts, please clean out my unconscious so that I can sleep in peace."

That night I only woke up three times, and when dawn stole in my window, I looked over at Christine who slept peacefully with her teddy bear, and suddenly remembered something. I had been my daughter's age when my best friend asked me to her house for cookies and hot chocolate. I promised to come, but that day a new girl on our street, older and admired by us all, offered to play with me. I had felt horrible guilt when I called my friend on the phone and lied to her, "Mom won't let me go to your house today." For weeks I had avoided my friend and felt greatly relieved when her family moved away. Now with the early morning sun painting Camelback Mountain in pastel shades the old guilt welled up in me.

"O God," I felt tears of shame. "It was wrong of me to lie. Forgive me." I felt strangely relieved.

After the children had left for school, I found myself singing as I stacked the breakfast dishes in the dishwasher. Gratitude swept through me—God had forgiven the wrong I had done so long ago. The memory had been hidden for nearly thirty years and festered like a sore inside me. Now it was exposed and healed.

It seemed almost too simple. The Bible promised that when I confessed my sin, God would forgive me.[4] I took the next step: "God, You showed me something I had hidden from myself because it hurt to remember. Thank You for Your forgiveness of my sin. Now show me if there are other hidden guilts I need to confess to You."

The next days and nights I felt as if I was on a journey backwards into my childhood and early teens. The memories popped up when I least expected them, but the pattern was becoming familiar. The sudden flash of thought, accompanied by a tightening in my chest and throat, a pounding of my heart or a rush of heat or cold while I was the involuntary spectator of a vivid and detailed, long-forgotten scene. Always I was the villain—lying, stealing, cheating, yelling cruel words in a fit of temper. Remorse and shame washed over me and I felt as if I couldn't bear to look at my own actions or motives for a second longer. I wanted to push the memory back where it came from yet, at the same time, I wanted to admit my wrong and take the consequences.

Sometimes the tug of war within lasted for hours—as when I remembered the time I lied to father about an incident in school. His disappointment was so great that he became ill for several days afterwards. My sense of condemnation was unbearable. I tried to push the thoughts away, busy myself with housework, even read my Bible, but there was no escape.

Finally I cried out, "God, I know I lied. It was awful. It nearly killed my father . . . Forgive me!" Instantly the heaviness lifted. I was still conscious of the great wrong I had done, but even more aware of God's love and forgiveness. Guilt was replaced by gratitude.

More than a week had gone by when I awoke one night with a sense of dread. Cold perspiration drenched me as I stared into the darkness. In my mind I was again standing in the doorway to mother's hospital room on my last visit before she died. The memory of the sickroom smell was making me nauseous. Mother's face was turned towards me, her skin gray against the white of the pillow, her dark eyes seeking mine. Again I felt the hardening inside against the urge to take her in my arms, rock her as if she was a child, and tell her that I wanted her to live, that I loved her. Instead, I turned and walked away—justifying it by saying that mother had hurt me too deeply—she had killed my love.

Now the veil of self-deception was torn away, and I was forced to look at myself as I had really been that afternoon eight years ago. I saw the helplessness and pleading for love and forgiveness in mother's eyes and the cruel refusal in mine. I had deliberately held back my love. I had wanted her to suffer. What a horribly evil thing I had done. Mother was dead. I could never ask her to forgive. The burden of guilt was mine forever.

I tossed on my bed. If I could only push the memory back into the darkness, yet having seen myself in the light of truth I could not hope to live with the knowledge of what I had done.

"O God," the words were a groan. "Forgive me . . . I deserve to die." An anguished sob rose deep within me and hot tears coursed down my face. I had not cried when mother died, now the pent-up dam gave way, and when the tears stopped, a heavy weight had rolled off my chest. I fell into a deep and restful sleep and did not awaken till Andrew tugged at my arm. "Mommy, we'll be late for school!"

The sun was flooding the room. The lightness was still within me. It wasn't just my imagination. Although David seldom came home till the small hours of morning and our front door remained unlocked I slept soundly night after night without a nightmare or a flutter of fear. My terrors had been caused by hidden guilt. Now I was forgiven and set free from the dark dungeon of my fears.

"I feel as if I've just begun to discover what life is all about," I told my neighbor.

Sue Ann usually came for a morning dip in the pool and a glass of iced tea.

Her gray eyes looked thoughtful. She had been raised a Catholic, but no longer attended church. Her husband, Jim Woods, was a successful real estate broker, but was seldom home and Sue Ann filled her empty hours with studies. She had returned to the university to get her teacher's credentials now that their two daughters were in the third and fifth grades. For several weeks she had been a non-committed and quiet listener to my excited outpourings.

Now she sipped her tea and her thin face broke into a smile. "Perhaps you can help David now that you've found help for yourself."

"You know David isn't interested in religion!" I felt a touch of irritation.

"I didn't mean that," Sue Ann's eyes had a somber look. "If, as you say, you've been forgiven for your past mistakes, perhaps you can now forgive David for his present errors." She hesitated for a moment, then added quickly, "He needs your love more than you may be aware of. I've seen him occasionally downtown dining with customers. He drinks a great deal."

"It's part of his job," I wondered why I felt on the defensive.

Sue Ann nodded calmly. "Did you know that I am a rehabilitated alcoholic?" She smiled at my astonished look. "Only my family and closest friends knew that I kept bottles stashed all over the house. I stayed intoxicated to overcome my shyness and sense of inadequacy. I've been dry four years now, and go to Alcoholics Anonymous weekly in order to stay that way."

I could only stare. It sounded incredible. Sweet, soft-spoken Sue Ann who was always neatly and correctly dressed, a drunk?

"Alcoholism is a deadly game," she spoke evenly, without emotion. "I think David is on the borderline already."

Heat rushed to my face. "David doesn't have a problem. He can quit anytime he wants to."

"Do you really believe that?"

I squirmed under Sue Ann's direct gaze and tried to push away the memories of countless incidents in the past. A pledge not to drink, signed and then broken. The horror of several-days-long bouts of drunkeness when we lived in Green River.

"So what do you want me to do? Tell him he's an alcoholic when he doesn't think he is one? It will only make him mad!"

"Don't tell him anything!" Sue Ann's hand touched mine in a quick gesture. "I just wanted you to know that David is suffering and that it may get worse. He needs love and support in action more than words of advice."

Our conversation had taken an unexpected turn, and I felt awkward. Surely Sue Ann was exaggerating. Just because she had been an alcoholic she thought everyone who took a drink was a potential drunk.

After she left I busied myself with dinner preparations and decided to put the whole matter out of my mind. David was no alcoholic. He had other problems; he was cold and unfeeling, and still hiding behind his mask. My words did nothing to penetrate it and we were getting nowhere. Every conversation deteriorated into a loud argument with the children as spectators, trapped in hell with us.

I had clung to the hope that David would change, but when he showed no signs of softening I caught myself wishing he would leave. Once I had been afraid of facing life on my own, now I had found an inner strength and source of help that could enable me to live without David.

When he finally moved out, I felt only relief. Without him, the children and I fell into a quiet routine.

David's demand for a divorce, however, caught me by surprise. Appealing to the conciliation court I hoped to force him to see the light. When that failed, I accepted the outcome with an inner calm that could only be explained in terms of my new relationship with God.

In my daily Bible readings I had come across a verse I copied to pin on the wall above my desk: ". . . to those who love God . . . everything that happens fits into a pattern for good." [5] It was hard to believe that a divorce could happen for good, but perhaps it would cause David to change at last.

I mentioned that idea to Pastor Borror, and he chuckled.

"I'm convinced that God makes all things fit together for good for those who trust Him, but right now your first concern should be with the good changes God wants to make in *you* through this experience, and stop anticipating what may happen to David." His blue eyes were suddenly serious and he touched the Bible on his desk. "There's a blueprint for marriage in here. Are you ready to do your part if David comes back?"

"I think I've done my part." My mouth felt suddenly dry. "What are you referring to in particular?"

Quickly Jim scribbled a few words on a note pad, tore off the page and handed it to me. "These are some of the specific references to marriage." His boyish grin had returned. "Take a look at them and tell me what you think."

Curiosity drove me to open my New Testament as soon as I got home. The passages were short and each made the same point. "You wives must learn to adapt yourselves to your husbands, as you submit yourselves to the Lord, for the husband is the 'head' of the wife in the same way that Christ is the head of the Church. . . .". [6]

Anger and disbelief mounted as I read the other verse. [7] They were simply too ridiculous to make any sense at all! I dialed Jim's office and fought to keep my tone light. "You can't be serious about those passages you gave me. They were written over a thousand years ago—by men who had never heard of equality of the sexes."

"Don't confuse equality with alikeness," Jim's voice was calm. "The writers you refer to considered men and women equal in the eyes of God—I can show you passages to prove it—but husbands and wives have been assigned different roles in marriage. It isn't as confining as you think, and it's the only system I know that works, or can you think of another one?"

Frustrated and still fuming, I hung up. There had to be another, better answer. For once the Bible was wrong or outdated, I thought. Marriage required mutual adjustment and, in our case, most of the adjusting had to be made by David. That was obvious.

My peaceful nights were disturbed once more. The words I had read swirled in my head: "Wives, adapt yourselves to your husbands. . . ." I threw off the covers and stepped outside on the pool deck where the warm Arizona night felt like an embrace. The stars were brilliant, but the beauty only added to my torment.

"I have just begun to discover a new freedom to be myself," I whispered. "Do You require me to give that up in order to adapt to a self-centered, tyrant like David?"

Bits of our old arguments were running through my mind. David's demanding voice: "I need your full support. You should take better care of the house. The meals. The children. Our needs come before yours." What about *my* individuality, *my* interests, *my* needs?

Summer vacation had started, and Sue Ann usually brought her girls along for a swim in the mornings. While our children splashed in the pool, we sipped iced tea in the shade and talked.

"It's too late to do anything about the past now," I said for the umpteenth time. "I did my best, and if I was wrong, David was even more to blame. The best thing to do is look ahead. I'm sure God has a wonderful plan for the future."

"Why are you always on the defensive?" Sue Ann's remark stopped me in mid-sentence. "Are you sure divorce is God's plan for you?"

"Unless David changes his mind I don't see how. . . ." My pulse was pounding furiously.

"Have you asked God to bring him home?" There was a shadow of a smile on Sue Ann's face.

"N-no, I never thought of it." My apprehension was growing, and Sue Ann laughed.

"You've been talking as if your God can do anything." The thin face was suddenly somber. "I don't mean to tease you, Sarah— You know I'm watching what is taking place in your life with great interest—maybe someday I'll get the courage to believe as well.

"If this God of yours is real, He can bring David home and help you become a better wife."

My mouth felt like dry cotton. "David doesn't want a wife, just a housekeeper."

"You're not being honest with yourself, Sarah," Sue Ann shook her head. "I've seen David with another woman—she looks like a younger version of you."

My cheeks burned, and Sue Ann continued, "David is looking for someone who can accept him and support him. He wants to be respected and loved. He needs you, Sarah."

The rest of the day went in a daze. When the children were asleep, I knelt by my bed. I had been on my knees only once before, but now it seemed necessary again.

"Maybe I'm the one who needs to change the most," the words were uttered with difficulty. "I still don't think a wife should adapt to her husband in everything. But I'm willing to compromise, if that is really what You want of me. Bring David home if you want to, and help me to support him more than I did before."

Crawling into bed I fervently hoped God had other plans for my future.

I awoke with the ringing of the phone and my hand shook as I lifted the receiver. I knew it was David even before I heard his voice, cold and businesslike.

"I am no longer with the company. I'm coming home this morning. We'll move to California and get our divorce there later."

The room swam before my eyes, and I felt numb. Somehow I got out of bed, dressed, and prepared breakfast for the children. When they had gone out to play I plugged in the coffee pot with fresh coffee for David. He always complained of my thoughtlessness when I forgot. In the back of my mind ran the thought: "God is bringing David home. I don't want to see him! Help me!"

When he arrived he looked very sure of himself and said, "I'm giving you another chance to prove your good will towards me." I swallowed the sharp words on the tip of my tongue and cried inwardly, "Lord, You can't expect me to endure this!" Somehow I stayed calm.

David retired to the bedroom where he spent the day resting and reading while I cleaned house and prepared a big dinner. Under my breath I recounted angry arguments about the unfairness of our situation. David had not said a single word of apology for his own behavior and obviously laid all the blame on me. I was seething with resentment, but underneath the turbulence was a quietness that somehow made it all bearable. As if a strong hand was keeping me in balance.

For two long days David remained behind the closed bedroom door, emerging only to preside at the dinner table and to watch a little television with the children. I remained calm on the surface, to my own amazement, and when he left for California before dawn on the third morning, I helped him pack the car and prepared a thermos of iced coffee.

"Have a good trip." I forced a smile. The self-assured mask on his face was still maddening to look at.

"Thank you," David's eyes met mine for a split second. "You've been almost pleasant these two days."

I was suddenly trembling. "If I'm different, it isn't me—it is God."

"Maybe so," David shrugged and turned the key in the ignition. At the end of the driveway he turned to smile and wave.

Back in bed all my pent-up emotions came out in a torrent of hysterical tears. Pounding my fists against the pillow I cried, "I can't stand it—it isn't fair—don't expect me to live the rest of my life like this. . . ."

David was gone for two weeks, and I alternated between despair and hope. When the children were asleep I allowed the tears to flow freely, pleading with God and reading my Bible with aching eyes, blinking to see the words clearer through the veil of tears. Gradually the roller coaster of emotions gave way to a calm acceptance of the inevitable. Life with David was not what I wanted, but if God was in charge, somehow it would work. "But please, God, change David soon, or change me so that I can bear it easier," I pleaded.

When David walked into the kitchen one morning in time for breakfast I looked at him and knew that something *had* changed. My dislike for him had faded. He was hugging Christine when his eyes met mine, and I felt a wave of warmth.

When the children had gone outside to play David talked eagerly between mouthfuls of food. Things didn't look good in California. There was a recession in the construction industry.

"We'll go to Green River and wait for an upswing in the national economy," he said. "I've already called dad. The lumberyard is doing fine and new industry has moved into the county." David looked confident, but I felt a pang of distress. Green River held painful memories. Then I reassured myself. With God in charge things were bound to work out for the best, wherever we went. Perhaps God was taking us back to the scene of our greatest suffering in order to bring about a new beginning in our marriage?

Chapter 5

Green River, Missouri

My father had aged and was pleased to see me back. I had gained valuable experience over the last five years and felt confident about the future of our business. Green River had prospered and seemed stable in spite of the fluctuating fortunes of the national economy.

My optimism received a bad jolt when the manager of the lumberyard quit as soon as I started back to work. With an associate he opened up a new lumberyard across town, taking along some of our old customers. Dad took the development with stoic calm; he had other business interests and could weather a temporary setback. My situation was worse. In order to make a living for my family I would have to raise the profit margin.

The only available rental in town was the old two-story house up the street from my parents, that had once belonged to my grandfather. No one had lived there for several years. I felt it almost as an ill omen, but with Sarah and the children pitching in, we scrubbed out old cobwebs and accumulated dirt, and hung our most cheerful pictures over the torn and stained places on the walls. Sarah was unaware of my despondency and chatted happily about plans to paint and renovate the old structure.

"It was once a showplace," she exclaimed. "We'll make it come alive again."

I was too exhausted to answer. At dusk I broke out a bottle of Scotch to chase away my sense of dread. Sarah and the children went to bed in the camper out in the yard while I tried to rest on the old blue couch that had once been my grandmother's prize possession.

Around midnight I woke up with violent stomach cramps. For the next forty-eight hours I could neither stand up nor straighten myself out. The agony was emotional as well as physical; I suffered a severe sense of depression. On the third day, with pain still gripping my insides, I returned to work at the lumberyard. I would not let myself be beaten by adverse circumstances. I still believed what I had told my old pal Mel Goodson when I last saw him in California, "We may lose a battle or two, but we'll win the war—there are blue skies ahead!"

I threw all my efforts into the business. A canvass of the community and old customers who were no longer buying from us, brought encouraging results. I reorganized and updated our inventory and hired a new manager. We were moving ahead, although I felt as if I was pulling a heavy load uphill all the way. My personal life was a daily trial, and hung like a threatening cloud over the future.

The only way I could relax after a hard day at work was to stop at the tavern or a restaurant for supper and a few drinks. Sarah spent most of her time away from home with church activities. Meals were seldom on time and the children went unattended. To top it off, she had started writing for religious magazines. Her religion was obviously a lasting fad.

When at last she began to take better care of things around the house, it was obviously under duress and it no longer mattered to me. I only wanted to be left alone. Co-existing with her was becoming unbearable.

An open break would upset the children and my parents. Sarah had reluctantly agreed to sleep in another room, but, after a few weeks, she insisted on moving back in with me—and I was forced to move upstairs. Sarah objected, claiming she *wanted* to be near me, but her words had a hollow ring. As long as I had known her I had detected cold rejection underneath an easy flow of words about love. Her attitude towards me had always been critical—and now, combined with pious platitudes of Christianity, it was more than I could stomach.

Fortunately, Leif at eleven and Andrew at eight openly preferred my company and spent as much time as possible at the lumberyard. I gave Leif his first driving lessons behind the shed where I had first learned to drive. Andrew was quick to learn how to sort nails or stack short pieces of lumber. He walked beside me with swaggering, grown-up steps, talked in a deep voice and considered himself a member of the working crew.

Ten-year-old John preferred to stay home with a book or roam the woods with the dog I gave him for his birthday. Christine was only seven and clung to her mother most of the time. It would be a while before all four of them were mature enough to be with me on a permanent basis.

Our second summer in Green River, Sarah and the children were invited to visit her family in Norway. I welcomed the reprieve. While they were gone I would move my things out of the house and establish my residence in the hotel.

I told Sarah of my decision just before they left.

"You have some good qualities," I tried to make my parting words as pleasant as possible. "But you've made my life very difficult. I find it impossible to go on living with you. When you return from Norway I will have moved out."

Sarah had been wiping the stove after supper, now she turned to me. Her brown eyes were hard. "Without me here as a scapegoat maybe you'll have to see that your biggest problem is between you and God."

"Shut up!" The words slipped out. Sarah had an uncanny way of prodding me to anger. "I'm sorry you've fallen for that Christian garbage. If you hadn't been such a fool, maybe we could have made a go of it." I emptied my can of beer and got another one from the ice box. "One of these days I'll prove that you and all Christians are nothing but phonies—I'll be another Saul of Tarsus, wait and see!" I pounded the table with my fist.

Sarah bit her lip, but I saw her quick, superior smile. "Don't you remember what happened to Saul?" Her voice was sickeningly sweet, and I felt sudden blind rage. She had trapped me into making a poorly-chosen comparison.

"Saul was a fool to join the Christians he had persecuted," I yelled. "I'll die before I change my mind!" Gulping down my beer I left the room without another word.

SARAH   *Green River, Missouri*

David and I seemed closer at first, then a barrier hardened between us. He was angry whenever I mentioned God or Christianity and scolded me for turning the radio to a Christian station or leaving Christian magazines or books around where he could see them.

"Quit pushing!" His eyes were dark under furrowed brows. "I can never accept the idea that man is evil and needs a 'savior.' I have to believe that man is basically good, or else we'll never get this world straightened out."

His words caused a tight knot of fear in my stomach. David could not see his need for God. What circumstances would have to come to open his eyes?

Green River was quiet and peaceful. The children found new friends in school and enjoyed the freedom to roam through the small town and surrounding woods and fields. We attended the old brick Methodist church on the corner, and I taught Sunday school and sang in the choir.

An upstairs room with a view of distant hills became my study, and I dug out the typewriter again. When I sold a couple of articles to Christian magazines, David muttered, "We can sure use the money!" I took his remark as an approval of my activities.

Work at the lumberyard took most of his time and his evening visits to the local taverns or cocktail lounges were increasing. When he came home he usually tried to ignore me. Our lives were once again taking on the nightmarish aspects I remembered from Arizona before our breakup.

I believed that God was in charge and that eventually David would change, but why did it have to last so long? It was hard to understand why the children and I were permitted to suffer for David's stubborn attitude. It didn't seem fair.

One day I chanced on a small book by Roy Hession, *Calvary Road*.[1]

One paragraph caught my attention. It stated that although it is wrong for someone to hurt you, God intends for the hurt to serve a good purpose in your life.

I left the book on the kitchen table and got up to fix myself a cup of tea. Spring had come again, and from the window I could see the sun shine over the yellow stubble of last year's wheat harvest. My thoughts were on what I had just read. If it was true, then it was no accident or oversight on God's part that I was suffering right now. Something very good would come from it in the end. It was the same principle I had discovered in my New Testament back in Arizona—that *all* things work together for good for those who love God and are His.

I leaned my head against the window pane and felt the sun warm me. How could I have forgotten that God would never let me suffer without good reason? I had allowed myself to indulge in useless self-pity. "Forgive me, Lord, and show me what You want me to learn through this." I reached for the little book and began reading again. Suddenly my pulse quickened. "You can't help your brother with the splinter in his eye until you get rid of the beam that protrudes from your own," the author quoted Jesus.[2] The beam, Hession asserted, is your criticism of whatever your brother is guilty of. You have no right to throw the first stone—you are never free from guilt yourself.

There was an uneasiness inside me. I was critical of David; did that make him the brother with a splinter in his eye while I had the beam of smug self-righteousness protruding from mine? It couldn't be. He was surely guiltier than I! Putting aside the book I started to prepare lunch, but the question still haunted me. "Are You trying to show me something?" I whispered.

The next day was Saturday, and the boys had gone to a movie. David was at the tavern—I had seen his car parked there—and I expected him to spend the evening. Already, waves of self-pity were mounting inside. I had looked forward to a special meeting at church. Instead I had to baby-sit with Christine.

At six-thirty, just as I was cleaning the kitchen after supper, David came in the door. I must have looked surprised, because he grinned, "You didn't think I'd be home early, did you? Always suspicious, always judging me in advance!"

He opened a can of beer and sat down at the kitchen table, spilling ashes from his cigarette on the clean table cloth. I could feel anger boiling inside. David was smiling broadly.

"Too bad you've turned into such a fanatic. Otherwise we could get along pretty well. . . ."

Suddenly the smoldering rage inside me exploded. "Shut up!" I heard myself yelling. "We never got along before I became a 'fanatic' and we wouldn't get along if I quit now. All these years you've been demanding and cruel, and I'm sick of it."

David was still smiling as if he was enjoying the scene, and I grabbed the nearest item, the empty bread basket, and threw it at him. The look on his face turned to bemused surprise. I rushed at him wanting to scratch the superior smile off his face, tear off the mask he had been wearing for so long.

He held out his hand to ward off my attack, and spoke calmly, as to an upset child, "Now, now, take it easy," but I was helpless to stop myself. Red streaks flashed before my eyes as my voice ranted on, harsh, ugly words. Somewhere inside was a rational me aware that my outburst was irrevocable. In ten minutes I had torn down whatever good the last two years had done in our relationship.

Out of the corner of my eye I saw Christine's pale little face as she clung to the door with both hands. I went limp. My mind was a gray void. In the silence after the blast I walked past Christine to the bedroom. My voice was hoarse and I could scarcely whisper, "I'm sorry!" Throwing myself face downward on the bed I only wanted to die.

Christine came in and put her small cool hand on my burning forehead. "Something bad got into you, mommy," she said. "You should ask God to make you nice again." I groaned and turned to the wall. How could I even get close to God again after what I had done?

David came to the bedroom door. "Don't worry about it; everyone is entitled to a few temper tantrums."

The front door slammed, and I heard the children's voices, Christine's high-pitched and excited, "You guys should have seen mommy scream and throw stuff at daddy. . . ."

I pulled the covers over my head and covered my ears. David put the children to bed. I heard him have a nightcap alone in the kitchen. Then he came to bed and within minutes was snoring peacefully while I tossed in the darkness.

Inside me was a gray void as if a clammy fog had descended on my soul. It was worse than nothingness. I had lost the awareness of the presence of God. Unless I could find my way back to the light I had lost, I wanted to die.

But how to find God now? My mind struggled to find a way. Could I sneak out of bed to a quiet corner of the house, throw myself face down and plead and cry for mercy? Or read my Bible until a light broke through? Or concentrate all my will power and lift my thoughts to Jesus Christ out of the darkness that surrounded me?

Even as I struggled to think of a way, I saw with agonizing clearness my own helplessness. I could do nothing to earn God's favor again. My inward struggle ceased and after what seemed like a long time, I became aware of a new quality to the silence around me, no longer a void, but a restful calm.

A thought pierced the darkness, as if a voice had spoken: *'You can do nothing to earn my forgiveness. The penalty for your temper tantrum and your hard-heartedness has been paid. Just as I've paid for David's rebellion. Only receive my love.'*

Warm tears trickled down my cheeks like melting snow into a spring brook. In the darkness beside me I could make out David's sleeping form surrounded by the faint aroma of stale liquor.

"I'm sorry," I whispered. "Forgive me for judging David when I've been guilty of something far worse. Forgive me my pride and my self-righteousness."

It felt as if a heavy weight was slipping from me. I was suddenly grateful for the ugly temper tantrum that had ripped my mask of "goodness."

"God loves me," I thought. "No matter how mean or ugly I am." Gratitude washed over me. David stirred in his sleep. "God loves you too," I whispered. The realization filled me with sudden joy. Some day David would be aware of it too.

Outwardly things continued to deteriorate rapidly. David ordered me to move out of the bedroom and the children were visibly upset.

"You and daddy don't love each other the way you should," John's brown eyes held reproach.

"You're right," I was aching inside. "But God is in charge of our family. It will work out in the end."

"I don't think daddy knows that," Leif shook his head.

"One day he will," I smiled at the four of them, huddled in John and Leif's bedroom.

"What if daddy leaves and gets a divorce?" Andrew's lips were trembling. He was more of a daddy's boy than the rest and held a fierce loyalty for David.

"That won't change God's plans," I said, outwardly calm. "Maybe daddy will need a time away from the rest of us. But God will work it out and bring him home." I wondered if it would come to that and shuddered at the thought. Andrew sighed deeply. "I just don't want to lose daddy," his voice cracked. "I'm glad we won't."

We were now leading separate lives under one roof, what the counselor in Arizona had called "the worst possible solution for the children." The emotional strain was hard on all of us.

One Sunday afternoon I was napping on my bed in Christine's room while David had taken the children to the creek. In a dream I saw myself as an old, wrinkled woman, lying immobile on a bed. Although I possessed the ability to get up, I had never stirred for twenty years, because I could not decide to rise up. Now it was too late. Hot tears flowed over my wrinkled, dry cheeks, while a sentence, like a banner, hung above me: "The Paralysis of Indecision."

The scene changed, and David was immobile on a bed while the children and I waited on him for twenty years. Whenever one of us strayed too far from his side, he called out, "Come back, or I'll get sicker!" The children were grown by now, and David and I were gray-haired. Another banner hung over the scene with the words: "The Tyranny of the Afflicted."

I woke up with a start. The afternoon sun shone pleasantly over Christine's books and toys on the shelves, but I felt a cold shiver as the words from the dream came back: "The Paralysis of Indecision" . . . "The Tyranny of the Afflicted."

"O Lord!" I spoke into the quietness of the room. "I'm undecided, and David is afflicted, and all of us are trapped!"

Burying my face in Christine's blanket, I sobbed. "Lord tell me what to do to break these deadlocks!"

In the silence the awareness came with sudden conviction; I had been hiding in Christine's room to avoid David's wrath, but I belonged downstairs with him. Resolutely I stood up and gathered my bedclothes. "Give me strength!" I trembled inside. David would be furious!

The pile of blankets were on my own bed once more when David came. "Your cruelty is appalling!" He stared coldly at me.

"I am your wife," my voice was pleading. "I belong here with you."

The sneer on his face almost made me waver. "You are forcing *me* to move!" In stony silence he gathered up his bedclothes and left the room. I heard his footsteps going upstairs. The confrontation had not done much good, I thought. Still I felt better.

Daily I asked God to show me what to do next, but whatever I did, David was always angry. My messy housekeeping had always been a source of complaint. Now I tried to improve. I rose early to prepare David's favorite breakfast—bacon and eggs with hot biscuits—but he staunchly refused to eat. I made sure his shirts were ironed and his socks back in the drawer before he had time to holler for them. I even scrubbed the old house from attic to cellar, painted the fireplace, and made new curtains for the living room. I thought he would be pleased, but he only accused me of putting on the role as super-housewife just to irritate him.

When school let out for the summer the situation became intolerable. Leif and Andrew sneaked off daily to the lumberyard without doing their chores, and when I reprimanded them, Leif retorted, "Daddy is the boss around here; you can't order us around."

If only we could get away for the summer. My Norwegian cousin Einar stopped by on his way home from the university in California. "Why don't you spend the vacation in Norway?" he suggested. I felt a twinge of hope, but shook my head. "It is impossible. It would cost too much."

A week later a letter came from Uncle Thor, Einar's father. "We are having a family reunion in August," he wrote. "We will pay your way if you decide to come with the children."

Tears of gratitude stung my eyes. "Thank you, Lord," I whispered. "You knew I could not have endured much longer."

DAVID   *Green River, Missouri*

Alone in the old house I felt more depressed than ever. John's dog whimpered through the night. He missed his young master, and somehow the dog's misery accentuated my own.

I tried to work in the garden, but twisted my ankle when I stepped on a hoe the children had left on the ground. Painfully I hobbled back to the house and for three days was confined to the living room couch. Kept awake by pain I listened as the wind made strange noises in the attic and behind the walls. The eeriness haunted me.

Wherever I looked were reminders of my failure: Sarah's book left open, a sweater hanging over a chair. The children's baseball mitts thrown hastily on the coffee table. And the old house itself where I had come as a boy to share my dreams with grandpa. In the porch swing or by the fireplace in winter, we had built my castles in the sky. Grandpa had believed in me and encouraged me. We had both been convinced that someday I would do important things.

Now grandpa was dead, and I was lying in pain on his faded couch, staring at the torn and stained wallpaper. My castles in the sky had been blown away by the wind.

Depression hovered over me, depression so dark that at times I toyed almost longingly with thoughts of suicide. Still, my pain was not as strong as my will to survive.

I had postponed thinking of the confrontation with Sarah, but one day came a letter addressed in her familiar handwriting. I experienced almost physical pain as I read it:

"Dear David:

I could choose to stay in Norway, but I *want* to come back to be your wife. I don't want to live under your roof without your love—that is hell for all of us. So much is at stake. Please, can't we try to love each other?

Your wife, Sarah."

How could she put on paper something so removed from the hopeless reality of our situation? Deliberately I ripped the page and watched the pieces go up in flames in the large ashtray on my desk.

I could no longer put off the move to the hotel. Life with Sarah was torture, her actions unpredictable, always upsetting my balance. I longed for stability to my days. Only then could I function and face the challenges ahead.

The hotel was old. The rooms had tall ceilings and were painted dismal green, brown, and beige. Over the years the old structure had housed traveling salesmen and the homeless, husbands estranged from their wives, alcoholics holed up for an extended drunk. There had been several suicides. But the place had a reputation for comfortable beds and good, home-style food, and Kay, the proprietress, was a kindly woman with the ability to listen with patience.

Now she welcomed me, clucking her tongue in sympathy. "Sorry to see it happen, Dave. Such nice-looking children."

"They'll spend quite a bit of time with me here," I spoke confidently. "I'm sure they'll appreciate your good cooking. . . ."

She smiled and smoothed her gray hair. "They're always welcome. I gave you number seven, upstairs in the corner. It is quiet with the best bed in town."

The children's homecoming was still a week off when Mel Goodson walked into my office one afternoon just before closing time. "I'm on my way to Denver," he grinned. "Thought I'd stop by."

Seeing him was a tremendous relief. "Welcome, cousin," I shook his hand. "I'm holding the fort, but in need of reinforcements!"

"Sergeant Goodson at your service!" Mel touched the rim of his sun visor in a smart salute, and we laughed together. I hadn't really laughed for weeks.

Over dinner I filled him in on the latest happenings on the home front. Mel understood. He was having similar problems. Mary had moved out six months ago, informing him that unless he stopped drinking, she would not be back. "So I joined AA and stayed dry for four months," Mel smiled sadly. "Until Mary let me know that she didn't like the 'dry' me any better. Now she wants a divorce." He lifted his stinger on the rocks. "I have decided to practice moderation. My new motto is: Drink less and enjoy it more."

"It seems we've both had the misfortune of marrying strong-willed women," I sighed.

"They would have invented Women's Lib if it wasn't already there," Mel chuckled. "Nevertheless, I'm convinced there are blue skies ahead, cousin. Good will triumph over evil in the end!"

With Mel around, the days went by with less tension. Even the constant noise in my ears subsided somewhat.

SARAH   Vestfjord, Norway

Cousin Einar was at the airport in Vestfjord. "Welcome home!" He hugged me and I wanted to cry and laugh. The United States and Green River seemed like a nightmare while this was reality. The gray mountains where heather bloomed, the familiar smell of fish and salt sea and Uncle Thor's nets hung to dry by the boat house.

Uncle Thor and Aunt Eldrid had not changed. "Welcome home!" They touched Andrew's and Christine's blond hair carefully. "How they resemble their grandparents!"

We stayed in the little house that had once been grandmother's. Christine and I shared the bedroom where I had slept often as a girl. Our window towards the fjord stood open and screenless letting in the fresh smells and the light of the northern summer. The familiarity of it all made me ache inside. This was where I belonged.

Day after sunny day my children explored the islands and mountains that had been my playground. Leif and John soon learned to row the boat and proudly brought home fresh-caught fish for dinner. "Why didn't you tell us about the caves on the island?" John looked at me with reproach. "Did Vikings hide out there?"

"I don't know," Uncle Thor answered for me. "But we know for certain that they sailed this fjord. . . ."

"Wow," the boys were awed.

In the forest behind Uncle Thor's house we found the hidden sunlit glades where wild raspberries and blueberries grew in profusion just as I remembered. Smaller than the domestic varieties, their taste was exquisitely sweet. Never had anything tasted so delicious in the years between. We returned to the house with mouths and tongues colored purple and our baskets filled to the brim. Aunt Eldrid served the berries fresh with cream or thick, yellow vanilla sauce—the favorite dessert of my childhood.

At suppertime the bells from the old church on the headland tolled out across the still fjord. The day was not yet over—the sunlight lingered in the northern summer night. The almost transparent dark did not come till near midnight. I could not—would not—sleep until the last of the day was gone, then I would wake up a few hours later when the sun returned from its short dip below the horizon. I wanted each sun-filled happy day to last forever.

The children didn't mention Green River or David. Andrew had not cried once since we left. I rested each night without the anticipation of unsteady footsteps in the dark. When the first bundle of letters from David arrived, Andrew and Christine were immediately tearful again, and I felt depressed. Green River was no phantom, and I had a return ticket to go there. Returning would hurt more, like going back into a dark, cold cave after having discovered the sun warm and beautiful outside.

At times came the strong suggestion that I ought to stay in Norway. If I was the free agent David so often referred to, there was no good reason why I should go back to expose myself and the children to continued pain. Finding work in my old profession would be easier in Norway than in the United States, and the welfare state with socialized medicine and pension plans offered greater material security instead of the uncertain future awaiting us on the other side of the Atlantic Ocean.

When the thoughts came I pushed them away. I was after all, *not* a free agent, since I had committed myself to be David's wife twelve years ago. Disregarding that commitment meant ignoring the specific instructions I had found in God's Word. Yet doubts persisted. Was I absolutely certain that God's Word was reliable? Wasn't it far-fetched to believe that God could change the mess in Green River into something good? Wasn't it more logical to assume that He had brought me to Norway and wanted me to stay there?

One night I could not sleep and was startled by three bats who flew in my open window and circled the bedroom looking for escape. Their wings and small bodies hit the walls in their desperate tries to return to freedom. Time after time they flew right by the open window without realizing it. I could tell by the frantic flapping of their wings that the small creatures were getting weary. When at last they disappeared out into the silvery summer night, I felt immense relief. "O God," I whispered. "Don't let me be trapped like that. Show me *Your* way to freedom."

Peace replaced my doubt. I *knew* in my heart God's way to freedom for me. The words I had read in my Bible months ago came back with renewed force: ". . . the Lord's command, is that the wife should not leave her husband." [3]

"I won't." The assurance swelled within me. "I trust You!"

In the morning Aunt Eldrid carried our breakfast tray out on the terrace overlooking the fjord. The children were already out in the boat with Uncle Thor, fishing. The surface of the water was without a ripple. The morning air was fragrant with the nasturtiums climbing the rock wall below us.

"You know there is always a place for you and the children here," Aunt Eldrid looked across the fjord instead of at me, and emotions were working in her face.

"Thank you." I was glad the question had been settled last night. "But right now my first commitment is to David."

"A wise attitude," Aunt Eldrid nodded with a hint of a smile. "Perhaps if you give all your time and attention to your husband and home for a while, things will be easier."

I stared openly at her. Aunt Eldrid had always been outspoken for women's rights, and had succeeded in combining an active career in local politics with homemaking and the rearing of children.

She smiled at the look on my face. "First things first. A strong woman has no more right to dominate a home than has a man. Be sure your strength doesn't threaten your husband. Especially while he is going through a difficult time. . . ."

Her gaze turned to Uncle Thor and the children in the white rowboat near the islands. There was a softness over her strong features.

"You're right," I nodded. "I've just begun to realize how important it is to take care of husband, home, and children first."

"I'm sorry you never learned that as a young girl." I thought I saw a hint of tears in her direct, gray eyes. "I guess I must take my share of the blame for always encouraging you in a career without mentioning the importance of learning your basics as a woman."

"Thank you for saying it now," I felt a new closeness between us. "I needed to hear that from you."

On our last day I rowed with the children to the island. While they searched for driftwood and shells, I found the narrow cleft in the rock where I had often sought solitude as a girl. The same white and pink flowers bobbed their tiny heads in the wind, and my eyes followed the massive silhouette of the mountain across the open expanse of the fjord. Gentle waves lapped against the gray rocks at my feet and seagulls swept overhead. The ache inside became a sob. How could it be that I did not belong here where I so longed to stay?

We said a tearful goodbye. Uncle Thor and Aunt Eldrid hugged each one of us. "Remember we love you . . . come back soon!"

Einar drove us to the airport where the big silver plane was waiting. When he hugged me Einar said, "Beware of the thin line between self-sacrifice and self-destruction. If you cross over you will not be able to help David or yourself." His eyes searched mine, then he smiled. "I believe you'll be all right. Take care!"

We had a last glimpse of the fjord, the islands, and the mountains. Then the plane swung out to sea. Norway became a blue line behind us, topped by ragged peaks, and slashed by fingers of the sea.

The steaming heat of Kansas City was hard to breathe and Vestfjord was already a dream I fought to remember clearly. At the motel the children ran for the phone to call David.

"Daddy will be glad to see you," Andrew said confidently. "It's been a long time now."

Fervently I hoped he was right.

DAVID   *Green River, Missouri*

I was in my room enjoying an after-dinner drink when the phone rang. The sound of Andrew's eager voice brought a sudden wave of emotion. "Will you meet us at the bus tomorrow?"

My throat thickened at the thought of facing Sarah. "No, son, I can't get away from the office."

The eagerness left Andrew's voice and I heard a sob. Hastily I sought to reassure him. "I want you to come to the lumberyard as soon as you get here, I'll be waiting for you."

I talked to the others in turn. Christine's soft little voice brought a lump to my throat. I had missed them more than I realized.

Before I could hang up, Sarah came on the phone. Tension knotted my stomach at the sound of her crisp, business-like voice. "Will someone meet us at the bus?"

"Yes, I'll see to it." I hung up feeling shaky, and poured myself another drink. Mother would meet the bus. I did not want to see Sarah.

When I called my parents, mother insisted, "You've got to meet your family, son. What will people say if you don't?"

People were already saying too much, and I agreed that it was best to give the appearance of normalcy.

The noon bus from Kansas City was always well-observed, but this time there was an unusual number of interested onlookers.

When the bus came to a whining stop near us, my throat thickened at the sight of my children's faces beaming through the window. They were first off the bus and yelled at the top of their lungs, "Daddy, daddy, we're home!"

Their strong, small arms clung to me. Mother embraced Sarah and I said, "Let's get your luggage and leave." Our welcoming scene was the center of attraction, and I shuddered at the thought of the endless versions to be told over the counters and kitchen tables around town.

Back at the house I put the suitcases in the living room and turned to leave. "You children can come down to see me at the lumberyard as soon as you change clothes."

Sarah stood still in the middle of the floor. Mother looked the other way to avoid the scene, and I said calmly, "I'm staying at the hotel."

Sarah went pale, and the children stared at me. Andrew's and Christine's eyes flowed with tears, John looked angry, and Leif's face was a blank. I meant to soften the blow, "I'm not mad at you or your mother. It is best this way and you can stay with me anytime you want." I started to leave. "I have a surprise waiting for each of you children at the office. I'll see you there."

Sarah's voice behind me was toneless, "What will happen next?"

"Why don't you wait and see?" I had not looked at her once and hurried to my car. It was time to get away.

SARAH   *Green River, Missouri*

When David had left, Christine hurled herself against me. "Oh, mom, I can't go on living like this!" Her thin little body shook and I wanted to cry with her, but steeled myself.

"Aren't you glad for our wonderful trip? God will make everything work out here at home too." I bent to hug her. "Now run along and change into your play clothes."

Grandma was still standing motionless in the middle of the living room. She tried to smile. "David loves you, Sarah, and he always will. He's just been terribly hurt." Her lips trembled. "We can only pray, and be as kind to him as possible."

Suddenly resentful I thought, "What about me? I'm hurt too. Who's going to be kind to me?"

Grandma touched my hand, and I felt her fingers icy cold in the sticky heat of midday. I thought, "God, she is suffering more than I am." My resentment melted. She looked so forlorn.

"We can't come to see you very often; David would misunderstand." Her eyes were pleading for my understanding. "But please let the children come to see us often."

"I will." I felt a wave of compassion as I watched her walk away, slowly, with stooped back and faltering steps.

Alone at last I sank down on the couch. My bags were still untouched in the middle of the floor. "I want to believe You're in charge, God, even in all this confusion." I struggled to stay calm. "Please help my doubts."

The children were playing with their friends outside, their voices sounding happy and normal. A quietness replaced the turmoil inside me. With David sleeping at the hotel, there would be less tension here at home. A turning point in our relationship was bound to come soon. In the meantime, this was the best solution.

Chapter 6

Davɪᴅ   *Green River, Missouri*

With the coming of fall rains and darkness my gloom deepened. I didn't enjoy drinking alone, but alcohol was a necessary tranquilizer to take the edge off the pressures of the day. I wanted the children with me as much as possible, but Sarah put obstacles in the way. In addition, bad weather kept the children at home; there was not much for them to do in the lumberyard or the hotel room. Nevertheless, Andy and Leif occasionally came with me on short business trips to nearby towns, and spent the night with me as often as Sarah would allow it.

Andy always carried candy cigarettes in his shirt pocket and held his can of soda just the way I held my can of beer. "I want to be just like you, dad, when I grow up." There was unmasked admiration in his blue eyes.

Leif was anxious to move in with me. "I like living with you; I'm too old to be mothered."

"We'll see, son." I hoped he would get his wish soon.

"You understand what a boy wants, dad," Leif winked. "You don't want to know where I am every minute of the day, and you know about cars and motorcycles. Mom just doesn't understand."

Sarah's attitude concerning the children's right to be with me whenever they wanted to was quite unreasonable, and in November I decided to take legal action against her. In my petition for divorce I asked complete custody of the children in order to protect them from the dangerous mental pressure of Sarah's fanatic religious beliefs. As soon as the matter could be settled in court I hoped that Sarah would have sense enough to pack her bags and return to Norway where she belonged. The children and I could build a better life without her.

SARAH   *Green River, Missouri*

With David out of the house I had hoped for greater peace. Instead, each day brought new difficulties. Andrew and Leif spent much time with David and resented my efforts to establish discipline at home. Leif was taking advantage of the situation; I discovered he was roaming around town when he had told me he was going to be with David.

David refused to talk to me face-to-face and sent word through an attorney that he wanted all four children each weekend, and the boys every afternoon.

"That's impossible!" I felt faint. "Tell him he can see them every second weekend. They are already torn emotionally, and we must have some time for a normal home life."

When the attorney had hung up, I pressed my hands against my temples. How could things have come this far? How could it keep growing, like giant waves tossing me about, threatening to crush me. Every day came a new blow. "I can't take it much longer," I moaned. "If You're really in charge, God, *do* something before we go under!"

All those promises in the Bible of peace and joy in the midst of troubles. I knew only glimpses of joy, glimpses of peace.

"Why don't I have it all the time?" I had been vacuuming when the attorney called. Now I picked up the power nozzle and pushed it over the rug. Peace was a gift, but it could only come in return for a surrender of all my worries and struggles into the hands of Jesus Christ. A total surrender—not a partial one.

I dropped to my knees by the couch. "O God!" I buried my face in my hands. "I have been carrying some of the load in my own strength. Forgive me. And please empty me of the pride that makes me want to be in charge. I *will* to surrender, Lord. Empty me of self and fill me with You."

I got up and resumed the vacuuming. The commitment I had just made was as final as the one I had made in Arizona two and a half years earlier. God had heard me then, and I was certain He had heard me now. I was not looking for feelings to prove it. I had allowed fears and doubts to upset me, yet looking back I could see ample evidence that God was in charge of my life. My suffering was caused by my own pride and rebellion. Only as I surrendered to God could He transform my pain into joy and peace.

That was what I wanted, at whatever cost. No more barriers between myself and God. I meant to give Him access to the innermost parts of me. I wanted Him to flush out every self-deceiving, or God-deceiving scheme I was clinging to. Steadily I pushed the vacuum cleaner over the rug. I had surrendered. The next move belonged to Him.

What followed was an unleashing of emotions, as if long-lost wells of pain deep within me had burst open. For three weeks it continued, waking me up in the middle of the night or overwhelming me with unexpected tears during the day. The process was similar to the one I had experienced in Arizona, re-living old guilts, except this time the hurts were deeper. Often I cried without knowing why, except that through it I was aware that old wounds were being healed.

One evening I went with a neighbor to a meeting in her church. The visiting evangelist spoke about the Holy Spirit and surrender. I sat transfixed in the pew.

"It isn't enough to simply ask God into your life. A lot of Christians stop there, and never come to know the true depth of love, joy, and peace God wants to give them. We must give the Holy Spirit access to our entire being. We must surrender our pride and our ego; allow the Holy Spirit to fill us."

He stopped speaking and began to sing in a rich baritone, "All to Jesus I surrender, all to Him I freely give. . . ."

My knees buckled under me as I stumbled forward to the altar. There the anguish poured out from the bottomless deep within me. I felt naked, stripped of all; and then, gradually, the raging ceased, as if calmed by a gentle hand, or as if oil had been poured on an angry sea.

In the absolute stillness something like a warm rain fell from above, suspending me, saturating me, in love and light and peace. I knew myself held in loving arms. Vividly I was conscious of my old circumstances unchanged: the separation from David, the children suffering, our uncertain future. Yet my eyes had been opened to a new dimension of reality. I could see God's love surrounding all of us. He was in complete control of our lives. I wanted to laugh at my old silly fears. My worries belonged to Him. I was safe and could rest in His perfect peace.

When I got up from my knees most people had left the little church. My neighbor was waiting by the door and put her arms around me. "You left some of your worries up there, didn't you?" I nodded. The intensity of what I had just experienced was too vivid for words.

Before going to sleep that night I read once more the words that had suddenly become so real to me: "Don't worry over anything whatever; tell God every detail of your needs in earnest and thankful prayer, and the peace of God, which transcends human understanding, will keep constant guard over your hearts and minds as they rest in Christ Jesus." [1]

The peace stayed solid within me for the next couple of weeks. If a question or doubt came, I only needed to remind myself that God was in charge. The problems continued but no longer concerned me. Our money was low, but just as we needed it, several checks came in the mail as payment for stories I had written. When we ran out of wood, a truck arrived with a new load before the stove died out. Grandpa had sent it without being asked. Stuffing newspapers in cracks where the icy November wind blew through the walls, we were warm and cozy by the fireplace. "God is taking *good* care of us, isn't He, mommy?" Christine snuggled close to me.

Then one morning, Ron Willis, the attorney, called to tell that David had filed for divorce and asked custody of the children. I felt the blood drain from my face, and fear shattered my peace. "It couldn't happen. God wouldn't allow it—or would He?"

"Can David get the children?" My tongue was nearly numb.

"There is a possibility." Ron's voice was businesslike. "If he can prove that your religious activities are emotionally harmful to the children, the judge might conceivably give him custody."

"O Lord!" My knees shook and I sank down on a chair. "What is your personal opinion?"

Ron chuckled, "If you were that much of a religious nut I wouldn't let my kids attend your Sunday school class."

I was relieved, but the fear would not let go.

"Don't worry," Ron tried to reassure me. "It is just as well this thing comes to a head. When it is over you can breathe freely and choose your own course for the future."

He hung up, and still in a daze, I sat down to write three brief notes. One to Pastor Borror in Arizona, the other to Jack and Lydia Morris, now in a theological seminary in California; and the last to Sue Ann Woods, my old neighbor from Arizona who had moved to Georgia where her husband had taken over the family farm. Sue Ann and Jim had both committed their lives to God a year ago, and their family was now on a solid footing. I thought they would understand my agony and know how to pray.

For the next two weeks I lived with fear and pleaded in vain for God to restore my peace. We were in December and the children wanted to celebrate Christmas. Somehow I went through the traditional preparations, fighting off the panic in the back of my mind; what if this was the last Christmas with the children in my custody?

Grandma and grandpa came for an early celebration before going on their annual winter vacation. "It is best if David doesn't know we came to see you," grandpa said anxiously before leaving. I closed the door after them and cried helplessly in my pillow. Our broken relationship was affecting so many others. Desperately I wished that it would soon be over.

The letter from Sue Ann arrived the next day. She wrote: "Why don't you come down to our farm over the holidays? Our kids would love to see yours again. The enclosed credit card is for your travel expenses. We feel this is God's way of providing for you. . . ."

Suddenly I yearned to escape the small town where David's presence and the pending divorce hung over me like a sword. The attorney secured the court's permission, and we planned to leave Christmas Day in the afternoon after the children had visited David.

DAVID   *Green River, Missouri*

We closed early on Christmas Eve to allow the employees time
with their families. After a lonely dinner at the hotel I drove
aimlessly through the deserted streets. The houses were lit for
Christmas, and I could see families gathered inside. Without
realizing it, I had slowed down outside Sarah's house. The tree was
lit by the front window, and I recognized the decorations the
children had helped make in years past. The fireplace was lit, and
Sarah and the children were by the piano, playing and singing.

A wave of self-pity engulfed me and I stepped on the gas. At the
tavern Christmas music blared from the jukebox. The air was filled
with smoke and noise. Paper poinsettias hung over the neon beer
signs behind the bar, and I drank deeply to shake my gloom.
Christmas had been bearable with the children. Without them it
was sheer desolation.

The evening faded into a haze. Vaguely I was aware that a fight
had broken out, and the sheriff came to remove the culprits. The
next thing I knew daylight was streaming in my window, piercing
my eyes with pain. I was fully dressed on my bed and it was already
9:00 A.M. I had promised to meet the children at eight o'clock at my
parents' house. Mother had put up a tree for us and left cookies and
a pie in the freezer.

A bottle of V.O. stood on the table, and I tried to swallow a drink
to stop the uncontrollable shaking. Immediately vomit filled my
mouth, and I lunged for the lavatory to let out the bitter stream.
Exhausted I fell back on the bed, my muscles aching and trembling.
It would be another half hour, at least, before I could hold any
liquor down.

Time passed on leaden feet till at last I dared to lift the bottle
with shaking hands and felt the jolt of liquid burn my throat. In a
few minutes the trembling of my muscles had ceased. I washed,
shaved, brushed my teeth, and bathed my eyes. It was already
noon. After one more shot of bourbon followed by mouthwash, I
felt and looked much better. My paleness could have been caused
by a touch of the flu.

The children were waiting in the driveway. I locked us in and lit the wood in the fireplace, then sank into a chair. The gifts were waiting under the tree, and as soon as I gave the signal, the children fell over them with shrieks of excitement. I had ordered large, expensive gifts, actually more than I could afford, but I wanted to make up for the pain they were suffering through our divorce.

Christine clutched her cuddly, stuffed Snoopy dog and climbed up on my lap, content to watch her brothers assemble their electric race car set. "Daddy," she looked up with hazel eyes troubled, "why don't you love mommy anymore?"

I felt a tremor in my stomach. "Your mother and I don't agree anymore about how we want to live," I spoke lightly. "But don't worry; I'll never stop loving you!"

"That's good, daddy." Christine settled back into my arms with a sigh of contentment. Her soft little hand caressed my cheek, and I looked at my daughter with a smile. A shadow crossed her pert face, and her small voice shook with sudden fear. "But daddy, what if you change your mind about loving me, like you changed your mind about loving mommy?" Sobbing, she buried her face against my shoulder.

Helplessly I stroked her soft blonde hair and murmured, "Honey, don't cry. I promise it won't happen."

Back at the hotel I had a quick drink and went to bed. Melancholy swept over me as I contemplated the unfortunate situation I was in. Sarah's cruelty was incredible. Depriving me of the company of my own children during the dreariest season of the year.

There was little to do at the office, and I spent most of my evenings in the bars, carefully avoiding the vicious circle of drinking that would take me to the hopeless impasse I had suffered Christmas morning. Alcohol was necessary to hedge against loneliness and depression, but I did not intend to let it overcome me again.

Thinking about the court confrontation with Sarah, I wondered if I had been rash in asking for custody of the children so soon. It would be wiser to let Sarah find out that she would be unable to handle the responsibilities alone. I was sure that after a few months the children would beg to come to me. My lawyer agreed to postpone the request for custody and go ahead with a simple divorce settlement. Our hearing was set for January 9 at 10:15 in the morning.

SARAH   *Oreola, Georgia*

Sue Ann's thin face had filled out, and her gray eyes held a new sparkle. "God is tremendous," she hugged me. "We're so happy."

Their 200-acre farm was on the bank of a quiet river, only fifteen minutes from Oreola, a bustling modern city of about thirty-thousand. Jim and Sue Ann were raising registered Duroc pigs for the new meat-packing plant in town. The sparkling clean farrowing houses were hidden from the main house by a grove of trees. The rows of pens held several hundred reddish brown pigs.

"It's a pretty efficient operation," Jim beamed with satisfaction. "And it makes selling real estate in Arizona seem dull by comparison."

The change in Jim was almost incredible.

"See what God can do?" Sue Ann winked at me. "You used to tell me there was no limit to His power. Now it's my turn to tell you!"

The family attended one of the largest Baptist churches in Oreola, and while the children were busy riding horses with Susie and Cathy and "helping" Jim with the chores, Sue Ann took me to a prayer-and-sharing group in town. There I met Naomi Holloway, the associate pastor's wife, a plump blonde with a contagious smile, and Audrey Kerns, a pretty redhead who led the fifteen-minute Bible study. Soon I felt as if I had known them forever. Sue Ann had already told them about my letter and prayer request.

"I think I know how you feel," Audrey's green eyes were compassionate. "I'm divorced and my ex-husband tried to take the children."

Naomi put her arm around me. "You're afraid of losing them, aren't you?"

I nodded, fighting back the tears.

"Don't you trust God?" Audrey's question was tempered by her smile.

"Of course I do!" I spoke defensively. "It is David I can't trust."

"Then you believe that David can do something without God's explicit permission?"

My face flushed. "I see what you mean."

"Think about it," Audrey's voice was soft. "Can you trust your children in God's care, even if David has custody?"

The awareness dawned on me. What a fool I had been. No wonder my peace had been replaced by fear. I had clung to the children as if they were *my* personal possession. "Forgive me, God," I buried my face in my hands and felt the trickle of moisture between my fingers. "The children belong to You. Do what is best for them, even if it means they must be with David." I felt physical pain as I spoke the words, as if at last I had cut an invisible umbilical cord binding the children to me. But the peace had returned.

"The fear is gone." I looked up. "I'm not even worried about the outcome of the divorce."

Naomi nodded, "Look out whenever the peace God gives you becomes upset. It usually means you are holding something back from God."

"I guess I have a lot to learn." I felt deeply grateful for my new friends.

"When the divorce is over, why don't you come back here to live?" Audrey looked as if she wanted me to take the suggestion seriously. I looked at the smiling faces around me and suddenly realized that the world wouldn't come to an end in the divorce court in Green River County, Missouri. Something akin to anticipation for the future stirred in me.

"Maybe," I mumbled, my throat suddenly choked. "If God makes it possible."

The old house welcomed us home, and I hummed a tune as I took down the ornaments from the Christmas tree. The phone startled me. It was Ron Willis. "David has changed his mind. He doesn't want custody. Just the divorce."

The gratitude welled up in me. "Thank God, Ron. That's wonderful."

Hanging up I repeated the words, "Thank God, thank God for letting me care for the children. Only don't let me forget again that they are Yours."

DAVID   *Green River, Missouri*

On the courthouse steps I buttoned my coat against the icy wind. It looked as if it was going to be a hard winter. I had waited outside the courtroom while our case was being settled. My attorney had represented me, and the whole thing was over in fifteen minutes. Now I was anxious to get away without running into Sarah.

At the table in a quiet corner of the hotel dining room I ordered a martini, then lit my cigar and tried to shake the depression. At least things would not be any worse from now on, I thought. Maybe they would be better. I had suffered enough emotional blows for a lifetime. From now on I would play it safe, no more deep personal relationships inviting pain.

It would be difficult enough to live in the same community as Sarah, having to avoid her daily. But I knew of no other way to maintain a close contact with the children. I stared out the window at the naked branches of the old oak tree in the parking lot. Failure. The word haunted me. I had always thought it happened only to people who were either stupid or careless. Yet here I was, no longer in control of one of the most vital areas of my life, my relationship to my own children. As long as they remained in the custody of the woman who had caused me endless pain, I was not free to pursue a life with my own family.

Snow flurries thickened outside. If it settled on the ground I would take the children sledding on Oak Hill in the morning.

The snow turned to sleet and rain during the night, and I was awakened by the phone. Leif's voice was breathless, "Dad, we're moving to Georgia. Can I stay here with you instead?"

His words came as a stunning blow. "When?" My mouth was dry.

"Saturday. Can't you talk the judge into letting me stay?"

Frustration choked me. "You better go with your mother now, son. I'll see what I can do later."

It had occurred to me earlier that Sarah might want to move to another community to escape the wagging tongues of Green River, but I had never suspected that she intended to take the children so far away that I could not see them daily.

Snow came the day they left. I walked through the rooms of the old house where piles of junk had been swept into the middle of the floor. The children's worn out tennis shoes and broken toys, some of my old books. I built a fire in the fireplace and sat on grandpa's old couch watching the last mementos of my broken life go up in flames. How could I go on living after this?

SARAH   *Green River, Missouri*

The white-haired judge looked perfectly cast for his role, but I kept thinking that we were only acting out a poorly-written soap opera. Any moment I expected reality to crash in and end our silly pretense. Instead, our marriage of twelve years was declared legally absolved, as if it had never been.

As in a daze I felt Ron take me by the arm and lead me across the courthouse square to the coffee shop. "That wasn't so bad," he smiled. "You are young. You have a whole life ahead of you."

"David may still come back some day. . . ." My voice trailed off and Ron shrugged. "It's your life. You can cling to any hope you like, but I think you're making a mistake. I've known David since we were kids. He won't come back."

Part of me wanted to believe him. The part of me that wanted to forget all about David. Still, in a corner of my mind I clung to what I had told Ron, that one day we would be together again. Not in a twisted, painful relationship, but sane and whole, able to accept and love each other. The words of the judge had changed nothing. I was still Sarah Van Wade, the mother of David's children. Somewhere, in a dimension untouched by the Green River County Circuit Court, I was still David's wife.

"Drink your coffee," Ron's voice shook me out of my reveries. "Remember, you are no longer David's wife. You are on your own, and responsible for the future of four children. Don't let them down."

Alone in the kitchen at home I stared at the snow flurries outside my window and fought a wave of despair. No matter how wrong

David was, I too had failed. *My* life and *my* marriage were broken. *My* children were suffering the consequences.

"O Lord," I put my head on the cold formica top of the kitchen table. "I've hurt David. I've hurt the children. I've hurt me. Forgive me, and teach me to be the woman I should be."

A single brown leaf clung to a twig on the walnut tree outside the kitchen window. "Just like me," I thought. "The old dead leaf still clinging. Why can't I let go and leave room for spring?"

The phone shattered the stillness. I recognized Naomi Holloway's voice. "We've been thinking about you this morning." She sounded bright and happy. "Audrey and Sue Ann are here, and we just wanted you to know that you're not alone."

"Thanks!" I felt suddenly lighter.

"There's a house for rent just three blocks from here," Naomi bubbled with enthusiasm. "Across the park from the church. Do you want us to put a deposit on it for you?"

"I don't know. . . ."

Audrey had taken the receiver. "You and the children need to get away from there. That little town is full of painful reminders."

She was right. In Green River I would always be "David's ex-wife." "Make the deposit." I felt a great relief as I said the words. "We'll leave as soon as we can get packed."

John and Christine were immediately anxious to go, while Leif and Andrew received the news with mixed emotions. "Leave daddy?" Andrew's lips trembled.

"He can visit you in Georgia, and you can spend part of the summer here."

Andrew brightened. "O.K. Let's move. I don't like it when people talk about our divorce all the time."

I called the moving van at once. For so long I had hoped for a miracle, that God would touch David and bring him back. Perhaps God had other plans.

I wanted to live a normal and quiet life with my children. Without any painful relationships. At thirty-five I was through with men. I belonged to God, and that was all I needed.

Chapter 7

Green River, Missouri

After Sarah and the children left I functioned mechanically, day after day, not looking further ahead than to the next hour. Painful memories surrounded me everywhere. I avoided the street where we had lived, but whenever I passed the school, the football field, or the baseball diamond, the faces of my children flashed before my inner eyes. I missed them terribly.

At Easter the despair caught up with me. For days I had been drinking continuously, fighting a sense of total failure and lack of purpose in living. Lying on my bed as dusk came to submerge me in darkness, I could not bear to face another hour.

Struggling to my feet I took out the small .32 automatic pistol from my dresser drawer. It felt heavy in my hand as I lifted it to my aching, throbbing head. My finger curled around the trigger. Nothing stood between me and the end.

A piercing thought cut the darkness of my mind: "Do you want your children to have a suicide for a father?"

"No!" The groan came from deep within me.

The hand holding the gun sank down. That avenue of escape was closed. All I had left to offer the children was my name, and I would not leave them with the shame of my self-inflicted death.

The bottle was on the bedside table. I held it with both hands as the liquid flowed into my throat and stomach, spreading a soothing glow. After several drinks I felt near normal again.

Days later I became aware that my outlook was better. There was a touch of spring in the air and business picked up. Soon it would be summer and the children would be with me for several weeks. In preparation I bought a boat and moored it at the Lake of the Ozarks. Each weekend I worked on it. Now I had something to look ahead to.

Mel sent me a book called *The World of the Formerly Marrieds*.[1] It made me realize that I was not the only divorced person who struggled with loneliness, guilt, and dejection. The author recommended a dose of self-acceptance and some new friends to break the pattern of defeat. Encouraged, I began to date occasionally. An attractive redhead became my most frequent companion. Laura was recently divorced, with three children. Unlike Sarah she did not challenge everything I said, but appreciated me for what I was. Neither was she demanding, and accepted our on-and-off relationship without promises for the future.

I decided to take her along on my trip to Oreola in June to pick up the children. The idea did not meet with the approval of my friend, Buddy Wilson, who regularly joined me for dinner and drinks now that his wife had left him. "You must really want to get Sarah's attention." He gave me a sidelong glance.

I protested, "You know I want nothing to do with Sarah."

"It sure doesn't look like it!"

The insinuation bothered me and to avoid an awkward confrontation at Sarah's house, I left Laura at a nearby motel while I went alone to pick up the children. They lived in a fairly new subdivision of Oreola, but the construction was shoddy and the hard-packed Georgia clay discouraged the growth of lawns and trees. I disliked the neighborhood at first sight.

A tall, dark-haired fellow with a too-friendly grin was there with Sarah and introduced himself as Russell Holloway, her pastor. He treated my children with obvious familiarity, and I had a strong urge to punch him in the nose. What business did he have with my family?

It had never occurred to me before that Sarah might show interest in another man. Of course she was in a vulnerable position as a woman alone with four children. I had anticipated that the burden of raising the children alone would be too hard for her, and had planned to take over custody myself at that point. Now it appeared that the situation might develop differently. The thought of another man as "father" of my children was repulsive.

Russell Holloway wore a wedding band, but the look in his eyes convinced me that he had an eye for lonely women. I only hoped that Sarah would not be foolish enough to fall for his line.

We picked up Laura at the motel, and the children were clearly unhappy to see her. Later they demanded an explanation.

"We already have a mother," John was firm. "We don't want another one."

"Then I don't suppose you want another father either?"

"Of course not." Andy climbed on my lap. "We like the one we've got."

Sarah   *Oreola, Georgia*

The life of a divorcee held perils I had not anticipated. There was the matter of credit. The gas and electric companies, the telephone company, and my landlord all demanded large deposits.

"But I've always paid my bills on time," I protested.

"Were the accounts in your name?"

"Of course not, my husband was the head of the household."

"Then as far as we are concerned, you have not established any credit."

The implication was only too clear. "As a divorcee you've proved you can't cope with something as basic as marriage—how do we know you can handle financial responsibilities?"

Naomi's husband came to my rescue and signed the application for a gasoline credit card. "Once you've established credit in your own name you'll be O.K.," Russell grinned and put his arm around my shoulder in a brotherly gesture. "Till then, be sure to let me know if you need any help." His even white teeth flashed in his slender face. "You have nothing to fear, Sarah. It's my responsibility as your pastor to look after your practical needs as well as your spiritual ones. That's what the church is for."

With most men I was tense and on guard, but I trusted Russell. He and Naomi were my Christian brother and sister. Almost daily I dropped by their house for morning coffee after the children had left for school. Their Christian love and acceptance provided a refuge from the buffeting I received in the outside world.

When enrolling the children in school, I had been asked to put a mark in the little square on the application blank where it said, "Parents: divorced." My children would now be looked upon as products of a broken home.

The manager of the nearest supermarket agreed to cash my personal checks, but suggested that I call him if I ever needed male companionship. "Don't be embarrassed. You won't be the first divorcee in that predicament." His blunt words and bold eyes made me blush, but I had learned a lesson. Never again would I volunteer information about my single status.

One morning my car refused to start, and a neighbor offered to check under the hood. Later his wife coldly told me to "lay off and do your manhunting elsewhere."

Hurt and tearful, I sought consolation in Naomi's kitchen. "I don't care if I ever know another man intimately," I confessed. "I've been bruised enough for a lifetime."

Only in the church community did I feel protected and safe and with my Christian friends, I gradually dared to relax some of my defenses.

Occasionally the children and I drove out to the farm to spend Sunday after church with Sue Ann and her family. The children had found a "big sister" in Joanie Stevens, a first grade teacher from Chicago who taught Christine's Sunday school class. Joanie dropped by the house several times a week to take the children to the park or the river.

All things considered, our new life was as good as could be expected, yet I was aware of a restlessness inside and a coldness, a reluctance to let anyone come close to me. I withdrew quickly from the touch when Naomi or Audrey put an arm around me, and one morning Andrew startled me by asking, "Don't you love me, mommy? Why don't you let me hug you anymore?"

David had often accused me of being emotionally frozen. Now his words haunted me. Even if I never wanted to give myself to a man again, I did not want to be frozen. My children needed my love. "Help me, God," I said aloud. "I want to be able to love."

Two days later I went with Naomi to a women's luncheon to hear a Christian writer from Florida. Dorothy Binford was an attractive woman in her early forties, and her words had an almost electrifying effect on me. With a soft voice and a radiant smile she confessed: "My biggest problem was that I didn't like to be a woman. I was a Christian 'neuter,' and closed my eyes to the fact that God deliberately made us male and female because He wanted it that way. Then I discovered that God wanted me to be a whole woman—whether or not I ever married."

My cheeks flushed and my eyes were riveted on the speaker. She looked so at peace, so thoroughly feminine in a wholesome way, different from anyone I had ever met before. It was difficult to believe she had ever been the cold and bitter woman she described.

"Only God can show you true womanhood." Mrs. Binford smiled and her eyes met mine for a split second. "Only then can you be the whole person He intends for you to be. Whole in relationships with others, with yourself, and with Him."

At home I threw myself on the bed and dared to admit what I had always denied: I had never *liked* being a woman. I had never been *glad* I was born female. I had never respected other women, but often thought of them as silly and empty-headed, and had wished I was born a man. As a little girl I had always wanted to prove myself in competition with boys, and as a teen-ager I had begun to think of myself as a "person," somehow a notch above the male and female delineation I thought only applied to the sex roles.

I shuddered as I realized that Christine was already following the same pattern. I had often heard her say that she wished she was born a boy, and she was always competing with her brothers, blushing with pride when they included her in a tough game.

"O God," I moaned. "I never stopped to think that You created me a woman because You wanted me that way. Help me to know what that means. Help me so that my daughter can grow up without the confusion and frustration I've always known."

The prayer turned the key to another hidden memory bank. As in Arizona and later in Missouri, long-forgotten hurts and guilts came welling up from the dark recesses of my subconscious. Now I saw myself with the boys and men I had known—always rigid, competitive, hurting, unable to love. How had it begun? Why did the hard crust first form? In self-defense? In fear of rejection?

Achingly, I saw the little girl I had once been, trying always to please my father, yet convinced that he would have loved me more if I had been his son. Looking back it seemed a silly notion, but it had always motivated me to try harder, to prove myself better than "just a girl."

While the children were in school I spent hours on my knees in the bedroom. My tears soaked the bedspread as I relived the hurts I had received, and the hurts I had inflicted. One by one I saw the faces of the boys and the men I had tried to love but always failed. Only as I asked God to forgive them—and me—and to heal the deep wounds within me, did a new peace and sense of relief replace my tension and pain.

"When will it end, God?" I was exhausted, but encouraged. At least I was not doomed to be an emotional cripple for the rest of my life. "Whatever it takes to crack the shell completely," I whispered with a shiver of anticipation, "let it come, God."

That night I dreamed that David moved back into the house. A mocking smile was on his face as he stood in the middle of the living room with a beer can in his hand. "I'm giving you another chance to prove your love for me." I woke up shaking, and the fear was paralyzing.

Audrey dropped by and found me pale and tense. "I'm scared," I confessed. "I don't want him to come back."

"So you are finally honest about it," Audrey gave me a quick hug. "I worried when you talked so piously about asking God to bring David home."

When Audrey had gone I wept bitter tears. "Forgive me, God. You know I don't love David. Help me. . . ." If I had been able to love him, he might have come out of his shell years ago. My hardness and crippled emotions had formed a wall between us. "O God, I've been so terribly wrong." The sobs racked my body.

After supper the phone rang, and I could tell by Leif's excited response that David was on the other end. He talked to each of the children, but didn't want to talk to me. I was glad. I could no longer pretend to be kind. If he would only leave us alone.

Audrey and Naomi came for coffee the next morning, and I confessed to them, "I'm unable to love. I'm not a whole woman. I want to be, but I'm afraid I'll get hurt."

Audrey was thoughtful. "Maybe the most difficult thing about being a whole woman is the vulnerability. To love and be loved and leave the protection of yourself to God."

I nodded. "The hard shell I'm hiding behind is self-defense; I want to let go of it."

"Then why don't you?" Naomi looked at me searchingly. "Your self-defense has proved to be a poor armor against hurt so far. Don't you think God can do a better job?"

I laughed in spite of myself. "Will you be my witnesses?" My voice was shaky. Naomi and Audrey nodded, and the three of us joined hands. In the stillness of the kitchen I felt the pounding of my own heart like a frightened bird flapping against the prison bars of its cage.

"Lord, take away the shield I've built around me. Set me free to love and be loved as the woman You made me and to trust in You only for protection." I felt the tears warm against my cheek, and a quietness inside told me that God had heard.

The next morning Christine climbed up on my lap at the breakfast table, and I discovered that I didn't want her to leave. I cradled her in my arms and smelled her hair, freshly shampooed.

"I love you, honey," I said, surprised at the strength of my own feelings. Christine wiggled loose and jumped down.

"Of course you do, mommy." She reached for her lunchbox and headed out the door. "I'll see you after school!"

I watched her skip down the sidewalk, her red dress a bright splash of color in the morning sun. The teen-age daughter of our neighbors came out of their house and smiled at her waiting boyfriend. They walked off holding hands, and I suddenly felt an intense longing for someone to take my hand . . . just like that.

At first, I did not understand what was happening to me. I was swept by sudden emotions: intense joy as I watched a beautiful pileup of puffy white clouds against the deep blue sky, or overwhelming sadness as I chanced to look at an old picture of my parents on the bookshelf. Tears sprang into my eyes as I realized how much I missed them.

I had always been able to control my feelings. Now their intensity—and variety—caught me by complete surprise.

"I can't trust myself any longer," I said to Audrey when she dropped by. "One minute I'm laughing, the next I'm crying; I'm as silly as a teen-age girl."

"You're thawing out," Audrey giggled and gave me a quick hug which immediately reduced me to tears again. "I like you better this way."

When she left I felt sudden panic. I was vulnerable now. Like a bird let out of its cage. The freedom was frightening. I was reacting firsthand to people and impressions, not filtering my responses through careful controls. I felt naked and exposed.

"O God, I'm scared," I whispered. "I love the way I feel, but I don't know how to handle it."

It was incredible, but the shell I had hidden behind was no longer there. I had read the promise in my Bible that Jesus Christ came to give us life more abundantly, but I had not anticipated *feeling* so alive. Like someone who has wakened from half-sleep, or as if I had been looking at life through clouded lenses, and now I suddenly saw and experienced it directly.

Over the next few days I felt pain and hurt more often than joy. Only a few weeks ago I had been relatively happy in my lot as a divorcee. Now my loneliness seemed unbearable, and the brokenness of our family an immense tragedy. I had been independent and self-sufficient, now I felt helpless and each minor crisis brought quick tears.

One morning the pilot light went out on our water heater. Cold water ran over the greasy breakfast dishes in the sink, and I felt as if a major disaster had overcome us. Nearly blinded by tears I dialed Naomi's number. Russell's voice, calm and dependable, reduced me to helpless babble once more.

He promised to come right over. "I'll have your water heater fixed in no time." Relieved I collapsed on the living room couch. Thank God for Russell!

The water heater was in the garage, and Russell lit the pilot without difficulty. I watched him from the doorway, aware of my swollen, red eyes, and flushed face. A wave of loneliness and self-pity swept over me. Russell was so strong, so capable. Why was Naomi the lucky one? He stood up and brushed dirt from his knees, then took me by the elbow and led me back into the living room.

"Now tell me what *really* hurts. Nobody cries like that over a water heater." His arm went around me, and the touch caused me to tremble. I blushed and hid my face against his broad shoulder. My feelings were unmistakable, and terribly wrong!

Firmly he lifted my tear-drenched face and his dark eyes seemed to look into the depths of my soul. I was sure he could read my secret. "I'm your pastor and friend. Let me help you, Sarah."

"No one can help me!" The horror of the situation hit me suddenly and the words spilled out. "God has thawed my emotions, and I feel sixteen instead of thirty-five. I even feel something for you! I want to be near you, and it's impossible!"

I expected Russell to look shocked. Instead, he pulled out his large, white handkerchief and wiped my tears carefully. His voice was kind. "I am glad you are honest with me. You see, I feel something for you too. I want us to be close; but don't worry, God will help us past the emotional turmoil into a solid relationship."

Had my ears played tricks on me? My heart was pounding wildly, and I looked into Russell's smiling eyes. Slowly he leaned forward and kissed me lightly on the lips. "Promise me you won't cry anymore. I'll be back to see you soon."

I watched him leave and my head was spinning. It had to be wrong—but why had God not stopped us? And why did I feel no guilt?

"I'm free," I thought. Not bound by fear or guilt. Free to choose between right and wrong. Delicious fantasies washed over me with an intensity I had not felt since I was a young girl. Half-heartedly I tried to push them aside. It was wrong to shamelessly desire Naomi's husband, but for so long my emotions had been numb. I wanted to savor the feelings for just a little while.

Sunday morning I sat on edge in the pew, aware of Russell's eyes seeking me out frequently from the pulpit. I was afraid our secret was written all over my face. At the door Naomi hugged me as usual. "Come over for pie and coffee this afternoon. I haven't seen you for days."

I blushed and mumbled, "I've been busy," and Naomi looked at me searchingly. Did she suspect something?

The children went with Joanie to the river and I was alone, torn between the desire to be near Russell and the fear of Naomi's probing eyes. The longing for Russell was stronger, and I almost ran the two blocks to their house.

We had coffee on the patio and talked idly about the weather while I savored the bittersweet mixture of feelings inside. When Naomi turned to me with her direct gaze and said: "What's wrong, Sarah? Is something troubling you?"

I blushed and stuttered, "It's the hard shell I used to carry around me, for self-protection. It's gone and it's frightening."

The air was suddenly tense. Three-year-old Deborah had climbed on her mother's lap, and Naomi glanced over her head at Russell and then at me. "I'll pray that God will help you through the frightening part."

In the awkward silence I felt a veil being drawn between Naomi and myself. Her round face looked less attractive now that her eyes were clouded by suspicion. Anger and resentment stirred in me. I could see clearly what I had heard rumored before: Russell and Naomi's marriage was unhappy, and it was her fault. Her voice had a sharp edge as she spoke to him, and her eyes looked at him coldly, without appreciation.

At home I bemoaned my tragic fate. "O God," I sobbed. "Why does she have the right to be with a man she doesn't love? It isn't fair."

Audrey came the next morning, and I could no longer hide my secret. She grew pale. "I was afraid something like that would happen, now that you're out of deep-freeze. Just remember that God melted your barrier. He won't let you down."

"I wish He would take away some of these feelings."

"How else do you expect to develop self-control?" Audrey's green eyes became misty. "I know you're going through a rough time. Call me when you need a shoulder to cry on."

Later I looked up the word self-control in the Bible. It was listed under the fruits of the Holy Spirit, as something that would develop and grow in the life of a Christian, not something that could be put on from the outside. Self-control, in the Christian framework, did not mean "control yourself!" but "allow yourself to be controlled by God, rather than by your emotions."

Self-control would be a meaningless phrase unless the self had the freedom to choose *not* to be controlled, I thought. "Thank You for this new freedom," I whispered. "You know I *want* to choose Your will. . . . Help me!"

Feeling a little calmer I sat down to my typewriter. Ten minutes later the doorbell rang, and Russell walked in without waiting for me to open the door. He carried my mail and wore a boyish grin. "I thought I'd save you a trip to the post office."

Self-control was not going to come easy.

"Cheer up," Russell laughed. "You don't look too happy to see me."

"I am, and I am not." My pulse was racing. "But I was just asking God to help me develop self-control. Every time I turn my feelings for you over to Him, they come right back. What am I going to do?"

Russell took my hands in his. The touch sent shock waves through me. "I'm glad you feel the way you do," he said softly. "I need you just the way you are."

"But Naomi. . . ."

Quickly he put his hand over my mouth. "If I had not been in the ministry, I would have divorced Naomi several years ago." He looked me deep into the eyes and I shivered. "Perhaps now the time has come."

I drank in his words. It was almost too good to be true.

Russell pulled me close. "Let's thank God for bringing us together. He alone knows what the future holds."

I leaned against him. "I was afraid I was doing something terribly wrong."

"I love you for your sincerity," Russell kissed the top of my head. "But don't limit God. His ways are higher than our ways, and His thoughts are higher than ours."

He was quoting the Bible but I had never thought the verse meant that God's ways and thoughts were higher than our interpretation of His commands. Now I felt a wave of relief. Russell was a minister. He understood God's Word and would never go against it. Happiness soared inside me.

Russell released me and pulled a large manila envelope from his briefcase. "This is a paper I hope to get published some day. Would you look it over and comment on it from a writer's point of view?"

"I'd love to—I'm just glad you need my help."

"God sent you to me because He knows what I need." Russell's arms went around me. "Naomi isn't interested in my work."

Eagerly I clung to him, then panic hit and I pulled away. "Let's wait till God makes it legal." My breathing was heavy. "You are still Naomi's husband."

Russell looked pained. Slowly he let go of me. "You are right. We'll wait."

Watching him leave, the happiness ached inside me. "O God, make it soon," I whispered.

I couldn't wait to share my joy with Audrey. She was silent for a long time, fighting back tears. "Oh Sarah," she hugged me. "I know God moves in mysterious ways, and Russell's marriage has been failing for years, but I hoped you would be spared the agony of waiting."

"I don't understand what you mean."

Audrey bit her lip. Her slender, ringless hand played nervously with a lock of red hair. "I guess I should tell you that I've been in the same situation for three years now."

"Three years?" I struggled to comprehend the meaning of Audrey's words.

Her cheeks flushed becomingly. "He is in the ministry. . . . His wife is a Christian. . . . God is teaching us to trust and wait patiently."

"For what? Why doesn't he get a divorce if God has brought you two together?"

The blush had left Audrey's cheeks. She looked pale and shook her head. "He doesn't believe in divorce. We believe God will solve it some other way."

The awful implications were slowly sinking in. "You mean through his wife's death?"

"Perhaps." The green eyes were darkened by pain. "Only God knows."

An icy chill made me shiver. Thank God, my situation was much simpler. Russell wouldn't hesitate. I was sure of it.

Our relationship occupied most of my time and thoughts. I looked forward to his daily visits as fervently as a prospective bride and yearned for the day when our feelings could be displayed openly.

A careful search of the Bible had convinced me that a physical relationship between us was forbidden. Under no circumstances did I want to spoil God's perfect plan for our future by disobeying Him now. It was difficult enough to understand why He would permit us to be "spiritually engaged" while Russell was still married. Occasionally I felt pangs of doubt and guilt, but Audrey had told me of others who were going through the same experience. The men were in the ministry or prominent lay leaders in churches. I told myself they could not all be wrong.

Russell and I always prayed together and read the Bible. We thought some passages spoke directly to our situation: "And I will bring the blind by a way that they knew not; I will lead them in paths that they have not known. I will make darkness light before them, and crooked things straight. . . .";[2] "Behold, I will do a new thing; now it shall spring forth. . . ."[3]

Our relationship was beautiful and pure. God had brought it about. It was a "new thing" and a "a way that we had never known before." God was not limited—not even by the old rules in His own book on divorce and re-marriage. It was just a matter of time before God would make our union possible.

In church and with Naomi I had learned to hide my emotions. I resented her "right" to occupy Russell's house and the pastor's pew. I belonged there. In God's eyes Russell was *my* husband, I thought.

Had it not been for Naomi and David our happiness would now be complete. David still appeared in my dreams and occasionally invaded my happy fantasies of a glorious future with Russell.

Audrey reminded me, "You can't escape the fact that you were David's wife for twelve years, and that he is the father of your children. I'm afraid you'll always think of him at times and feel compelled to pray for him."

David called when school was out in June to say that he would come for the children. I had pushed away the realization that the children had to go with him. Now the old fears surfaced. Would they be safe? Would he drink?

The night before they were to leave I could not sleep. "God, the children are Yours, not mine," I prayed. "Go with them and take care of them." At last I felt peace and was able to rest.

Russell came to give me moral support during the farewell scene. David's face was a grim mask and he avoided my eyes. The car took off with screeching tires, and I stared after the children's smiling faces and waving hands through a mist of tears.

Inside the house Russell put his arms around me. "You'll miss them, but you've got me." He wanted to kiss me, but I pushed him away. My own reaction surprised me. "I think I want to be alone with God," I said slowly. "Please go!"

He looked hurt. "O.K. . . . If you don't need me, I'll leave."

I stared after him, trying to sort out my feelings. Never before had I wanted Russell to leave me alone. Something about it made me feel ill at ease.

Chapter 8

DAVID   *Green River, Missouri*

The children enjoyed being back in Green River with their old friends. At the hotel, Kay treated them like favored guests, and at least once a week we dined with mom and dad who were overjoyed to see their grandchildren.

The daily discipline was harder than I had anticipated. Sarah had not taught the children neatness and responsibility. Left alone at the hotel, they turned my room into a shambles, and I often returned to find them all jumping on my bed. At such times it was hard to keep my temper under control.

They obviously needed the firm hand of a father. As the boys grew older, Sarah would be less qualified to handle their problems. I shuddered at the thought that she might choose to marry again to provide them with a substitute father. A better alternative would be for me to keep them. I could hire a housekeeper and establish a home for us again.

To investigate that possibility I arranged for an appointment for us with the judge. "How long will it be before these children can choose to stay with me permanently?" I asked.

The judge looked at each of the children in turn. "The mother has custody. She will have to consent to any new arrangement. It will be several years before the children are considered old enough to make their own choice."

Frustration boiled inside me.

"Of course you may petition for change of custody," the judge continued, "if you have convincing evidence that the mother is unfit."

John took a quick step forward. "Your Honor, she's doing O.K."

There was a flicker of a smile on the old judge's face, then he shrugged and looked at me. "For the time being I think you will have to make your arrangements directly with the mother."

The system was so unfair, so obviously stacked in favor of Sarah. Talking to her would be useless unless she changed radically.

Leif wanted to remain with me till the beginning of school.

"I won't be any trouble, dad." He tried to look older. "I can take care of myself while you work, and I'll be company for you in the evening."

Leif, at twelve, was more independent than the other three. He liked to spend the entire day on his own, and I had allowed him to stay overnight with friends several times. I was certain that part of his motivation for wanting to remain with me was the greater amount of freedom he enjoyed in the small town. Still, having him here would knock the edge off my loneliness.

"That's a great idea, son," I smiled. "Provided your mother agrees."

"I'll talk to her," Leif was confident. "I can usually get what I want."

He dialed Sarah's number and spoke rapidly. "Mom, how are you? I sure miss you." He winked at me and I smiled. Leif was quite a salesman. "Will you let me stay here till school starts? Dad really needs me. Gosh, mom, I'm twelve, and you know I can get into a lot more trouble in Georgia than in this little town. Grandma and grandpa want me to stay too."

He turned from the phone. "Mom wants to talk to you," he was apologetic. "But I think she's gonna say 'yes.' "

Sarah's voice was nervous and loud and caused the familiar twinge in my stomach. "I don't want Leif to have too much freedom, but if you really want him, I guess I'll let him stay." Her voice sounded hesitant.

"Of course I want him. I'll send him down the first week of September." Leif let out a loud "Yippee."

I hung up before Sarah had time to say more. Hearing her voice had been painful.

With the other children gone, Leif and I settled into an easy routine. He was on his own till five o'clock, but often reported to me at the lumberyard during the day. I figured if he got into any kind of mischief the news would soon reach me.

We had dinner together at the hotel or at mom and dad's. Afterwards we watched television in the hotel room, or Leif went with his friends to a ball game or the show. I enjoyed his company and we had some good talks.

"You know, I like your way of life better than mom's," he often told me. "You're free and you do what you like. It's a man's life, and I'm too old for mothering."

"Would you like to stay with me through the school year?" I had considered the idea seriously.

His face lit up. "Gee, dad, that would be great!"

I submitted a petition for the change of custody, stating that a boy of twelve needed the companionship and guidance of his father. Hopefully, Sarah would not make a fuss.

My optimism had been misdirected. Sarah called late one night and was almost hysterical. "I want Leif home immediately," she sobbed. "If I'd known you would pull this trick on me I wouldn't have let him stay."

There was no use arguing. "I'll put him on the plane," I consented. "But I'm sorry you want to deprive us of a relationship that we both need."

Leif had tears in his eyes.

"I guess that's it, son. Your mother insists that you come home." I fought to hide my disappointment.

"Will you ask the judge again?"

"Sure," I slapped him on the shoulder. "And if things get too rough in Georgia, you can always come here."

"Thanks, dad." Leif smiled tremulously. "Don't be too surprised if I turn up soon."

I put him on the plane the next day and my hotel room seemed lonelier than ever. There was no sense in pursuing the petition for custody with Sarah opposing it. The judge would obviously side with her.

I told Buddy Wilson what had happened, and he shook his head. "You sure go to great lengths to keep Sarah riled up," he said.

"If only she'd let me pursue my own interests."

Buddy's round, perspiring face broke into a wide grin. "That's what you keep saying, but you act like you want to make sure she won't forget you."

"That's an interesting point—but you're wrong." I was suddenly irritated.

"So why don't you make up your mind? Go down to Georgia and have it out with her, or forget about it and start building a life of your own."

Buddy's red-rimmed, watery blue eyes were sincere, and it dawned on me that he was right. I had spent too much time reacting to Sarah. It was time to concentrate on my own future.

SARAH   *Oreola, Georgia*

The house was terribly empty without the children. I had hoped to catch up on several writing assignments. Instead I moved restlessly from room to room. What had happened to the peace I had felt a few months ago, even in the midst of the divorce?

Russell came daily, and my emotions were on a continual roller coaster, soaring heavenward when he was with me, and plunging to near despondency when he left. Joanie came one afternoon and barely missed running into him. She looked around the quiet house and plunked herself on the couch.

"Tell you what," her brown eyes sparkled over her upturned, freckled nose, "my roommate has moved, and I'm rattling alone in that big apartment. How about letting me move in here? We can split the rent, and when the kids come back I'll play big sister."

For a moment I was torn. Having Joanie meant less opportunities to be alone with Russell. On the other hand, my emotions were almost getting out of hand, and I feared that I might be tempted to do something foolish.

"That's a great idea," I smiled at her. "How soon can you move?"

Joanie seldom walked, she skipped or ran, and her enthusiasm usually bubbled into whistling or singing. The house was suddenly full of life, but that did not remove the restlessness inside me. The double life I led was wearing me down.

I lived only for the future with Russell. Most of my life, it seemed, I had lived like this. Either clinging to memories of the past, or hope for the future. Only once, a few months ago, had I glimpsed what it meant to live in the present. It had been glorious. I had felt so alive, and Jesus had been so real. Now I was right back in the old pattern. Even the presence of God seemed to have faded. I still believed in Him as strongly as ever, but my suffering was now almost as intense as before I knew Him.

Why did not God break the deadlock we were in? I complained to Audrey who smiled sadly. "Are you willing to accept whatever time plan God chooses?"

"As long as I don't lose Russell in the end." Fear tugged at me.

Audrey looked suddenly worn. "Can you pray for God's perfect will in yours and Russell's life," she spoke slowly, "regardless of what that may be?"

Her words stayed with me long after she had left. Could I pray for—and accept—God's will, even if it meant that He would heal Russell's marriage and leave me alone once more? "God, You wouldn't do that to me," I sobbed with sudden pain.

Opening my Bible I found a verse Russell had underlined for me: "For I know the plans I have for you, says the Lord. They are plans for good and not for evil, to give you a future and a hope. In those days when you pray, I will listen. You will find me when you seek me, if you look for me in earnest." [1]

We had been so sure that the good plans were for us together. Now I stared at the words in anguish. "If that isn't Your plan, God," I whispered, "then You must have something else in mind that is good, even better. O God, Your will be done, not mine!"

Being in church, with Russell on the platform and Naomi in the pastor's pew, was torture.

"Let's visit another church," I suggested.

Joanie looked at me a little strangely. "What's the matter? Why are you so touchy when we're in church?" Her eyes would not let go of mine. "Why don't you visit Naomi anymore? And why does Russell bring your mail here every day?"

I swallowed hard.

"I don't like it, Sarah," Joanie's voice was firm. "Gossip starts easily, and it is no secret that Russell's marriage is a little shaky. There have been rumors about him and another woman once."

"I'm sure they were unfounded." I bit my lip.

"Just assure me that any rumors about you and Russell would be unfounded as well."

Sudden tears stung my eyes, and Joanie threw her arms around me. "I'm sorry, Sarah," she said softly. "But I love you and I don't want you to be hurt."

"I'm already hurt. . . ." Suddenly I was sobbing like a baby in Joanie's arms. "I love Russell, and he loves me. He's planning to get a divorce and we'll be married, but the waiting is horrible."

Joanie had gone pale. "Oh my God," she whispered. "I'm so sorry."

"It will work out. It has to work out. God is in it."

Joanie shook her head slowly, "Honey, it can't work out. God does not permit adultery. He tells you not to covet another woman's husband."

"You don't understand." I searched for a convincing argument. "God allowed it with David and Bathsheba. David even murdered her husband, but God blessed their marriage and their son was the wise King Solomon."

Joanie's eyes were brimming with tears. "Honey, don't try to twist God's Word. He did not permit David and Bathsheba to do wrong. Only after David confessed his sin did God forgive him."

"We're not bound by the old laws anymore," my voice shook and I felt sick inside. Joanie didn't answer. "You know I don't want to do anything wrong." I spoke defensively. "I wouldn't feel this way about Russell if it were wrong."

Joanie pushed my hair gently out of my eyes, and I cried unashamedly again. "It can't be wrong," I sobbed. "It's the most beautiful thing that ever happened to me."

"I understand, Sarah." Joanie rocked me gently. "I had no right to judge you. Please forgive me. And I'll be glad to go with you to another church."

We went to a service across town, and I missed Russell horribly. Back home I stayed by the phone and when he called Joanie left the room discreetly.

"What's wrong? Are you sick?" He sounded anxious.

"We went to First Baptist."

"Will you be back where you belong for the evening service tonight?" There was an edge of impatience to his voice.

My heart was pounding. "I don't belong in your church, Russell," the words came with difficulty. "It isn't right for me to care for you as I do and appear in front of Naomi and the entire congregation. It is dishonest and sullies the beauty of our relationship."

Russell was silent and when he spoke, his voice was angry, "There is nothing dishonest about our behavior in church. I love you and want you for my wife one day. I need you near me now."

His words made me weak, then I pulled myself together. "Please let's play this by God's rules. I don't want to see you again until you're free to marry me. I don't want to be 'the other woman' in your life."

"You've got a twisted perspective of our relationship!" Russell was shouting in my ear, then he restrained himself. "O.K., we'll do it your way, because I love you. I'll be waiting for the day I can claim you publicly as my own."

"I'm waiting too." Sadness was choking me. "I pray it won't be long."

His voice changed, it was smoother now. "Naomi will wonder why you don't come to church. Is it O.K. if she and I drop by for a visit once in a while?"

"I guess so." His eagerness pleased me. "Just as long as you and I aren't left alone, even for a minute."

I hung up feeling relieved. No more make-believe, no more pretending indifference in front of others. I breathed deeply. Joanie had at least been partially right. I had no right actively to covet Naomi's husband. I would step aside and wait quietly for God to make the next move.

The days were long and empty while Joanie was in summer school. I struggled to concentrate on my work, but my bouts with depression were almost reminiscent of the days before I made my initial step to accept God at His word. Reading the Bible did not bring the assurance and encouragement it used to. Passages that had once been vividly real seemed vague and distant, as if they no longer concerned me.

More than three years ago, in Arizona, I had decided to accept what I read in the Bible as fact, regardless of my up and down feelings. I had *known* His Word to be true and what it was like to have peace inside, that deep abiding peace underneath all ups and downs. Now the peace was gone.

What had Naomi said the day I first met her? "When the peace

God gives us is upset—look out. Something is usually wrong between you and God!" What had I done wrong? Each day I had pleaded with God to not let me go against His will. Russell and I had been very careful not to let passion carry us too far. So what could be wrong?

The thoughts gave me a headache. Joanie's words kept coming back. "Honey, it can't work out. God tells you not to covet another woman's husband."

I walked the floor and stared out where the Georgia sun had burned the last scraggly bits of lawn to a pure yellow. It was true that I was coveting Naomi's husband. Even lusting. Was that the reason for my lack of peace? Was that why I no longer knew the presence of God? Was the wall between us of *my* making?

My own pale image stared back at me from the mirror on the wall. Distress and tension were etching new lines around my eyes and mouth. Waiting was hard, Audrey had warned me. But I would wait. I would force my thoughts from coveting, concentrate on my work, and someday my torment would be over. Russell would be free and our love consummated.

Joanie chaperoned a group of youngsters on a weekend trip and came home with stars in her eyes. Her cheeks colored as she talked unceasingly about a Peter Donelly who was youth director for the little town of Sunrise Beach half way down the east coast of Florida. Already the first weekend after Joanie's return he drove all the way to Oreola to see her. A lanky young man with an engaging smile, he was obviously as much in love with Joanie as she was with him.

Watching them together was a bittersweet experience. They were so *right* for each other. Their relationship was open and natural. I saw them holding hands, laughing, and running with the children, and my heart ached.

They planned a Christmas wedding. "We feel this is God's plan for us," they told me. "We are willing to commit ourselves to each other and to Him for the rest of our lives."

They had not complicated their lives with wrong choices and a difficult relationship the way I had. That was why their love could be so simple while mine was so complicated. I told Joanie how I felt, and she looked up from the pillowcase she was embroidering.

"I think you're mistaken. God can take the confused and complicated messes we've made out of our lives and make them straightforward and beautiful. Your problem is different. A relationship with a man who is already married can never be simple. Even if he gets divorced and marries you, there will be broken and confused relationships around you. It can't be avoided." Joanie looked down and her quick fingers pushed the needle back and forth in the colorful floral pattern.

"Think about the children." She didn't look up, and I was grateful. I didn't want to see her eyes. "Think about the difficult relationships with step-sisters and brothers, with double sets of parents and grandparents and in-laws." Joanie paused, then added softly, "The Bible says that God is not the author of confusion, but of peace." [2]

Of course I had thought about it. But God could bring order, even into a difficult situation. He would have a perfect plan for Naomi and little Deborah as well, just as He had a perfect plan for Russell and me. Did it not make sense that a gifted Christian leader needed a spritually-understanding wife in order to reach his full potential in God's service? If his present marriage was a hindrance, was he not justified in getting a more suitable wife? This was the case in each of the situations Audrey had told me about. I was sure I could be a better help for Russell in his ministry than Naomi who seemed to care only for her house, her potted plants, and Deborah.

Searching the Bible, I tried to find further support for my conviction. But the verses Russell and I had underlined no longer seemed as comforting: ". . . for you have been given freedom . . . for the whole Law can be summed up in this one command: 'Love others as you love yourself.' " [3] "For Christ blotted out . . . the list of His commandments which you had not obeyed . . ." [4] Did those verses *really* mean that we were no longer required to observe God's commandments? Reading the passages in the context where they belonged, I was no longer sure. The writer had been referring to laws concerning religious rituals, special diets, and observances of special holy days, made obsolete by Jesus Christ.

I was almost afraid to read on. Several passages I had never noticed before seemed to leap at me from the pages: "A pastor must be of blameless reputation, married to one wife only, and be a man of self-control and discretion, leading a disciplined life." [5] My cheeks were burning. Were those instructions meant for the first century church only? But if parts of the Bible were obsolete, how could I know what to believe, what to trust in?

That night I tossed on my bed, wrestling with my thoughts. "O God," I moaned. "I *do* want to believe You. Show me what is right and wrong."

With the coming of dawn I crawled out of bed. Still in my pajamas and robe I knelt by the bookshelf and pulled out my Bible and the well-worn copy of the New Testament John Conlan had given me three and a half years ago in Arizona when I had taken my first uncertain step of faith and it seemed valid. I had dared to believe promise after promise, and they had proven true.

Now it seemed I had come to another crossroad. With throbbing temples and aching eyes I scanned the heavily underlined pages, tear-stained here and there. The words of Jesus himself: "You must not think that I have come to abolish the Law . . . You have heard that it was said to the people in the old days, 'Thou shalt not commit adultery.' But I say to you that every man who looks at a woman lustfully has already committed adultery with her—in his heart." [6]

The words were swimming on the page. "It was because you knew so little of the meaning of love that Moses allowed you to divorce your wives! But that was not the original principle. I tell you that anyone who divorces his wife on any grounds except her unfaithfulness and marries some other woman commits adultery." [7]

"O God!" I leaned my forehead against the sharp edge of the bookshelf and sobs racked my body. In flaming letters the words were etched across my mind: *"Do not commit adultery!"*

The verdict was painfully clear: In God's eyes my love for Russell was wrong. In a flash of anger I thought, "Why did God let it happen?" I had pleaded with Him to keep me in His will, yet He allowed me to fall for the oldest trap in the world. The relationship with Russell had seemed so "pure." Now it was shattered and sullied, like a precious porcelain figure crashed against a dirty floor.

Hot tears flowed down my cheeks, and in a twinkling I realized that all was not yet lost. I could still love Russell. God would not stop me. Lightning would not strike me dead. The liberty to choose was mine!

It was as if I was balancing a narrow line between two futures.

Russell was on one side, surrounded by golden sunshine, laughing with arms outstretched, waiting. Even an illicit love would fulfill my longings. Russell was real, a man of flesh and blood.

On the other side was the lonely path of obedience to God, dull and gray by comparison, and I felt myself drawn towards Russell.

"God, help me!" The cry forced its way past my clenched teeth. Instantly the vision of Russell dimmed while the narrow path on the other side seemed less dreary. Strong forces were battling for my will, as if in a gigantic tug of war. My throat felt constricted and it was difficult to breathe. Mustering all my strength I cried, "God, Your will, not mine."

The struggle ceased all at once and I slumped to the floor, drained and empty. Before my inner eyes stretched the gray future without Russell. It was all over. I felt as if, at thirty-five, my life had ended. But inside was an all-encompassing peace. Months ago it had left me so subtly that I had not even noticed at first. But now it was back, thank God.

Wearily I crawled on hands and knees back to bed. When Joanie woke me up, the afternoon sun was slanting in my window.

"Good Lord, Sarah, what happened?" She stared at my swollen face.

My voice was a hoarse whisper, "I finally realized that my relationship with Russell was wrong. How could something so beautiful be sin?"

Joanie knelt to hug me. "You would never have done it if it had been obvious and ugly. Temptation clothes itself in beautiful garb sometimes."

"Why didn't I see it before?"

"I think you did," Joanie's voice was soft. "But you wanted it so desperately. You rationalized."

I nodded. I had deliberately put blindfolds on. It was all so clear now. "I almost rejected God." It was a horrible thought.

"Don't condemn yourself." Joanie picked up the New Testament from the floor where I had left it. Her voice shook as she read, "If we refuse to admit that we are sinners, then we live in a world of illusion and truth becomes a stranger to us. But if we freely admit that we have sinned, we find God utterly reliable and straightforward—He forgives our sins and makes us thoroughly clean from all that is evil." [8]

Gratitude swelled within me. "Thank you, Joanie." I felt myself drift towards sleep again. "I really love you."

"I love you too, sister." Her eyes shone. "Now rest." She lifted the phone off the hook and tiptoed out of the room. I knew she was thinking of Russell's frequent calls.

Anger rushed through me as I thought of him. As a minister he should have known better. And what of Audrey? And the others she told me about? Were they really blind? Did they really believe that adultery was permissible in special cases? If they had not led the way, I would not have let myself be fooled. It was really their fault, and God's, for not stopping me.

The bitterness disrupted the calm I had felt only minutes ago. The urge was strong to reach for the phone and confront Russell and Audrey with the great wrong they had done. Then, in the back of my mind, a voice spoke distinctly; "Let the one who has never sinned cast the first stone." [9]

"O God!" I buried my face in the pillow. "What am I doing? Forgive me." I had no one to blame but myself. I had let my feelings override God's clear direction.

"Please, God," I stared out the window at clouds chasing each other across the sky, "teach me not to rely on my feelings again!"

Joanie woke me up after dark. "Let's go out for hamburgers!" She looked cheerful, and I felt refreshed.

At the restaurant I looked across the room at a handsome stranger and was suddenly swept with physical desire for the man.

"Dear God!" I clutched Joanie's arm. "What's wrong with me?" I blushed with shame. Then the significance of the moment hit me. "Thank You, God," I whispered inwardly. "I see now that I can't trust my feelings." As quickly as it had come, the desire left, and I breathed a sigh of relief.

My feelings for Russell did not evaporate overnight. They came over me like waves after a passing storm. But I fought against them, refusing to let them linger as in the past. At night, when the full moon shone into my bedroom, I walked the floor singing from the hymnbook or reading aloud from the Psalms. King David had written them after he had committed adultery with Bathsheba, and his penitence and words of praise for an all-forgiving God echoed in my heart.

Gradually the attacks of longing were reduced in strength and frequency. When Russell called, at last, my pulse beat a little faster, but my voice was steady, "We've been wrong. Please forgive me for leading you on. We had beautiful feelings for each other, but now I know that only Naomi has the right to love you as a wife."

Russell was silent for a long time, then spoke hoarsely, "We weren't wrong, Sarah. There is nothing to forgive."

I ached inside for him. "Please understand that this is goodbye," I fought to control my voice. When he hung up, I cried. In spite of everything, I still missed him.

When the children returned from Missouri, we decided to move at once with Joanie to Sunrise Beach, Florida. I felt an urgent need to establish a life and a future of my own. No more foolish entanglements with men. I felt I had at last outgrown that stage.

Chapter 9

Without Leif, I no longer wanted to live in the old hotel in Green River. I needed to establish a new life style, and looked for an apartment in Springfield, thirty miles away. I could easily commute the distance, and in the prospering university town I hoped to avoid the dangerous rut I had been in last winter.

I installed my stereo, my books, and a few pieces of art in a modern apartment near the campus. Most of my neighbors were singles associated with the university, and I soon found congenial companions for a game of chess or a few drinks. I thought things were going to work out, but I was mistaken.

As the November winds whipped the last brown leaves off the trees, I felt myself slipping back into depression. Business was slow and held no incentive. I drank more to hide the emptiness inside.

There was no sense in kidding myself any longer. Without the children, my life held little purpose. If I could not have custody of them, the next best alternative would be to live where I could at least visit them on weekends.

Sarah had moved to Florida, a more promising area of employment for me than Georgia. By mid-December my plans were firm. I would pack my things in the boat and pull the trailer south for Christmas.

I called Sarah to tell her, and her voice sounded less stern than I remembered. Perhaps she would be at least civil, allowing me the relationship with my children I needed so desperately.

Christmas Eve I pulled into Chattanooga, Tennessee, and called Duke Massey, my old bachelor friend from California. He had not been very successful in the movie business, and had moved back home. Duke was an expert guide to the cocktail lounges of his city, and two days later I continued south nursing a giant hangover, but with hopes for the future.

The warm Florida breezes and sunshine would soon get me out of the dumps I had been in the last couple of years in Missouri.

SARAH   *Sunrise Beach, Florida*

Our house was an older one, surrounded by a generous garden of overgrown fruit trees, within the sound of the surf. A small guest cottage in the back was nearly hidden under climbing bougainvillaea. Flaming hibiscus bushes surrounded the patio and goldfish pond. Our sub-tropical paradise was on the outskirts of town near an isolated stretch of beach.

"It's the neatest place we've ever lived," John declared after having made a careful inspection of the jungle-like garden. He had picked an armload of oranges, lemons, avocados, and mangoes. Even Leif admitted that living near a year-round surf spot had its advantages. "I'm getting a paper route and will have enough money for a surfboard in no time," he announced.

I drew a sigh of relief. His attitude had been sullen and rebellious after returning from Missouri. This was the first time he had indicated an interest in staying in Florida instead of returning as quickly as possible to live with David.

Joanie lived in the little cottage. She and Peter spent much time with the children, and I was grateful for their influence. Frankly, I did not quite know how to handle the discipline on my own.

My desk was piled high with a book assignment and several unfinished articles. I worked hard to forget what had happened in Georgia. In church I volunteered as Sunday school teacher and youth leader. I was busier than ever before, and assured myself that I was happy.

Still, in rare, quiet moments I was aware that I was hiding something from myself again. On lonely walks along the beach I felt the restlessness of the sea echo inside me.

"I think you're drawing back into your cocoon," Joanie looked concerned. "You're surrounding yourself with groups of people, but you're afraid of relationships with individuals. I feel it."

Her words struck home. "I'm afraid of getting hurt again."

Joanie put her arms around me, and the touch made me shiver involuntarily.

"You need to talk it all out," her warm brown eyes registered alarm at my reaction. "Why don't you see Dorothy and Richard Binford? They live over near Tampa."

I remembered Dorothy, warm and soft-spoken, from the luncheon meeting in Georgia where I had gone with Naomi. It seemed ages ago.

"They have a solid marriage," Joanie went on. "And they're not off on an emotional, spiritual tangent. You can trust them."

I called and Dorothy told me to come over right away. I drove across the Florida peninsula into the sunset. The Binfords lived in a small, unpretentious bungalow on a quiet street. Dorothy's kitchen smelled of fresh apple pie. Her engineer husband greeted me with a firm handshake and an open smile. I felt comfortable under his steady gaze.

"Tell us why you came," he said simply.

It felt good to pour out the whole, sad story. The years of hurt and frozen emotions—and a release from rigidity when I dared to trust myself as a woman to God after hearing Dorothy's lecture. "And then I fell for the first man I saw," I blushed, "a married pastor!" It hurt to talk about it even now.

"I'm retreating back into my old shell, afraid to come close to my children and my friends. I realize this is my own rigid self-defense, and I want to trust God instead. I just don't know how." I looked at Richard helplessly.

He smiled. "Is that all?"

I blushed again. "Not really. My biggest fear is of men. I don't think I can ever trust one again."

"I understand," Richard's eyes were gentle. "But I believe there is a cure for that. When you first trusted yourself as a woman to God, you obviously held something back, and it was that something which caused you to stumble when you first experienced a desire to be near your married friend."

"What do you mean? I was sincere in my commitment."

"Sure you were," Richard looked thoughtful. "Sometimes when an army surrenders, soldiers hide out in caves refusing to believe that the war is over. We are like that when we surrender to God—part of us may still be in hiding, afraid to come out. We may have to ask God specifically to bring us out. Do you want to do that?"

I nodded, suddenly overwhelmed with emotion.

Dorothy put her arm around my shoulders, and Richard took both of my hands in his. I felt their love surrounding me.

"Dear God," Richard prayed. "As a man I ask You to forgive the men who hurt and bruised Sarah, making her afraid to be loved again. Forgive her the hurts she's inflicted on the men in her life. Let there not be a single, dark hiding place in her soul where fear and guilt may bind her. Cast it all out and set Sarah free to be the woman you created her to be."

A tingling sensation began in my fingertips and feet, spreading rapidly throughout my body. Something like a giant coil tightened in my abdomen and chest. I could not move. Breathing was painful. I tried to open my mouth, but my face was stiffened in contortion and my throat was paralyzed. I looked up into Richard's eyes; his were steady and without alarm. He spoke calmly, "Don't be afraid, Sarah. It can't hurt you. God is more powerful than the evil that has bound you. It has to leave now."

Richard held my rigid hands in his. I could see them; the skin looked whitish gray and the fingers were twisted and bent, like the hands of a paralytic. My entire body was like that, rigid and bent, and an icy cold was moving up through my limbs.

"I'm dying," I thought desperately. Richard looked into my eyes and spoke in a suddenly stern voice:

"In Jesus' name, let go of Sarah. She belongs to God. You have no power over her."

There was a convulsive struggle inside me, and I thought I was going to lose consciousness. Yet at the center of my being I was aware of a light, an oasis of calm. I repeated the thought over and over again: "Jesus is saving me. His power in me is stronger than the force I feel."

Slowly the grip loosened. A warmth spread from Richard's hands into mine. Gradually the rigid muscles of my arms and legs were relaxing. The coil around my stomach and chest left and I could move my facial muscles again.

Sinking limply back into the chair, I felt drained of all strength. There was total quietness and light inside.

"If it hadn't happened to me I wouldn't have believed it," I whispered. "I had no idea evil could be so real. It would have killed me!"

"Yes, one way or the other," Richard nodded. "The battle between good and evil is no parlor game."

"But I was a Christian!" I shivered at the thought of how close I had been to destruction.

Richard shrugged. "I don't profess to understand it all. In many cases I am sure Christ makes a clean sweep when he first comes into a life. In other cases, like yours, old rebels hide in caves, refusing to recognize that the war is over. But it is certain that evil can't get that kind of foothold in our lives, unless the practice of wrong has been an ingrained habit. You were a rebel for years and engaged in the wrong kind of relationship, even after you became a Christian."

He smiled and patted my hand. "It's all over now. This paralysis has kept you from being a whole person for a long time, but now you are free."

Gratitude overflowed in me. "Thank you, God," I whispered. "Thank you."

Dorothy and Richard invited me to spend the night. I was too physically exhausted to make the trip home. The next morning birds sang joyously in the lemon tree outside my window. I stretched in bed, wonderfully relaxed, as if I had been tied in knots for years and now had been released. My hands looked young and strong, the skin tanned from the sun. I shuddered at the memory of their ugly appearance only a few hours ago. Never had the concept of "being saved from death" seemed more real.

What an incredible journey I had been on since that first timid start back in Arizona. I had not arrived yet—there would be lessons to learn as long as I lived—yet the change from the old was noticeable and significant. God's promises were real. I felt a shiver of excitement as I thought about it. I was no longer afraid of the future, and the past was safely behind me. It was good to be alive today!

At home it was easier to relax with the children and talk openly with Joanie. Somehow my relationship with God was more solid. The acute sense of loneliness I had felt since leaving Georgia had disappeared.

I had written Audrey a note, telling her that my deception with Russell had finally exploded. I had not been able to face her before leaving Oreola. I had admired her and trusted her advice. Her humanness had angered and shocked me.

My doorbell rang one morning, and Audrey stood outside, her eyes holding the question I had dreaded. She had lost weight and the soft red hair framed a face that looked somehow more transparent and vulnerable. Standing there I felt the old bitterness melt away. I opened my arms, and suddenly we were laughing and crying together.

"Can you forgive me?" Her voice shook.

"Can you forgive *me?* I judged you so harshly."

"If only I could have seen my own mistake in time to warn you."

"It wouldn't have made any difference," I shook my head. "I only heard what I wanted to hear, once I had begun to deceive myself."

Audrey laughed with some of her old sparkle. "Now that we don't have to pretend we're perfect, we can at least be honest friends."

"I shouldn't have put you on a pedestal."

She giggled in the old way. "It feels good to be off."

Audrey stayed for lunch, and we could have talked forever. It was such a relief to have no pretense between us.

"When you live a lie it distorts every other area of your life as well," Audrey brushed a strand of hair from her eyes with the quick gesture I remembered. "I came so close to accepting a counterfeit for truth."

Audrey was leaving Georgia to return to North Dakota. "Chuck, my ex-husband, is still there," she blushed becomingly. "I want the children to have an opportunity to see him more often."

"Then you're less selfish than I am," I shuddered involuntarily. "I keep dreaming that David comes to move in with us, and I resent it terribly. I don't want him to interfere with the children or with me."

Audrey was silent for a moment, then looked straight at me. "Those are dangerous feelings to cling to. They can only harm you in the end."

I felt uneasy. "I know—and I'm O.K., as long as I know that he is in Missouri and I'm here in Florida. But whenever I think of him coming to see the children I get goosebumps and want to run and hide."

"I know what you mean," Audrey nodded. "I felt the same way." She reached out to touch my hand. "But Sarah, we've learned something about the unreliability of feelings. What you *feel* for David shouldn't keep you from making a deliberate commitment to love him as a Christian."

"It's so hard."

"That's how God loves us," Audrey's voice was barely audible, "not because we're lovable. He does it deliberately, intentionally, because He wants to. That's what *agape love* really means. It's not something we feel, but something we decide to do."

I groaned. "In theory I know all that . . . but to practice it!"

"God will teach you," Audrey hugged me, and her cheeks were wet. "If you are willing to let Him."

My ideas about love—even God's love—had always been vague. I wanted to love my children and love my friends, and I had always assumed that somehow I would *feel* love for them. I had also assumed that unless I *felt* this vague something, I did not love them.

Now it dawned on me that this was not what the Bible taught about love. Jesus commanded His followers to love God and to love one another. And you can't *feel* something on command. Obviously Jesus meant something other than feeling.

The more I read my Bible the more I realized that love was something tangible, practical, and deliberate, and that, according to the criteria listed, I was very unloving.

The discovery was depressing, but also gave me hope. I could see now that I had never loved my children, or anyone else, as I should. But I also saw that love was something I could learn to do. It was not a mystical feeling that I had to wait for.

I could not *make* myself loving, but I could admit it when I acted unloving, and ask God to make me more loving. Little by little, He would make the change real—I had seen enough evidence of His power to be sure of that.

As a daily reminder of my need to grow in this area I made a list of some of love's attributes and taped it to my bathroom mirror. My list read:

Love Is:
Patient and kind, loyal, always believes,
expects the best, defends the loved one,
and rejoices when truth wins out.

Love Is Not:
Jealous, envious, boastful, proud, haughty,
selfish, rude, demanding its own way,
irritable, or touchy. It does not hold
grudges, notice when others do wrong,
and is not glad about injustice.[1]

Until I compared my behavior to the ideal presented by Paul, I had not realized how impatient, touchy, irritable, and selfish I was with the children. I had justified my actions on the basis of my busy schedule and the children's lack of self-control. I had been terribly wrong.

Leif was the hardest to handle. He missed no opportunities telling me that I had no authority over him. "You can't boss me around, mom," his dark eyes were defiant. "I'm going back to dad as soon as the judge will let me."

Always his words caused a twinge of fear. "You have to obey me as long as you live here," I countered.

"You can't make me!" Leif flashed a confident smile and headed for the door. "I'll see you later. I'm going surfing."

He was drifting away from the rest of us. The other children enjoyed staying home and always wanted me to join them in games or projects.

"I like it when the whole family is together," Andrew hugged me. "If only dad could be here too." His face looked suddenly wistful. "We'll never be a *real* family without dad."

"Why don't you get married again, mom?" John questioned me. "You could meet a fellow in church, someone who likes to fish and hunt with boys."

Christine climbed up on my lap. "I think you should wait till dad becomes a Christian," she said gravely.

"That only happens in books," John was impatient. "I want a daddy before I get too old to enjoy him!"

Such discussions no longer upset me. I did not intend to remarry, and being alone did not distress me anymore. The closeness of Christ was real to me now. I had no need of a man.

We attended a small, friendly Baptist church with Joanie and Peter. The children, except Leif, participated enthusiastically in all the programs for their age groups. Leif came along under duress. I made him go because I thought that was better than letting him stay at home by himself. When Peter brought me a note in Leif's handwriting, I got a sinking feeling in the pit of my stomach.

"I intercepted it in Sunday school," Peter's usually clear blue eyes were clouded with concern. "It could mean trouble."

My hands shook as I unfolded the crumpled piece of paper: "Dear Patti. Can you get me some stuff Wednesday? . . . 'L.' " Patti was a deacon's daughter who had been in trouble with the police for smoking marijuana. She and Leif often sat together in the last pew in church.

Peter's arm went around my shoulder. "Don't worry about Leif," his voice was gentle. "Only God can get through to him. Your job is to love him—with authority."

"I feel so helpless."

Peter's grin was encouraging. "The more helpless you are, the more help God can give you. Just try to accept Leif as he is. Don't push, don't preach."

My smile was tremulous. I had always pushed too hard—and preached. It was not easy to change now.

When I talked to Leif that afternoon the old pushiness reasserted itself in spite of my efforts to tone it down. "Be honest with me, and with God," my voice had a demanding, hard edge.

Leif's eyes avoided mine. "Patti was going to get me a couple of rings, that's all."

"You're lying!" Anger and fear fought inside me. "Go to your room and stay there until you're ready to tell the truth."

Leif's face froze into a mask of hostility. "You'll regret saying that, mom!" He slammed the door to his room, and fear spread inside me. I had done the wrong thing.

"God, please take over," I whispered inwardly. "You see I can't handle it."

John was the one who discovered that Leif was gone. The window in his room was left wide open. "I bet he's gone to dad." I instinctively knew he was right. I visualized the skinny twelve-year-old alone by the side of the road with his thumb out. He had to be stopped before he got himself into serious trouble. Quickly I lifted the phone and dialed the police.

The officer who came was young and sympathetic.

"Children in a broken home often run away to the other parent." He noted Leif's description on his pad and borrowed a recent picture. "We'll find him before he gets out of Florida. Don't worry."

I tucked the other three into bed; they insisted on sleeping in the same room. We prayed for Leif's safety and for God to bring him home soon, but our little family had been ripped apart. We all felt the hurt. Andrew and Christine cried openly.

When they were finally asleep, I sat by the fireplace in the living room and allowed myself a good cry. "Forgive me for being such a poor mother," helplessness swelled inside. "Teach me to love."

When the phone rang, I jumped. It was near midnight. A man's voice said, "I live fifty miles up the beach from you. Your boy just knocked on my door and wants to come home."

The relief was wonderful. "Thank God," I breathed. "Someone will be there to pick him up right away."

I called the police station, and the young officer informed me that Leif's disappearance had not yet been reported to the highway patrol, so there would be no official record. "But I would like to pick up your boy and have a talk with him. We don't want a repeat performance."

After a nervous couple of hours, I opened the door to a subdued Leif escorted by a stern looking uniformed police officer.

"Next time you will have to go before the judge!" It was an ominous promise. "I am sure you would rather work out your problem at home."

"Yes, sir!" Leif was impressed. "I won't do it again."

When we were alone, my son looked at me uneasily, and I struggled to control my emotions. "Do you want to tell me about it?"

He nodded, relieved. "I planned to go to dad in Missouri, but I stopped to rest on the beach, and when I looked up, there were millions of stars in the sky. It made me think of God and how He didn't want me to run away from home." Leif blinked back tears, and when I put my arms around him he did not push me away.

"I was wrong too, son," I whispered. "I've been pushing you too hard instead of realizing that you are old enough to make some choices of your own."

"I've made some wrong ones," Leif pulled away to walk into the family room. I heard him open and close a cupboard. When he returned, he wore an embarrassed smile and carried a half-empty package of cigarettes. He put them in my lap. "I've been smoking on my paper route every morning, but I want to quit."

My heart was beating loudly. "I was hooked on cigarettes once," I tried to sound casual. "It is hard to quit."

"I'm gonna try."

"What about Patti?"

Leif's cheeks reddened. "I've tried pot."

"I thought so." I felt strangely calm, grateful at least for the openness between us. "It is dangerous, you know."

"Don't worry, mom." Leif shook his head. "It wasn't that great."

"I can't make your choices for you," I spoke carefully. "I remember what it was like to be your age and trying some things. I tried some wrong ones and was sorry later."

Leif put his arms around me, and I realized he was not a little child anymore. "I'll be all right." He smiled his old confident smile. "God stopped me from going to Missouri, didn't He? He'll stop me if I go too far with other things, too."

"Don't count on it." Leif didn't know his own vulnerability, and I wondered if he would believe my warning. "God gives us a free will. When we deliberately do something we know is wrong, He may not stop us. He may let us do it and learn from the painful consequences."

"Did He ever let you go ahead with something wrong?"

"I'm afraid so." The memory was painfully fresh.

Leif yawned. "I'm not worried about that. Come tuck me in, mom. I have to get up with the paper route soon."

I sat by his bedside, stroking his thick, brown hair, and he reached out to touch my hand. "I was a little scared, mom—it's good to be home." With his eyes closed, his face looked as I remembered it when he was quite small. He smiled and murmured, "Don't go away, mom. I like it when you're there."

I bent to kiss him. He was still my little Leif, struggling to grow up.

"Watch over him," I whispered. "Help him to trust You."

In response I felt a quiet assurance, as if a voice had answered, "I hear you; don't fear. Leif is Mine."

I believed it—but I had heard the same promise for David over a year ago. Between the promise and its fulfillment could be years of rebellion and hurt. Leif's problems were not over yet. I could see it in his eyes. But at least he had come home. I had been given another opportunity to love him.

Peter and Joanie were married a week before Christmas. Naomi and Russell were at the wedding, and my heart beat a little quicker as I watched them from a safe distance. Naomi came to hug me after the ceremony. Her smile was warm and guileless. She looked radiant in a bright red dress with a soft, white collar.

"Pray for us, Sarah," she said. "We are being honest with each other for the first time in our marriage, and it's wonderful!" Her eyes sparkled through tears, and I felt a rush of happiness for her mingled with shame. How could I ever have wanted to see her marriage destroyed?

Peter and Joanie would be gone on their honeymoon till after Christmas. The house was quiet without them, and I stood alone in the kitchen baking Christmas cookies, resisting attacks of loneliness and self-pity. In contrast to the happiness of the newlyweds my own life was a dismal failure. I would never know a fresh new beginning after all the wasted years. I had made my wrong choices years ago—and had to live with the consequences.

I was cracking eggs into the mixing bowl when a little thought began way back in my head: "Remember that all things fit together for good for those who love God . . . All things are made new . . . Lost years are restored. . . ." I stared at the cooky ingredients lined up on the counter, and the self-pity gave way to a rush of joy. What a picture of my life! All those ingredients waiting to fit together into a tasty cooky—but first the wheat had to be ground, the eggs cracked, the sugar refined, the salt mined, the oil squeezed, not to mention the blending together, the forcing through a cooky-press, and finally the hot oven!

I chuckled to myself. "If I'm going to come out a tasty cooky in the end, I see that all those painful processes were not wasted as I thought. They were necessary!"

"Thank You, God," I said out loud. "For the dead-end streets that taught me where You aren't. For teaching me the things which do not work in a marriage. Even for the affair with Russell—now I know that feelings can't be trusted, and that love is something much more reliable."

The warm drops running down my cheeks were a joyful expression of my gratitude. "Thanks for the failures that drive me closer to You."

After supper, we sang Christmas songs, decorated the tree, and finally rested by the fireplace with mugs of hot chocolate and a tray of cookies. After the children were tucked in bed, I stayed by the fire, plucking the strings of the guitar, and humming phrases from a favorite song.

The phone interrupted my pleasant thoughts. It was near midnight, and my hand shook as I lifted the receiver.

David's voice sounded close in my ear. "I am moving to Florida to be near the children. I'll be there a day or so after Christmas."

The iron hand of fear grasped at my throat. Why did God let him come? I fought to regain my balance. My reactions were wrong—I knew it only too well. David's coming must be a necessary ingredient in the re-shaping of my life. I should be grateful.

When he arrived, he looked pale and sick, but his eyes had the old look of icy steel. He backed his boat-trailer into our yard and prepared to park it there. It was like my recurring nightmare. David behaved as if he had the perfect right to do as he pleased on our property without consulting me. The old paralysis of indecision nearly strangled my voice, but I managed to say, "You can't do that!"

"Why not? I plan to use the boat with the children." He looked indignant, and I trembled under his gaze.

"Our lives are separate now." I forced myself to look him in the eyes. "Your boat doesn't belong in our yard. Please remove it."

He hesitated for a moment, then gave in with a shrug. "As you wish, but I had at least hoped you would show me Christian kindness."

His words stung. Leif had overheard our conversation. He tossed his head in anger. "Boy, you sure know how to be cruel, mom."

After David had left, I closed the door to my bedroom and cried into my pillow. "Oh God. Do what You have to do—in my life and in David's—to bring an end to this pain."

Chapter 10

Miami Beach, Florida

In the face of Sarah's hostile attitude I didn't want to stay in Sunrise Beach. Besides, the small town held few employment opportunities, and I needed a job right away. I had left Missouri with only a few hundred dollars in my pocket, and they had dwindled dangerously. I told Sarah I would look for work in the Miami area. "I'll be back every second weekend to be with the children."

"Just as long as they don't miss church."

Her remark struck me as ludicrous. "What's more important, church or a relationship with their father?"

"Frankly, what they need most is a relationship with Jesus Christ." Her face was defiant.

"Have you absolutely no feelings at all?"

She did not answer, and I was glad to get away.

In Miami the employment situation was worse than I had anticipated. This was a serious complication as I had an expensive habit to support. I was now dependent on a fifth of bourbon a day to keep going. Each day it required more of an effort to hide the obvious signs of alcohol in my system: the bloodshot eyes, the puffiness under my skin, and the fine network of veins visible on my nose and cheeks. I always shaved and dressed neatly and made the rounds of employment offices, but invariably I gravitated towards the inexpensive bars in the low-rent west side of Miami. I could not afford to drink or sleep anywhere else.

A bartender had referred me to an Italian who owned a duplex in a once-fashionable, but now run down, neighborhood. I could only pay part of the rent, but on the promise of paying up as soon as I got a job, the owner allowed me to move in. My accommodations were simple; a single room with a bath separated from the rest of the house by a thin plywood wall. All day and night I was treated to a continuous stream of loud cursing and quarreling in Spanish by the Cuban family who lived in the front.

The heat was oppressive. Drenched by perspiration I would lie down in the breeze from the noisy old table-top fan by my bedside. Opening the small window only increased my torment, letting in the full blast of the incessant croaking of big bullfrogs who lived in the old cracked swimming pool directly outside my door.

Stinking, brackish rainwater had collected in the deep end of the pool where the frogs had found a home among the junk and trash thrown out by the tenants. The noise kept me from sleeping and nearly drove me out of my mind. I still had my gun, and when I could stand it no longer, I stepped out on the pool deck and pumped bullets into the stinking green water. I never killed any of the slimy creatures, but in the short interval of silence following my barrage of gunshots, I at least clung to my sanity in a demonstration of mastery over those damned frogs.

It was a struggle to sober up completely every second weekend to make the long drive north to Sunrise Beach. I could not afford a motel room and slept on my cot on the beach. The children sometimes joined me with their sleeping bags, but our visits were strained. I only allowed myself one or two beers the entire weekend, and abstinence was painful.

Sarah accepted the fact that I was out of work and could not give her any money. She actually seemed kinder after I told her, and offered me a sandwich.

"Don't worry about us," she assured me. "God has provided enough writing assignments to keep us going."

The glimpse of kindness was offset by her continuous harping on my need for God. I avoided her as much as possible and kept the children with me on the beach. The trip back to Miami was an ordeal. About forty miles down the road from Sunrise Beach I had to stop to vomit, always at the same spot on the road. The attack usually lasted thirty minutes before I could continue south to Vero Beach. There I stopped at a roadhouse for several stiff drinks. Only then could I face my inevitable return to the little room and the horror of the frogs.

I was not ready to admit defeat. This was not the end. I would find a way out and up. I *had* to. My last bottle was less than half full and I had only a nickel and a dime left in my pocket, when there was a knock on my door late one evening. Outside stood Mel Goodson. He did not seem to notice my two-day old stubble beard and was undaunted by the chorus of the frogs behind him.

"Good evening cousin, may I come in?"

He stepped into my dingy little room as if it was a first-class suite in a hotel, and placed himself in my only chair with a cheerful grin.

"These are just temporary lodgings," I said lightly. "There are blue skies ahead."

"Of course, cousin," Mel interrupted my apologies. "I came to ask your advice in a business matter. Could we talk at dinner?"

Over the first good meal I had eaten in days, in a plush restaurant in Coral Gables, I felt back to normal again. Mel was serious. He needed advice about investing in some property in Missouri.

"You know the area better than I do," his tone was businesslike. "You have nothing to win or lose by telling me the truth about it."

I lit a cigar and felt at ease for the first time in months.

"Your investment will be well-placed," I nodded approvingly. "You can plant the land with pine and get a nice return on your money, if you have time to wait."

"I have time," Mel nodded. "I've inherited a small sum from an uncle in Wyoming." He smiled. "Besides, I believe in keeping America green."

Then he leaned forward: "Cousin, I'm concerned about your health. You look too much like my dad just before alcoholism killed him."

I smiled uneasily. "I've had a few hard breaks. Work is scarce, but I expect to have things under control and moving forward soon."

Mel sipped his drink. "I see," he said slowly. He pulled his checkbook from his coat pocket and tore out a check he had previously filled in. Folding it carefully, he handed it to me.

"There may come a time when our roles are reversed," he said gravely. "This is meant as a loan. It will get you out of the rut."

I glanced down at the four-digit sum and felt a lump in my throat. Mel had driven a couple of thousand miles, not to ask advice he really did not need, but to hand me a ticket to the future! It was an incredible thing—completely unexpected. Nothing like it had ever happened to me before. I struggled to find words to thank him, but he stood up and said brusquely, "Well, cousin, thanks for the advice, I'll have to get on my way."

We drove in silence back to the dingy street where I lived. There Mel shook my hand while I mumbled a "thanks for everything." As soon as he drove off I walked into my little room and started packing my suitcase. I was going to waste no time getting out of there.

The next morning I paid what I owed on rent and drove north towards Sunrise Beach. It was Easter—a good time of the year for a new beginning, I thought. I would give Sarah some money and tell her I had a job and then head for the Florida Keys where I would spend a month or two relaxing and regaining my strength. After that, I was sure I would be able to find a job without difficulty.

SARAH   *Sunrise Beach, Florida*

Between David's visits I worked on my attitude, asking God to make me kinder. Yet each time David drove up, somehow I froze. I watched his face carefully for signs that he was changing, but he always wore the same emotionless mask. He was pale and still had not found work. I hoped that when the circumstances got hard enough, he would turn to God for help.

When he brought me five hundred dollars on Easter weekend I felt oddly disappointed. David looked more self assured. He had a job and was not in such obvious need of God.

Easter Sunday I took the children to the beach after church. I was dozing on my blanket when Christine suddenly yelled, "Look mom, daddy is here!"

David settled himself a few yards away and nodded wordlessly. My heart beat as I closed my eyes against the bright sunshine. Why had he come so close? And what did he want?

I waited in suspense for something to happen, but the only words he said to me all afternoon were, "may I borrow your suntan lotion?" and "thank you." The children ran back and forth between us, but when the sun sank below the tops of the palm trees David gathered his things and left without a word. I felt a curious letdown.

Monday morning he waited till the children had left for school before coming to say goodbye to me. I felt a sudden compulsion to tell him, "Sooner or later you'll have to face God; you know that, don't you?"

He glared at me. "Why do you always act as if you're personally responsible for saving me? Why can't you just be kind and sweet?"

My eyes were stinging. "One of these days it will be too late." I still felt the urgency of the moment. "God has a plan for your life, but if you keep on ignoring Him there comes a point of no return. Your time will be up."

"You make me sick!" David spat the words out. "I hope you return to reality before it is too late."

He drove off in anger, and the lump stayed in my throat. How could two people be so totally out of touch with each other?

It was the morning of our weekly prayer and Bible study group, and when the women arrived I told about my frustrating encounter with David. "We are in a complete deadlock of communication; one of us might as well be speaking Chinese or Hottentot."

Catherine Perkins, a youthful, energetic-looking mother of five teen-agers, cleared her throat before speaking. "You know, David makes a lot of sense sometimes."

"Not to me!" I looked into Catherine's bright blue eyes, and she returned my gaze with a slight smile, as if to soften the impact of her words.

"He's right on one point, at least. You do take the responsibility for 'saving' him too personally. I think you're missing the point. Only God can save him. So why don't you relax and let it happen in its own time? And accept David where he is in his struggle right now."

She paused, and I looked at her strong, almost heavy features, surrounded by thick, dark hair streaked with gray. I had liked Catherine from the day we met in the church library. She was vivacious and outspoken, and I had learned to respect her sensible, well-thought out opinions. "David is suffering, you know—he needs acceptance and Christian love."

There was truth in her words. It was almost funny how God put outspoken friends in my path to point out what I needed to hear. Sue Ann had used almost the same words back in Arizona, and here I was four years later, and I still had not learned to stop pushing David and the children and just loving them instead.

When it was time to pray, I heard Catherine's voice: "Dear God, speak directly to David, and help Sarah to trust You more."

Catherine was the last to leave, and before climbing on her bicycle, she smiled with the look of a conspirator. "Perhaps I ought to warn you—from now on I will be praying for God to heal your marriage."

"That's the last thing in the world I want!"

"I know," Catherine laughed heartily. "I'm glad you admit it, but you know God won't bring David back unless it is a good thing. Don't you trust Him?"

"In theory yes, but in practice. . . ." Inside I was trembling.

"Relax, honey." Catherine touched my arm. "Why don't you and the children come for dinner tomorrow? We'll have a chance to talk some more."

Catherine lived in a two-story house right off the beach. Her engineer husband was on night duty that evening, and Catherine was alone with her five children. The oldest was nineteen, the youngest thirteen, and they were all remarkably well-behaved. After the meal the children cleared the table and did the dishes without fussing.

In contrast the manners of my children were noticeably bad. I had not paid too much attention to it before. Now I felt suddenly embarrassed.

Catherine must have read my thoughts. She carried our coffee cups into the living room where the ocean shimmered in the sunset just outside the big windows. "My house wasn't always running this smoothly," she began. "I had to learn something about priorities first."

"And I suppose I haven't." She was touching a sore point, and I was not sure I liked it.

"You are a gifted writer and a good teacher in Sunday school, but that means nothing if your home and children are neglected."

"I'm better than I was."

"I'm glad." Catherine's face broke into a smile. "But I've seen enough of your house to know that David had considerable grounds for complaint. If God is going to heal your marriage you may have to do most of the changing."

"Aren't you exaggerating a little?"

"I don't think so," Catherine shook her head. "So much of the well-being of the family depends on the woman. Did you ever read Proverbs, chapter thirty-one?"

"Sure." I could barely hide my irritation. Catherine was going too far in implying I was ignorant as well as incompetent. "I'm doing my best, but it isn't easy to be alone in charge of four children."

"Please don't be offended," Catherine caught the defensive tone in my voice. "You are a great deal like me. I am just trying to help you avoid some of the mistakes I made." Her eyes were kind, without condemnation.

My resentment melted away as I looked around the comfortable living room. It was neat without being antiseptic. The potted plants and warm colors made a visitor feel immediately welcome. "If you were ever like me, you've come a long way," I said slowly. "I would like to know your secret."

"It lies in accepting God's prescription for a well-ordered, happy home." Catherine sipped her coffee. "Ask God to change your attitudes where you know they are wrong, but don't sit around waiting to *feel* different. Start doing the obvious things. Go on a regular schedule. Just because there isn't a man at the head of the table doesn't mean you can shirk on a meal." She smiled at my expression. "Your kids will love it and accept more of their own responsibilities too."

"Maybe you're right." I smiled in spite of myself. "As a divorcee I have allowed myself a carelessness I would never have gotten away with if I was married. To be honest, I've enjoyed my freedom."

Catherine laughed. "I'll pray that you won't be able to drag your feet any longer."

I drove home in a thoughtful mood. The children were fussing in the back seat as usual, but I did nothing to stop them. Catherine had pinpointed an area of my life that had never been quite right. There had been some improvements since I began to turn things over to God, but I had been wrong in settling for anything less than the orderly plan for a home I had glimpsed in the Bible. That should have been first on my priority list a long time ago.

I pulled into our driveway, and the children spilled noisily out of the car and raced each other to the front door. There was a persistent little thought in the back of my head: "How can you expect your children to learn proper order if you do not submit to order yourself?"

When they were all in their pajamas, I gathered the children for a talk. "I'm sorry I've been so busy with my own activities that I've let things slide around the house." I spoke firmly to hold their attention. "From now on we're going to operate on a regular schedule." I hit my fist against the palm of my hand and the children were sitting bolt upright. "I promise to have dinner ready at six every evening, and I expect you to be here on time. You are responsible for keeping your rooms neat, helping with the dishes, and carrying out the trash. I am responsible for getting your clothes washed and ready when you need them, and for keeping the rest of the house in order. Is that clear?"

Leif let out an enthusiastic "Yippee! I'm sure glad we're gonna eat at the same time every day. Now I know when to come home!"

"Our friends always eat at six. We can go home when they do." I felt a new wave of remorse as I looked at John and Andrew's beaming faces. I had not realized the hardship I had caused my children.

With regularity, things improved remarkably. A written schedule for mealtime and major household chores, pinned to the kitchen wall, kept me more or less on time, and the children were outspoken in their appreciation. Christine hugged me and bubbled over. "We're more like a *real* family now that everything is neater and we eat always at the same time." The children even responded better to discipline.

My daily Bible reading focused on the references to the role of women and wives, scattered throughout the Old and the New Testaments. I had read most of the passages before, but now they made more sense. I still didn't *like* some of the things I read, but the last year had taught me that my *feelings* on a subject could lead me to draw the wrong conclusions.

Inwardly I was relieved that I did not have to submit or adapt myself to a husband. If that requirement ever came up in the future

I would have to deal with my own reluctance. Just reading some of the passages made me shudder. Especially in the amplified form:

"You married women, . . . subordinate yourselves as being secondary to and dependent on them, and adapt yourselves to them . . . You are to feel for him all that reverence includes—to respect, defer to, revere him; revere means to honor, esteem, appreciate, prize, and in the human sense adore him; and to adore means to admire, praise, be devoted to, deeply love and enjoy your husband. . . ." [1]

"I don't think there is a man in this world I could do that for!" I complained to Catherine. "How can any woman submit to any man like that without losing her own identity?"

"Relax!" Catherine smiled patiently at my agitation. "You are forgetting that this is a three-dimensional arrangement. You are not just submitting to a man, but to God. If you submit wholeheartedly to Him, you can trust God to be in charge of the man, however imperfect he may be."

"I'm scared. If I tell God I am willing to be a wife in the Biblical sense of the word, He might let me get married to some tyrant."

"You know better than that!" Catherine laughed at my expression. "It really boils down to whether or not you believe God when He says that His plan works. Do you, or don't you?"

That was really the heart of the issue I had struggled with for several years. Was I willing to trust myself *completely* to God's plan for me as a woman? The decision could not be postponed indefinitely. My feelings were dead set against it, but unless I surrendered wholeheartedly to God's plan, I would remain forever on the outskirts of a promise. If I held back from trusting Him, He could not bring His plan to fulfillment in my life.

I felt the pounding of my heart. I *wanted* God's plan. I *wanted* to be a complete woman. Suddenly I realized the intensity of my longings. I *wanted* to be loved by a man—in God's way.

I grasped Catherine's hand. "Please be my witness." There was still a struggle inside, but deliberately I spoke the words: "God, I do submit to Your plan for me as a woman. My *feelings* say no, but I say yes, Lord. I trust Your Word. I want Your way, not mine."

When it was over, I felt light inside. The fearful agitation was gone, and something like excited anticipation filled me. It was as if I had cut the moorings of a vessel and set sail on a marvelous journey. I could not—I would not—turn back, and I felt as if the unknown land beyond the horizon was the one I had always longed for.

Catherine held both my hands firmly. "I don't think the real-life situation of submission will be as rough as you fear," she said softly. "I think the worst part is already behind you."

I fervently hoped she was right.

Chapter 11

The Florida Keys

I pulled my boat-trailer up in front of the old Beach Club and got out of the car. The heat and humidity seemed less here with a breath of air blowing from the ocean. The club had been the setting for a Humphrey Bogart movie years ago and still looked charming in a decaying sort of way. The small boat marina was in the back, and lush tropical vegetation grew everywhere.

I went inside for a drink, and the lady behind the bar smiled at me. "You're new around here?"

I nodded. "I'm looking for work and a place to live."

She pointed towards a balding young man eating a sandwich at the other end of the bar. "Art is my cook and bartender. He's leaving to go back north for a few months. Maybe you can rent his place. Then come back and see me." Her smile was open and friendly, and I suddenly felt optimistic. This would be a good place to stay and rest for a while. Pleasant setting, relaxed atmosphere. I slid my drink over and introduced myself to Art. It turned out he was a school teacher who had come to Florida to "re-group after my divorce," he told me.

"I know what you mean," I nodded. "I'm in the same boat."

Art was willing to sublet the little cottage he was renting within walking distance of the club. The owner, an elderly widow, lived in a bungalow in front of the property, and was glad to see the cottage occupied by "a nice young man," as she put it.

Pink flamingos walked in the shallow water of the lagoon just a few yards away, and flaming red hibiscus and bougainvillaea grew by the cottage wall. It was the picture of the perfect Florida idyll on the postcards. Quite an improvement over my miserable quarters in Miami.

Back at the club, Cora, the manager, hired me as Art's replacement at twenty-seven dollars a week. "With meals and all you can drink free," she added.

I gratefully accepted. My needs were small. Now I could continue to give Sarah the regular support money on my bi-weekly visits to Sunrise Beach. I did not tell her I had moved from the Miami area, and she still thought I was working as superintendent on a construction project. When Mel's money ran short I would tell her the job was over.

My intentions were to drink less. Instead, my daily intake increased. The other employees and the regular customers were all heavy drinkers. We kept one another going almost around the clock. By now sleep was nearly impossible for me anyway.

The effort to sober up for my bi-weekly visit to Sunrise Beach was more of an ordeal each time. By early June Mel's money was almost gone. I took four hundred dollars to Sarah and told her that the job was over. I would not come to see the children again for a while. "I'll be looking for work," I felt uncomfortable under her searching gaze. "I'll let you know when I can come back."

"Don't worry about us, but how will you live without an income?" Her concern seemed sincere for once. We were sitting side by side on the stone steps leading to her garden. The sun filtered through the branches of the tree above us, making Sarah's face look almost soft. For a desperate moment I wished that things were different between us. Then the reality of my life back at the club crashed in on me. There was no possible way that Sarah and I and the children could get together again.

The pain was almost unbearable. I stood up. "I'll manage. I have enough to last me a couple of months. Things will get better, I'm sure."

Sarah waved and smiled as I drove off. I tried to smile back, but could not. This time when I pulled off the road to vomit, I thought that I would not be able to make it to the bar down the road.

My life without the children held no meaning. Yet knowing the hopelessness of my own condition, I could not bear the emotional anguish of seeing them again for a while.

SARAH   *Sunrise Beach, Florida*

I had no particular worries about our finances. I could make ends meet with the advance payment on a new book assignment, co-authoring the story of a heroin addict who had been healed through a personal conversion to Christianity. Sonny Gonzales was now a pastor in Los Angeles, and the publisher paid my way out to interview him. I was impressed by the dramatic change in his life. If God could do it for him, why not for David?

Sonny smiled confidently. "Don't worry. God will touch David before long." Why could not my faith be that simple and strong?

Jack and Lydia Morris invited me for dinner. Jack's faith seemed as unswerving as Sonny's. "It is just a matter of time," he rubbed his balding head. "Are you prepared to be his wife when God brings him back?"

I felt uneasy. "*If* God brings him . . . maybe."

"Invite us to the wedding." Lydia hugged me.

"Don't expect it." Our conversation seemed strangely unreal to me. "It doesn't look promising."

"It's always darkest before dawn," Lydia's smile was undaunted.

Back in Florida I worked hard to transcribe my tapes and make an outline for the book. It was difficult and I felt restless.

One morning I took off from work and went house-hunting. Without David's support money and with Joanie gone, I really could not afford to keep such a big house. My search was half-hearted and when I found nothing to suit us, I at last exclaimed, "God, if You want us to move, where is the house?"

In the silence that followed, an odd thought came into my mind. I "saw" a large, two-story, white house on a hillside with a view over a city and what looked like a Norwegian fjord. There were tall, snow-capped mountains on the other side. I had an "inner view" of the house, the kitchen, and a breakfast nook I "knew" had once been a sun porch.

I could not remember ever having seen a house quite like that, and certainly not in Sunrise Beach. Slightly bemused I said, "If *that's* our house, God—where is it?" I really had not expected an answer, but the thought that came into my mind was clear as a bell: "Seattle, Washington."

Turning my car resolutely towards home, I decided to forget about the house hunting. I was not going to move cross-country on a foolish impulse. By careful managing I could afford to stay on in the house we had all come to love.

The mail had arrived—just a magazine and my Norwegian paper. Opening the magazine, my eyes fell on a by-line: Delores Weissbaum, Seattle, Washington. I felt a flutter in my stomach. I had not heard from Delores for years but we once had attended a writing class together in Arizona. I put the magazine away and opened my newspaper. There, on the front page was the picture of a familiar face and the caption: "Lars Asvoll makes good in Seattle, Washington." Lars and I had been classmates in high school. Now, I read, he was an executive with a large Seattle firm.

"Coincidence, pure coincidence," I muttered to myself. There would have to be something far more substantial before I would even consider the idea of moving my household thousands of miles away. Yet it *could* be that God's plan for our future included a move to Seattle. If that was the case, I would be willing to go.

"Show me," I whispered. "I won't do anything until You convince me."

Putting the question of moving out of my mind, I went to work on the book outline and got nowhere. There simply was not enough information on my tapes. Frustrated, I called Sonny in Los Angeles.

"I just don't remember enough details of the early years," he was apologetic. "I wish you could go to Seattle and interview the guy who used to be my assistant."

The restlessness I had felt all day was suddenly replaced by a great calm. The promptings to move to Seattle had not been random thoughts out of nowhere. I was not losing my mind. The pieces were beginning to fit together.

"I think I'll do that," I told Sonny. "I'll be in touch." Hanging up the phone I said aloud, "I'll go, God, if that is Your plan for us. But You'll have to arrange the circumstances and the financing of the move."

The children seemed enthusiastic when I told them, and neighbors who heard of our move came to ask if I wanted to sell any furniture. Soon my aging refrigerator, beds and tables, chests and chairs were gone, and we were reduced to what could fit comfortably into a rental truck. The proceeds from the sale covered the expense of the move.

Gerald Tunney, one of Peter's friends who often came to play basketball with the boys, asked if he could drive the truck cross-country for us. Gerald was an ex-marine and ex-drug addict whom the children admired greatly. They listened in awe as he told how he got the bright red scar on his left cheek: "In a knife fight when I was drunk—before Jesus changed my life."

John was allowed to touch the scar with his finger. "Man," he breathed, "I never knew anyone who was that bad!"

That evening there was a new expectancy in the children's prayers. "Thank You for changing Gerald, God. Please change daddy right away. We know You can do it."

I felt a flicker of conscience as I thought of David. He had looked pale and wan on his last visit. What would he say when he heard that the children were moving so far away?

"God, You are in charge of our move and of David," I whispered. "It must be part of Your plan for all of us." Actually I felt tremendously relieved that we were going to be too far away for David to upset our tranquility by regular visits.

My conscience was greatly eased when he called to tell me that his own plans would prevent him from coming to see us anytime soon. It probably made little difference to him where we lived.

Then at dawn a week later, on the morning of our departure, my phone rang again. In half sleep I heard David's voice: "I'll miss you." He slurred his words.

"You mean you'll miss the children."

"No—I'll miss you."

Silence hung between us and, I heard the twitter of a bird in the gray dawn outside my window.

"Tell me the truth, do you love me?"

My mouth was dry and I was shaking. "As a Christian, yes, but as a wife, no."

I had to strain to hear his muffled reply. "I just wanted to know. Have a good trip."

"Thank you, good luck to you too."

There was a click in the receiver, and I turned back to the wall and restless sleep. My alarm went off an hour later. Everything was packed and ready to go. I jumped up with the excitement of the trip. The memory of the phone call at dawn brushed past me and faded away. It probably meant nothing. David must have been drunk.

DAVID   *The Florida Keys*

After the phone call I don't remember how I made it back to my little cottage. There I collapsed on the bed, and heavy sobs shook my body. It was all over now. I had seen Sarah and the children for the last time. I was physically incapable of ever going to see them again. There was nothing left for me to do but wait for the end.

My days blended into one another. Somehow I functioned in my job. On my off hours, when I was sober enough, I sometimes took the boat out for a fast spin, or drove my car at breakneck speed for hours. I expected to die and wished it would come soon.

Often, when I was drinking hard, my conscious mind faded out, and something else—a power greater than my own—took control over my body.

I had been a realist all my life, and had not believed in a reality beyond the physical universe. Yet now I experienced crossing the boundary lines over into something else. The power and terror I felt was real, all right. It existed and it was about to devour me.

At times I was conscious during those hours that something other than myself was operating in my body. It was as if I, David Van Wade, was gagged and bound in a corner, helplessly watching while something—or someone—was speaking with my voice and moving with my arms and legs. Other times I knew nothing of the activities of my own body until friends told me the next day.

I was not consciously aware of taking my two drinking partners Lou and Bud on a night ride down a narrow bridge highway between the Keys. I drove at 100 miles an hour on the wrong side of the road and with my lights off. My two friends had been scared sober, but a week later Lou tried the same stunt. He hurled himself into a head-on collision that left him paralyzed and blind.

Neither was I aware the early morning when I pounded on the

door of a girlfriend's apartment. She avoided me for days after that and I finally forced her to say why. "I opened the door and didn't recognize you at first," Helen turned white at the memory. "You looked like the devil himself, your features horribly contorted and eyes glowering with an eerie light." She hid her face in her hands with a sob. "Go away Dave, and don't try to see me again, ever."

So I was turning into some Jekyll and Hyde monster. Vaguely I remembered standing outside my door trying to fit the key into the lock. The moon was bright over the lagoon, and I was making so much noise that the old lady in the front came out to ask if I needed help. I turned and saw terror change her face into a mask. She ran back to her own house, and I heard the door slam and the bolt fasten on the inside. Obviously I had frightened her terribly. She never spoke to me after that. The following day a carpenter came to fix up a room in the garage next to my cottage. Soon a renter moved in. Apparently the old lady was afraid to ask me to leave and afraid to be alone with me on the property.

My own terror was worst in the hours between unconsciousness and wakefulness in the mornings. I knew myself hurtling on a one-way ride to hell, with someone else at the controls. There was no way out.

Ken Johnson was the sturdy-looking skipper of a lobster boat. He brought his wife to the club for dinner whenever he was in port, and we often talked. One evening Ken said, "How about coming along on our next lobster-run, Dave? We could use you as a cook. There's good money when the catch is big."

"Sure." His idea struck me as a good one. "When are you leaving?"

"Thursday. I'll pick you up at five in the morning."

The next day was Wednesday, and I determined to keep my drinking to a minimum to be in shape for the trip. Instead, I became terribly drunk. I was conscious, but no longer in control, and cursed my misfortune as I staggered over furniture, spilled drinks, and fell sprawling to the floor. It was three o'clock in the morning when I finally stumbled down the path to my cottage. Mustering all my efforts, I managed to set my two alarm clocks near the head of the bed where I would be sure to hear them go off. Then I fell in a stupor on my pillow.

When the alarm went off I was shaking so hard I did not think I could stand up. But I felt an almost obsessive desire to go on that trip.

Ken did not come to pick me up as he had promised. He had probably heard that I was too drunk to stand on my feet. I grabbed a bundle of clothes and made my way down to the dock. Ken was about to loose the moorings; the "Annie K." was ready to take off. I could barely put one foot ahead of the other to cross the gangway, and Ken looked as if he wanted to put me back ashore. But he grinned instead.

"Glad you could make it. Put your clothes in the forward cabin. You'll be sleeping on deck."

As we moved slowly out of the small harbor I felt a tremendous sense of relief. I was sick, but I had made it. Somehow the accomplishment was important.

Had I known that the "Annie K." was heading for seven days at sea without a drop of liquor on board, I might not have come at all. Towards the end of the first day I had the shakes bad, along with trying to balance on a moving deck in the narrow galley. The second day was worse, and the third day I would have swum ashore if we had been within sight of land. But on the fourth day I felt better. The salt air, the movement of the boat, and the quiet routine on board were invigorating. I felt better than I had for months.

We reached the Cay Sal Banks, and Ken set his 200 traps. The weather was beautiful and the water calm. We were anchored in only forty feet of water, so clear you could see the grains of sand on the bottom. It was like being afloat in a giant aquarium.

The other crew members were experienced scuba divers. After a full day of pulling lobster traps, we all went diving. For me, it was like entering a dimension of life I had not known before. Underwater, with the strange sensation of weightlessness and surrounded by colors and shapes unlike the world I knew above, perspectives were suddenly and unpredictably altered. Once I turned my head and stared into the unblinking eyes of a shark silently poised by my shoulder. Ken had warned me not to make any quick movements below, and slowly I turned and swam towards the boat. The shark did not follow. Later, panting on the sun-warmed planks of the deck, I realized that I had not been afraid. Death could have come quickly, the end I had waited for.

The only reading material on board was a machinist's manual

and an old salt-stained Bible someone had once given Ken. When I could find nothing else to do I read a few lines here and there, but they did not impress me much. The Bible still seemed as quaint and remote from reality as I had always found it.

One morning I awoke at sunrise, and sat up on a coil of coarse rope to watch the shining disc rise out of the sea. Our boat was only a tiny speck on a vast, empty ocean, but with the warming rays of the sun and the gentle rocking of the boat under me, I felt an aliveness and at-homeness in the world that I could never remember having felt before. I had lived with pain from one moment to the next for so long. Now I was suddenly aware of an absence of pain, at least for the moment.

Something appeared to flash over the ocean to my left. I turned and saw a brilliantly white sea bird flying towards me, directly out of the sunrise it seemed. My eyes followed the perfect lines of the big white bird as it turned in a graceful arc towards our boat. Then I caught my breath in surprise, because there, coming towards me, were not one but three birds flying side by side in perfect precision.

They circled the boat and disappeared as small specks in the western sky. I sat motionless staring after them. Somehow their appearance had shaken me. I had been so certain that there was only one bird—yet there were three.

I sat there in the warm sunlight, barefoot, and wearing old faded jeans. Suddenly I became intensely aware that beyond the gently rocking boat and the vast shimmering ocean lay my shattered life. My family, my position, and my money were gone. My pride, my dreams, and my hopes had vanished. I could do nothing more to restore them or even to help myself survive.

Within me rose a wordless cry. If there existed a personal God and if He cared for me I wanted to know about it.

It was not a cry for help because I did not know if there was anyone to cry to. But for the first time in my life I acknowledged the possibility that He might be there. Beyond that I had no thought of what might or might not happen. I sat there on the boat deck, willing to accept that God was really there. That was all.

Our catch was exceptionally good, and my share of the money amounted to a substantial sum. The trip had been an accomplishment and significant, although I could not tell exactly what made it that way.

We hit port at four o'clock in the morning. I felt good as I made my way home and went to bed. No problem sleeping. The next morning I got up and went over to the club for breakfast. Everything was the same. I had not expected it to change, yet somehow I felt different. I wanted to leave and go someplace where I could get along with less drinking. With my old buddies I knew that was impossible.

When I told Cora I was leaving, she looked distressed. "You don't steal from the cash register. I'll give you more money and responsibility if you'll stay."

"My ex-wife and kids are on the West Coast," I told her. "I want to go where I can see them once in a while."

Somehow I was not able to leave right away. It seemed as if every time I tried to get away, some inner force I could not understand propelled me to the bar where rounds of farewell drinks left me physically disabled again. Each morning I struggled to hold on to a couple of hours of near-sobriety after I had repaired the previous night's hangover and before I had begun drinking seriously for the day. Those hours were my only hope for a getaway.

Finally, one night, I was able to get some sleep, and the next morning I was steady enough to pack. Without going to the club to say goodbye, I left and headed north, stopping only for gas and avoiding the gas stations near a bar. I wanted nothing to prevent me from leaving Florida. In Louisiana, on the second day, I pulled into a motel and headed for the cocktail lounge. I was tense and tired and got quite drunk, but rested enough to get up early and head on west. Something drove me on. A determination I could not identify—but it kept me going.

SARAH

Seattle, Washington

I had written Delores Weissbaum to tell her we were coming. She had found a house for us on a hill overlooking the city and Puget Sound.

"Most of the Norwegians live in this section of town." Delores smiled. "I thought you'd feel at home."

The air was fresh after a summer shower. The gardens along the street were ablaze with color. The grass and the trees were intensely green. The sun glittered on the water, and beyond rose the majestic Olympic Mountains.

"It's beautiful," I whispered. "So much like home." I felt a quickening of my heartbeat. And so much like the vision, I thought.

There was only one thing wrong. The house Delores had found was really too small for us. It was painted green and had only a partial view. The house I had "seen" had been white with a gorgeous view.

I was strangely disappointed. Almost reluctantly I paid the twenty-five-dollar deposit. Before we could move in, I would have to look for beds, tables and chairs, a stove and refrigerator, but I felt less than enthusiastic about it.

Delores served iced-tea, and her gray eyes were serious behind the dark-rimmed glasses. "What's bugging you, Sarah? Is it the house?"

I nodded. "I had such a beautiful vision back in Florida." I told her all about it, and she looked upset. "Why didn't you tell me in the first place?"

"I didn't want you to think I am a complete nut."

"I'm disappointed in you," Delores smoothed her long plaid skirt. "How can you settle for second-best when God has promised you a better house?"

"You're right." I suddenly felt ashamed, but somehow the gloom of the afternoon had lifted. "I'll call the realtor back and cancel our deal, even if I lose the deposit."

The realtor offered to return the money, although he had first told me it was not refundable. While I was on the phone, Delores scanned the Sunday paper and discovered a promising new ad. "Listen to this." She was excited. "Large home for lease, partly furnished, view."

Anticipation stirred in me. "Let's call!"

The man who answered the phone described the house: "It's a two-story with a view of Puget Sound, five bedrooms, dining room and a breakfast nook." He hesitated for a moment, then added, "The breakfast nook is actually a converted sun porch."

I did not need to hear another word. "Please don't rent it to anyone before we get there!"

The man laughed at my eagerness. "O.K. lady, just hurry."

We drove to the northeast section of Seattle and I would have recognized the house without the address. It was the white, two-story house with the pillars in front I had "seen" in Florida. The spacious rooms were furnished with everything we needed, including a spare bedroom for Gerald who planned to stay for a while. There was even a small study, complete with bookshelves, large desk and typewriter table. I had to pinch myself to make sure I wasn't dreaming.

In the breakfast nook I stood alone for a moment, looking out over the roofs of the houses, across the blue expanse of water to the white-topped Olympic Mountains rising majestically in the distance. Happiness mingled with awe inside me. How incredible that God had brought me all the way across the country directly to a house He had picked for us.

The owner of the house was a Swedish engineer who had taken his family along on an eighteen-month assignment overseas. The kind man who showed us around the house was a neighbor, Mr. Swanson, whose blue eyes and thinning blond hair told of a Scandinavian background as well.

"What's the rent?" I suddenly realized I had not asked and felt a flicker of fear. The house was so big and nice, what if I couldn't afford it?

"Two hundred a month, including utilities."

The little green house had been two hundred and twenty-five, without utilities. I felt a mixture of gratitude and shame tug at me. How could I have doubted God's concern for every detail?

When the rental agreement had been signed and the first month's rent paid in advance, Mr. Swanson extended a large hand to shake mine. "Welcome," he smiled broadly. "I hope you like fruits and vegetables. The wife and I love to garden, but we have much more than we can eat. Send the boys down with a basket." He touched his faded blue cap with his finger and went out the back door where a small gate opened in the fence between his house and ours.

Leif let out a shout, "Yippee! We sure are lucky."

"Let's thank God." I resisted the urge to leap and shout myself.

Down the hill we discovered a Norwegian bakery, grocery store, delicatessen, and restaurants where the people spoke Norwegian or broken English. We wore the Norwegian sweaters I had knitted and received friendly nods from our neighbors. The small weekly newspaper was full of Norwegian names and ads for Scandinavian products and gatherings. We were as close to "home" as it was possible to get on this side of the Atlantic.

The children loved Norwegian food. Christine's favorite was fish soup, made from fresh cod, while the boys relished "pølse," dinner sausage, served with mashed potatoes and melted butter. Our budget was slim, but I was learning to prepare food with less expensive ingredients from the cookbook. No more package mixes or frozen dinners.

Gerald found a job in a hamburger stand a few blocks away, and brought his small weekly check to me. He was "big brother" to the three boys, and established a firm daily schedule of exercise and Bible study. Every morning they jogged around the block, then did push-ups and sit-ups and spent half an hour studying the Bible. The discipline was good for all of them.

One of our neighbors was an elderly Swedish widow I first met in church. "Aunt" Adah let me know that her door was always open, whenever I needed a heart-to-heart talk. Her face, softly framed by gray curls, was wrinkled, but the blue eyes held a lively sparkle. In her cozy living room, where potted plants framed the view of Puget Sound and her cat purred loud contentment on his pillow, I felt at home. On my very first visit Aunt Adah announced that she would pray daily for David. "God will reach him," her smile was confident. "Just wait and see."

David was thousands of miles away, and I preferred not to think about him. He was no longer involved in our lives. He was not providing any money for child support; my small income was sufficient, and slowly increasing. I was dependent on God and secure in the knowledge that He would supply everything we needed. He had demonstrated that in the past.

For the first time in my life, I liked being me and living the way I did. It was good to be independent of a man. Of course there were still problems with discipline of the children and minor crises in the household. But I was learning to cope, and things were better than they had ever been.

Chapter 12

Los Angeles, California

By the time I reached Phoenix I was worn out. I stopped at Kirk Pickens' house, and he took one look at my bedraggled face. "Man, come on in. You need to rest!" His wife fixed me a solid meal of pork chops, beans, and biscuits. Kirk drank his beer and talked while I ate. He had left my old employer and was doing well selling refrigeration units. "In this part of the country anything cold sells." He wiped the beads of perspiration off his gleaming red face.

With Florida far behind me I could relax with an ice-cold beer and tell Kirk of my plans to settle in California once more.

"You can make it." Kirk slapped me on the back. "The divorce was a rough break, but I always said you can do anything you put your mind to, Dave. Good luck!"

I was no longer as sure of that as I had once been, but Kirk's enthusiasm gave me a much-needed boost. Rested after a few hours sleep, I got up before dawn to cross the desert into California. I was more optimistic about the future than I had been in a long time.

East of Indio, a car coming towards me crossed the center line into my lane. Thinking the driver had gone to sleep, I blinked my lights to alert him. Instead, he veered crazily and increased his speed, heading straight for me like a Kamikaze pilot zeroing in on his target. I felt strangely calm, knowing that the end might be near. With only seconds to spare, I drove off the road, heading up the steep embankment and turning my car at an angle to avoid head-on impact. Then I turned off the ignition and crouched in the front seat.

The other driver hurled into me at top speed, and I heard the sickening thud and screech of metal against metal as he careened off the side of my car and on down the road. I climbed out to inspect the damage. My front fender had been pushed in and there was a scratch along the side of the car, but the engine started up without hesitation, and I pulled back onto the road.

The first glimmer of dawn was breaking over the desert. Only a few weeks ago I had hurled my own car down a highway on the wrong side in an unconscious search for the end. With a flicker of surprise I realized that this time I had acted to stay alive—I *wanted* to live.

In Los Angeles I called my sister Jane who was glad to share her apartment with me while I got settled. I had a little money left from the lobster catch, but I needed a job right away.

In response to several newspaper ads, I landed job interviews with two large building products manufacturers. They were encouraging and told me to wait for their final decision on hiring. To kill time I tried to contact old friends in the area. Most had moved away, but Cliff Barnhouse was still selling stocks and bonds in Riverside. We met for lunch, and he looked better than I remembered. His old baggy suit, frayed at the cuffs, had been replaced by well-fitting slacks and an expensive looking sports coat. I glanced at his fingernails. They had always been dirty with oil and grease from his car engine. Now they were clean, and Cliff smiled as he caught my glance.

"Things are different, old friend." He looked confident.

"So what are you drinking?" I beckoned for the waitress. "It sounds like we've got cause to celebrate."

"Just plain ginger ale."

"Come on," I was disappointed. "We've had some good times over drinks before. How can we have a reunion if you don't join me?"

"Sorry, Dave," Cliff's blue eyes didn't waver. "But I haven't had a drink for two years."

"How's that?" I was vaguely curious. "You were hitting the bottle harder than I did."

"I know. It nearly cost me my health, my job, and my family." Cliff leaned forward with his old eagerness. "Alcohol had me licked, Dave." His eyes were glued to mine. "Then a friend took me to an AA meeting. They don't have a magic cure, but they have a program that works. Are you interested?"

I gulped my drink. "Wait a minute. I may have a bit of a problem, but. . . ."

"I'd like to see you get out of the rut, old friend." Cliff's concern was touching, but I shifted uneasily in my chair. He handed me a card from his wallet. "Does any of that fit you?"

The card held a list of questions, and I glanced at them reluctantly. I had heard about Alcoholics Anonymous, a bunch of ex-drunks who got together to brag about who had been worse off. It wasn't for me. But the questions on the card were right on target:

"Do you gulp down your drinks quickly when you are bored or restless?"

"Do you ever have blackouts, not remembering what happened after you got drunk?"

I had seen enough. "You know my answers as well as I do," I tried to smile. "I won't deny that I have a problem, but I'm learning to live with it. AA isn't the answer for me. I don't like sharing the details of my personal life with groups of people."

"I don't mean to push you, Dave," Cliff was apologetic. "I'd like for you to come along to a meeting, just to see what it is like, but it's up to you. We're friends either way."

We ate our meal while Cliff did most of the talking. He was excited about his new way of life without alcohol. Apparently he was doing better financially as well as personally.

"Why don't you come to the house for dinner tomorrow?" he said. "Alice would love to see you."

"I'd like to." Seeing Cliff at home would tell me more about the validity of his sober way of life.

Bits of our conversation stayed with me as I drove back to Jane's apartment. Cliff had told me he could not get along without the twice-weekly AA meetings.

"I can't fight this battle alone. I get so thirsty for a drink I can't stand it. Alcohol used to be my lifeline, I couldn't go a day without the stuff."

For Cliff the case seemed clear-cut. He was the kind of person who thrived on group activities, and he was probably a little weak on will power. I was a loner; I could handle it myself. Besides, I did not want to cut out alcohol altogether. I needed it to function. It was like medicine for the diabetic, I told myself again. It would not be realistic for me to go the AA route. I could not imagine myself living like Cliff with a burning, unsatisfied desire for alcohol for the rest of my life.

My last visit to Cliff's house had been eight years ago. It had looked neglected then, the yard unkempt, full of toys and debris, the paint on the house peeling, the furniture inside worn and food-stained.

The contrast was remarkable. Today the house had a fresh coat of paint, shrubbery and flower beds bordered a well-manicured lawn. Inside, the furniture and wall-to-wall carpet looked new and spotless. The children greeted me politely and were quiet and well-mannered at the table. I remembered distinctly that they had been terribly rowdy before. But of course, they were older now. Alice was pleasant and served an excellent meal. After dinner she left us alone with our coffee in front of the fireplace. Cliff was eager to talk. "It isn't easy to stay sober, but it's a lot better than being drunk."

"So you've chosen what you feel is the lesser of two evils, enforced sobriety instead of dependency on alcohol?" I asked and Cliff nodded.

"Those are the only two alternatives available to an alcoholic. You can be a sober or a drunk alcoholic, but you've got to face that you're an alcoholic." He sat quietly absorbed in thoughts for a moment.

"Two years ago I was a drunk, and all I cared about was to maintain my supply of booze. Today I'm sober. I've paid my bills, fixed up the house, my family is doing better." He sipped his coffee and I was silent.

"You know there's even more at stake," Cliff's eyes probed mine. "It's really a choice between life and death. The drinking alcoholic thinks he can control his drinking, but we know he's kidding himself. Soon he loses his job and his family, his physical and mental abilities deteriorate. He's headed for a miserable end."

I remained silent. There was nothing to say.

"Tell you what," Cliff said cheerfully. "There's a meeting just a couple of miles down the road. Why don't you come along and listen in? You don't have to say anything. The program is based on voluntary participation."

"O.K." I suddenly realized that I wanted to see for myself.

The meeting was held in the recreation hall of a local church. Fifteen or twenty men sat around a table, talking. They looked up and nodded a greeting as we came in. No one paid special attention to us, and I sat down gratefully.

I had expected the men to look like drunks. Skid row types. Instead they were neatly dressed. Some even looked quite prosperous.

A fellow about my age, wearing a suit and tie, spoke up. "Before we begin, let's introduce ourselves. I'm Bob and I'm an alcoholic." The fellow next to him nodded and said, "I'm Rex and I'm an alcoholic." With a sinking feeling I realized that the turn would soon come to me. I got hot under the friendly gazes of the others.

My throat was dry and I forced out the words, "I'm Dave . . . and I'm an alcoholic." I had never said the words before. The friendly faces around the table registered no shock. Hearing myself say the words aloud made the fact suddenly and inevitably established.

Until now it had been my personal problem. I had even thought of myself in a unique position. But these fellows around the table all identified. I listened in silence as they talked back and forth among themselves and I was impressed. Around the table were a bank president, a truck driver, a schoolteacher, a salesman, a realtor, a plumber, and a newspaper writer. They all admitted that they had used alcohol as a crutch and that it had finally licked them. Now they were committed to helping one another stay sober and cope with the kind of pressures that had once triggered their drinking.

Admitting your own helplessness was the first step, I was told. The second step was to believe that what they called "a Higher Power" could help overcome your weakness.

"It isn't some mysterious force outside you," Cliff explained with a smile. "The way I see it, we're all born with it. All we need is to learn how to release it."

That was the kind of positive thinking I agreed with wholeheartedly. I always thought I had the power for successful living within myself. I had just never hit the right formula for using it. Perhaps if I tried harder it would work.

"We don't promise *never* to drink again," Cliff explained. "But anyone can fight the urge for a determined amount of time—say fifteen minutes or an hour. You walk a mile by taking one step at a time, you stay sober for a year by doing it an hour at a time."

The thought of fighting the desire to drink for a limited time was far more reasonable than attempting life-long abstinence.

"You can tell yourself that you may drink after the hour is up," Cliff read my thoughts. "But for that one hour you've made an unbreakable contract. Later you can extend it or drop it."

"It makes better sense than I thought," I nodded. "Maybe I could try for a short while, anyway."

"Wonderful!" Cliff slapped my shoulder. "There's a meeting somewhere every night if you need it—sort of replaces the visit to the bar—and you can call an AA member near you anytime the going gets rough."

His arm remained around my shoulders. "If you slip nobody will criticize you for it. We've all done the same thing. You can even come to the meeting drunk, as long as you don't disturb the proceedings."

Driving home I dared to be more hopeful about the future. The men I had met led successful lives. By using the program I should be able to get back on my feet and someday have something to offer the children. Not being able to contribute to their support was one of the most painful aspects of my present circumstances. It was futile to attempt to build a good life without them. Perhaps with the help of the AA program Sarah and I could begin to communicate again.

Jack and Lydia Morris were still in seminary and invited me for dinner regularly. Their home held an atmosphere of quiet peace that always had a calming effect. Jack was anxious to see me get in touch with Sarah again.

"What those kids of yours need is a Christian home." His deep-set blue eyes showed concern. "When are you going to accept that God has a better formula for living than anything you can figure out for yourself?"

Jane had a Bible on her bookshelf, and I looked up some of the passages Jack referred to about the Christian home. I was pleased to find something I agreed with: that the husband should be the head of the wife. If Sarah would agree to submit to me in the way the Bible recommended, we could perhaps build a workable relationship.

Jack was skeptical. "It's the right formula, but it won't work unless you both accept the basic premise of faith in a personal God."

Disregarding his warning I carefully composed a letter to Sarah.

Dear Sarah:

I have been studying the Bible, and the formula for marriage I find there makes a lot of sense. Read Proverbs, chapter 31, and I Timothy, chapter 2, verses 10 and 11. If you are ready to take God's command seriously, we can perhaps discuss further our joint responsibility for our four children who need a complete home.

In light of these Bible passages I hope you can also see your errors of the past. . . .

Sincerely, David.

P.S. I need the full support of a loving wife. Your competitive attitude in the past caused me much suffering, and I could not endure it again.

————————

SARAH   *Seattle, Washington*

My hands trembled as I opened the letter postmarked Los Angeles. Why had David followed us to the West Coast? I felt a tightening in my throat as I scanned the typewritten page. Proverbs 31 was familiar, but what had Paul written to Timothy? I found the passage in my Bible: "Christian women should be noticed for being kind and good. . . . Women should listen and learn quietly and humbly." [1]

Despair nearly choked me. "O God, please not this! I know I promised to submit to Your plan for me as a woman and as a wife, if I should ever marry again, but is this what You require of me?" A chilling fear made me shiver.

With the crumpled page in my hand I ran down the street and burst breathlessly into Aunt Adah's quiet house. She read the letter carefully, then looked calmly at my red eyes.

"Don't be afraid. God loves you and doesn't want you to suffer. Thank Him for this letter. At least David is reading the Bible. Maybe next he'll understand what God is saying to *him*."

"I'm terrified—what do I answer?"

"Don't write till the terror is gone. Ask God to give you love and wisdom to tell David what you honestly think without hurting his feelings."

"Then you don't think this means I have to marry him?" Hope leaped within me.

Aunt Adah's blue eyes were twinkling merrily. "Don't jump to conclusions. David isn't asking you to marry him. He just wants to know what you think about the Biblical formula for marriage. That's all."

Leaning back in Aunt Adah's big chair I felt weak with relief. Of course, God was still in charge, and I could trust Him. With a surge of assurance I leaped up, kissed Aunt Adah, and stepped back outside where the sun shone on the colorful flowers in the gardens along our street.

A squirrel scurried up the white birch in our front yard and I drank in the fresh air. How silly of me to panic like that. So much had happened in my life since I turned over the management of my future to God. Everything had worked together for good. I was happier and felt more alive than ever before. How could I think that even David's letter and his nearness in Los Angeles posed a threat?

In the quiet of my little study surrounded by the books and pictures I loved most, I felt at peace as I wrote to Catherine in Florida:

Dear Sister:

David has followed us to Los Angeles and wrote that he wants to know what I think about a Christian marriage in light of Proverbs 31 and I Timothy 2:10 and 11. At first I panicked, but now I have peace. Please pray. . . .

Love, Sarah.

Putting David's letter aside, I went to work on my book manuscript. I would write him when I knew what to say; I felt no urgency about it.

Catherine's answer came by return mail:

Dear Sarah:

I wondered how long it would be before David showed up in your neck of the woods. I'm sure Jesus is drawing him to Himself. Are you prepared to do your part? I am really excited about the latest development. I can almost *see* God at work in your situation.

Love, Catherine.

A slow irritation tugged at me. Who's side was Catherine on anyway? She asked if I was ready to do my part, but what about David's part? I stared at the blue peaks of the Olympic Mountains where the angle of the sun was creating an intricate pattern of light and shadow between the ridges and valleys. At other times of the day the mountain range looked like a solid, majestic wall, but now each individual crag and ridge was sharply defined in a fascinating depth dimension.

Unexpectedly, tears popped into my eyes. God did not look at our lives in the single dimension of "my side" or "David's side," but from His perspective, seeing it all. From God's point of view we were both wrong in insisting on our rights. It was true that David had a right to expect his wife to do her part, but he had overlooked the fact that God also had a role for him as husband and head of the family. Now I knew what to write him.

Dear David:

I've been thinking about what you wrote. I believe the formula for marriage in the Bible is valid today. However, I don't think it works unless both husband and wife submit to God's plan.

That means that Christ is the head of the man, just as the man is the head of the wife, and the man is told to love his wife the way Christ loves us.

I don't think I am ready to discuss marriage yet, although I hope someday I can be a wife for someone in the way God intends.

We are all well and pray for you daily.

Sincerely, Sarah.

I hesitated, then added:

P.S. I don't want to be married to a man who doesn't like me—and you never did. I'm sure such a marriage would end in another failure and much pain for both of us.

I felt tremendously relieved. I had been able to tell David the truth and hoped he would be able to understand.

It was only a question of time before the children would need the firm hand of a father with proper authority. But David was hardly the right one yet. In Florida his presence had only fanned the rebellion that smoldered under the surface, especially in Leif.

Gerald had returned to Florida, and the children missed him, but I shuddered at the thought of a closer relationship with David right now. Hopefully my letter would make him realize how incompatible our lives were.

Chapter 13

Los Angeles, California

I had turned down a job selling building supplies in Nevada in order to wait for a management position with a firm in Los Angeles. I wanted to stay in Southern California, and Frank Lavarte, my future boss, said it would be just a matter of days before the job would be mine.

Waiting was hard, and I found it difficult to control my drinking. I could manage fairly well during the daytime, but dusk always made me restless. As long as I could remember, the early evening hours between daylight and dark had affected me adversely. The pressure was real enough to chase me into a bar or to the bottle at home.

Chuck, an AA member who lived nearby, had given me his phone number to call in emergencies. As long as we were talking, I could hang on. Chuck said:

"My worst time is the early morning. Once you pin down your roughest time of day it's easier to fight."

That was not true for me. Instead, I began to anticipate the onset of depression and anxiety early in the afternoon. I decided to spend the evening in an AA meeting, but when I could not find the address, I ended up in a bar. Discouraged, I tried to start all over again the next morning, but so far I had not been able to stay off the booze for a single twenty-four hour period.

"Hang in there," Chuck encouraged me. "Remember you're not going to lick this thing alone. Admit that the alcohol is stronger than you, and ask for help from the Higher Power. And lean on the rest of us whenever you need to. That's what we're all doing."

More and more I found myself going to Jack and Lydia's in the evenings. There I felt less of a pressing need for alcohol. They welcomed me warmly even when I showed up with a few under my belt.

Jack's idea of a Higher Power differed from Cliff's and mine. "There's a Higher Power, all right," he scratched his balding head and looked thoughtful. "But if it exists in each of us and is a power for good, how do you explain the conflict with evil we all seem to experience?"

"I wish I knew. . . ."

Jack's gaze was penetrating, but his thin lips curved in a smile. "The only explanation that makes sense to me is the one I find in the Bible: the Higher Power is God who exists separately from us, and Who created us with freedom to choose between good and evil. I see each of us caught in a tremendous power struggle between God Who is good and an evil which is also real and powerful. We're faced with the choice of surrendering to either side."

In a flash, I remembered the terror of the in-between world I had experienced in Florida, but I pushed it aside. "I'm sorry, Jack," I shrugged. "I've tried to make sense out of the Bible, but it doesn't ring true."

Jack's smile was undaunted. "Don't give up on it yet. God is real, and I'm convinced you'll encounter Him soon—if you really want to."

"Maybe." The thought was not so incredible as it once had seemed.

When I told of writing Sarah, Lydia's warm brown eyes seemed to light up from within. "In time you two will be together. I'm sure of it."

For once I wished I had her sense of certainty.

When Sarah's answer came, I tore open the envelope and scanned the typewritten note. The disappointment was heavy inside me. She had not understood or accepted what I had to say, and responded with some nonsense about "Christ being the head of the man!" I had hoped she was mature enough to drop that religious double-talk.

Time hung heavy on my hands without any word from the company in Los Angeles. They were still waiting for some high-level decisions. I had nothing to do except straighten up Jane's apartment and do the cooking. I held off my first drink till I started in the kitchen, usually about eleven in the morning. I had switched to wine because it was cheaper, and hoped the lower alcohol content would keep me from getting drunk.

In the evenings I usually went to a bar to avoid a scene with Jane who frequently blew her top about my "stupidity," as she called it.

"How can you waste yourself?" she yelled at me. "You sit here day after day doing nothing except getting drunk. What kind of a life is that?"

Her words echoed in my mind as I drove down the freeway. Jane was right. I was leading a rotten kind of life. It would be better to end it. I had an insurance policy for $25,000. The suicide clause was invalid by now. Besides, who would know the difference if I drove into the concrete divider of a freeway underpass? Sarah and the children would be cared for, and I would be beyond pain.

Into my fogged-up brain came the reminder of the job waiting for me. I slowed down and felt a little better. I would call Frank again in the morning.

But when I called, Frank's voice was apologetic. "Tomorrow, Dave. I'm sure we'll have some definite news tomorrow."

I hung up and downed my glass of wine. Tomorrow was a long way off.

The next morning I had a piercing wine hangover and Frank's voice was muffled by the increased ear noise. "I don't know how to tell you this, Dave, but you are aware of the sharp decline in building starts. The company decided not to expand. There is no job." A black hole seemed to open under me, and Frank's voice rang as in an echo chamber, "I was looking forward to our association. Keep in touch, Dave. Maybe we'll have a chance to work together in the future."

"Fine, Frank." I was surprised at the steadiness of my voice. "I'll let you know what I decide to do."

After a few more polite phrases Frank wished me luck, and I hung up to run for the bathroom where my stomach cramps exploded into sour vomit.

There was no longer any reason to delay plans for suicide. By evening I was quite drunk in a bar a few miles down the freeway. I intended to demolish the car and myself against the concrete pillar of an underpass on my way back to Jane's apartment. I knew exactly where, and the whole thing would be over in seconds. The decision firm, I staggered out to my car and fumbled in my pockets for the keys. They were gone. I looked everywhere, in the bar, on the floor by the stool where I had been sitting. No one had seen them. In the end I had to call Jane and ask her to bring the spare key from my dresser drawer.

"Are you kidding!" Her voice was shrill in my ear. "You're so drunk you can't talk straight. I'll come and bring you home before you end up in jail."

I had never seen my sister so furious. Her pretty face was contorted, and a stream of angry words rushed over me as we drove towards home. "You're not fit to ride a tricycle." She grimaced with disgust. "I thought my big brother was moving in to help me; instead, I end up taking care of you." Her eyes flashed fiery darts sideways at me. "You're always saying you're so smart. Why don't you prove it? You can't sit in my living room drinking for the rest of your life."

She bit her lips to stifle a sob, and her hands whitened around the steering wheel. I felt sorry for both of us.

"I'll leave if you want me to," my tongue was thick in my mouth. "I don't want to be a burden."

We had pulled up in front of the apartment, and Jane put her hand on my arm. "Don't be a fool, David," her voice was suddenly soft. "I don't mean to yell at you. I just don't know what else to do. I don't understand what's going on with you."

Inside the apartment I poured myself a glass of wine and tried to explain about the job.

"Oh, I'm so sorry!" Jane hugged me impulsively, and her pert face was lined with concern. "I guess you were upset about that. What are you going to do now?"

My head was heavy and I leaned back against the couch. "I'll think of something." I didn't believe my own words, but Jane looked relieved.

"Good! I know you can if you try hard enough."

The next days flowed together in a nightmare of drunkenness and pain. At night I could not sleep and tossed on my bed waiting for dawn. The grocery store on the corner opened at nine, and I was there a few minutes earlier, waiting to buy my two quarts of wine. I could not even hold off till I got home, but had to stop down the block to get my first sip out of the bottle in the brown paper bag.

Five days and nights without sleep. The shadowy world of terror and pain was closing in on me. I no longer managed to stay half sober for a couple of hours at midday. The force pulling me downward was stronger than anything I could put up against it, and the end could only come in insanity and death.

The morning of the sixth day I staggered into the kitchen, too sick to hold another drop of liquor. I knew I was licked. My body was burning. The darkness of depression and panic rose to a pitch inside me. This was the end. I had tried everything: seeking in vain to release the "Higher Power" within me, the AA program. There was nothing left to do or think or try. I was chained, bound, worse than dead, and every fiber of my being cried for release.

Without thinking, I sank to my knees by the kitchen table and leaned my head on my arms on the brown formica top. Heavy sobs started deep within me, and I heard my own voice cry out hoarsely: "God, I give up. I'm sick. I hurt. Help me, God. I don't care what You do with me, just that You do it. Let me die now, or do whatever You want with what's left of my life. I'm Yours."

On the deck of the lobster boat I had cried out to a God I was not sure was there. Now I *knew*. In the depth of my pain, in the pit of my soul, something told me that God was there and that He heard me.

Over and over I cried the words of surrender. I meant it to be total and as honest as I could ever be with myself, my Creator or anybody. God had put His breath of life into me at the beginning. Now I meant to give it back to Him to do with as He wished. It was not that I expected anything to happen. I only wanted to surrender. I was sick and tired of life in my own strength. I had looked over the edge of the bottomless pit of oblivion. Now I meant to turn myself over to God, without reservations, hopes, or expectations. I was ready to die right there on my knees in Jane's kitchen, if that was God's will for me.

Time and space seemed suspended. Slowly I became aware of sunlight streaming in on the bright yellow walls. The floor was hard under my knees, and I noticed milk and cornflakes spilled on the slick table top after Jane's hurried breakfast. Empty and exhausted, I pulled myself up and walked into the living room. Weak and sick,

I only wanted to sleep. Sinking down on the couch, I leaned my head against the pillows and closed my weary eyes.

I woke up when Jane slammed the front door and turned on the light. She glanced quickly at the cluttered living room and kitchen where dirty breakfast dishes were stacked in the sink.

"Been out of it all day again!" She looked disgusted and dropped a bag of hamburgers and french fries on the coffee table.

"I figured you weren't in shape to cook. Help yourself to some food—if you can keep it down."

Blinking against the light I stared at her. Slowly the incredible fact sank in: I had been asleep all day without a drink! For months I had only been able to sleep two or three hours at a stretch, and then only after enough drinks to make me relax. This morning I had fallen soundly asleep although I had been too sick to drink at all.

How or why this amazing thing had happened I could not imagine, but I was glad that it had. I bit into a hamburger and realized that I was hungry. Jane was already absorbed in television, and I was glad she did not want to talk. My body was still weak and aching all over, as if I had the flu.

"I think I better go to bed," I mumbled and Jane looked up in surprise.

"Already?" She munched her french fries. "You *must* be sick."

She was probably right, I mused as I tottered in to my room where a deep, dreamless sleep immediately overtook me. The sun was high when I awoke again. From the silence in the apartment I knew Jane had already left for work. Still weak and sleepy, I dressed and made myself a cup of coffee. Not that I really wanted to be wide awake. I was glad to be resting as much as possible. Soon I would probably feel worse again—back to my old "normal" self.

For twenty-four hours I had not taken a drink. I was not making a conscious effort *not* to, and assumed I would drink again when I felt the need to, but for the moment the pressure was gone. In a remarkably relaxed way I felt myself to be stripped of pressures, reduced to nothing, zero, empty. I felt no pain. There was no struggle inside. I was just resting.

Days slipped by. I lost track of them. Like a convalescent recuperating from a long illness, I slept most of the time. My appetite had picked up and occasionally I drank beer with my supper. But never more than two or three. It was not an effort to keep the amount down, I just did not want anymore. If Jane noticed a change, she did not say so. As usual, she was gone from dawn till after dark.

When I was not sleeping or resting, I read. The Bible suddenly held a curious interest. In short order I read through the Phillips translation of the New Testament and then tackled the entire Bible from the beginning. Before, it had been a closed book. I had forced myself to read and it had been boring or difficult, even ridiculous. Although much of it was still beyond my understanding, I made the startling discovery that what I *did* understand held a ring of truth. It was as if I stood on the threshold of a new dimension of reality brimming with new concepts and ideas. I had not yet had time to test or verify them, but they carried a strong implication of probability.

The supernatural element in the Bible had before struck me as contrary to reason. My view of the universe had always been strictly naturalistic. Now as I read of a universe *both* natural and supernatural, the idea seemed suddenly quite plausible. As an amateur radio operator I had accepted the "realness" of invisible radio waves flowing through the visible tubes of my receiver and transmitter. If there was an invisible half to the physical universe— why should there not be a supernatural aspect of the total reality as well? This was a concept of the universe far more complex than I had thought while I considered only the natural half of it, but there was nothing really incredible or mystical about it. Why had I not realized that before?

The strongest objection for me, the self-determinist, had been directed towards the Bible's picture of man as incapable of doing good in his own strength. But now the experiences of my own life supported that view. I had obviously been incapable of saving myself from total destruction. If there was a solution to my dilemma, it *had* to come from beyond myself.

The Bible held that lost, rebellious men could only be reconciled to God through a surrender to God's solution, not through men's own efforts. It seemed utterly fantastic, the epitome of all contradictions, that the surrender of the ego, the "I" that I had cherished and struggled to maintain, should be the key to the birth of the real person I was intended to be. Like the classic picture of the seed surrendered into the ground in order to give birth to the new life of the plant.

That morning, at the kitchen table, I had surrendered myself into the hands of God without a clear picture of who He was or what He was. He had no identity as the God of a particular church or religion. Now the question was forming in my mind: Had I spoken to the God of the Bible? As I read, the vague God began to take on character and personhood. The Creator of the universe who still maintained an intimate, personal relationship with His creatures; was He the one who had heard me and responded?

At the moment of surrender I had not been conscious of a turning point in my life. I had simply been at the end of my rope and cried for help. Exactly what had happened was still a mystery, but looking back I was aware that some things in my life had changed. There was a lot less pain, I was not compelled to drink, and I was able to rest.

Sitting in Jane's lawn chair in the back of the apartment, looking at the sky or the birds playing in the sprinkler, or the bright red geraniums along the fence, I experienced a measure of peace unlike anything I had known for years.

On my first visit to Jack and Lydia's I felt awkward under Jack's intense gaze, but his handshake was warm.

"You look good. What have you been doing?"

"Mostly resting." There were no words to describe it.

Jack's narrow face broke into a happy grin. He seemed to know without being told that things were different, and put his arm around my shoulder in a gesture that brought a sudden lump in my throat.

Lydia had prepared my favorite meal, roast beef with plenty of gravy over the potatoes, but our conversation at the table moved unusually slowly. At last, I put down my fork and cleared my throat.

"I guess I've never really thanked you two for being such good friends." There was an unfamiliar feeling of warmth expanding my chest.

"Don't thank us," Lydia's motherly face was beaming. "We're just glad God brought you here; friendship is a precious gift."

The lump in my throat prevented my speaking, and Lydia leaned over to give me a quick hug. "Oh, David, we can see God is doing something in your life!"

A month ago her remark would have annoyed me. Now it seemed reasonable enough. "Perhaps He is," I nodded. "I don't understand it, but something is happening."

"Are you reading the Bible?" Jack asked.

"Yes—and some of it makes a lot of sense."

His next remark threw me off balance. "When are you going to see Sarah and the children?"

"I don't know." Tension tugged at my stomach. "I don't think I am ready to face Sarah yet."

"I think you are." Lydia handed me a plate of hot apple pie covered with slices of cheese. The look in her eyes defied argument.

Before I left, Jack asked if I would object to a word of prayer. Not wanting to offend my old friends, I nodded and remained standing uneasily by the door while Jack and Lydia knelt together.

"Dear God," Jack spoke as if the listener was in the same room. "Thank You for what You're doing in Dave's life. Continue to show him the truth he is looking for, and when the time is right, bring him to his wife and children. We pray in the name of Your Son, Jesus Christ, who made our relationship with You possible."

There was an unaccustomed stinging behind my eyes and I left in a hurry, before Jack and Lydia could see that I was deeply moved. Driving home over the freeway I relaxed in the seat and suddenly realized that the ear noise I had been troubled with for years was almost gone.

Incredibly many aspects of living were better. Still I was cautious about drawing the conclusion that I was actually embarked on a new way of life. On a daily basis I was grateful to experience less conflict and pain, but I dared not think in terms of a permanent change. The future was still unknown.

For the time being I was free from the clutches of alcohol. Freedom was the only term to adequately describe it. For so long I had been forced to plan all activities around my drinking and the inevitable limitation of physical and mental capacities—like a man who has been immobilized for a major portion of every day in an iron lung, and now is suddenly released to go and come as he pleases. Not being used to the freedom, it was almost frightening. I could even think of traveling north to Seattle, *if* I wanted to. That was an open question.

A confrontation with Sarah had always been painful in the past. Would seeing her again destroy the new peace I was experiencing and throw me off balance?

Still, the urge to see the children was too strong. I called an airline and found that I could fly to Seattle for the weekend for a reasonable round-trip fare. John and Christine's birthdays were coming up and I decided to go.

With some trepidation I dialed Sarah's number, and Leif answered. "This is dad." My heart was suddenly pounding. "I'd like to speak to your mother."

"Are you sure you want to speak to her?" Leif sounded hesitant.

"Please call her to the phone."

Sarah's voice was calm. "It's been a long time. Have you been all right?"

"I'm fine. I'd like to come up for John's and Christine's birthdays. Would you mind?"

She seemed to hesitate. "Of course not. Do you want me to find you a motel room?"

"I don't have much money. Is there a reasonable one nearby?"

"Don't worry about it," she answered quickly. "I'll talk to some friends. We'll find you a private room."

"My flight arrives Friday at 4:30 P.M.," I kept my voice businesslike. "I'll take the bus to town and call you from there."

"Fine. See you then."

Afterwards I wondered if I had made a mistake. Was I strong enough to take the pressure of a whole weekend with Sarah? I scarcely dared to hope.

SARAH   *Seattle, Washington*

My calm lasted through our phone conversation, but as soon as I hung up I felt as if I was going to fly apart. Leif was watching me.

"What's happening, mom? Is dad coming?"

Nodding, I swallowed my fear. "Let's not tell the others yet. Let it be a surprise for their birthday." Somehow I could not bear the thought of the children's happy anticipation of David's arrival.

Leif grinned and winked. "Sure, mom. It'll be a blast to see their faces when dad gets here."

As soon as I could, I ran down the street to Aunt Adah's.

"David is coming!" Panic was stalking me, and I allowed the tears to flow freely. "I feel as if he's coming to put me in prison!"

"Nonsense!" Aunt Adah smiled. "You're forgetting Who's in charge."

Breathing deliberately slowly, I leaned back in the chair and felt the tension gradually disappear. "I don't practice much faith, do I?" I said sheepishly. "I've got to get over my instant negative reactions."

"You know very well that David would not be coming unless it is meant to work out good for all of you," Aunt Adah scolded me. "The sooner you accept that, the better." Her kind blue eyes were patient, and I felt a surge of gratitude for her faithfulness.

"There's one small problem. He can't afford a motel. I have to find him a room." I glanced down the hallway where the door to Aunt Adah's empty guest room stood ajar. She followed my eyes and shook her head.

"I think God has other plans, Sarah. He can't stay here."

"Oh." I felt bewildered. It was unlike Aunt Adah to refuse hospitality to anyone. Then I remembered that Harry and Evelyn down the street had a spare bedroom as well. It would be better if David could stay with them. Harry had been an alcoholic and drug addict before he became a Christian. Perhaps David would listen to his story. With renewed optimism I hugged Aunt Adah and ran home.

Harry and Evelyn agreed to house David over the weekend, and I drew a sigh of relief. Now all I had to worry about was my own attitude. What if the subject of a Christian marriage came up again? I trembled inside at the thought. It would be difficult to be firm with him face-to-face.

Friday morning Evelyn called. "I'm terribly sorry, but Harry has been called out of town this weekend. I don't feel right about having David here while I'm alone."

Suddenly I was frantic. Why did David's presence always trap me one way or the other? I called Aunt Adah hoping she would change her mind and offer her guest room after all. Instead, she said, "You've got a spare room yourself, Sarah. It looks to me as if that's the alternative you're left with."

My knees were shaking and I gripped the receiver. The trap was closing around me. "I guess you're right. Just pray for us. . . ."

Aunt Adah laughed confidently, "I think you'll have a very special weekend."

Now that it was settled I felt calmer. If this was God's plan, somehow it would work. I told Leif who immediately looked worried.

"You and daddy always fight. He never wants to be around you."

"I've tried to find him another room, but I can't. God must want him here."

"O.K.," Leif still looked a little doubtful. "If God's doing it, maybe it will work."

At the last minute I decided to drive out to the airport to meet David there. It would save him the limousine fare to town. We told the other children that we were going to pick up a special package arriving by air. They were sure it was a gift from daddy and agreed to wait with me in the car while Leif went into the terminal to pick up the "surprise."

Butterflies were busy in my stomach, and my hands were perspiring on the steering wheel. Under my breath I kept repeating, "Thank You for what is happening. Just keep me calm and kind."

Chapter 14

DAVID   *Seattle, Washington*

It was drizzling when I stepped out of the plane at the Seattle-Tacoma airport. The anxiety I felt about the weekend ahead was mild compared to the pressures I remembered from my visits in Florida. I was startled to see Leif's beaming face in the waiting crowd. He waved.

"Hi, dad, how-ya-been?"

Other than needing a haircut badly, he looked his old bouncy self and pumped my hand excitedly.

"Mom's in the parking lot with the kids. We didn't tell them you're coming. It's a birthday surprise. They think I'm picking up a package." Leif giggled and led the way out of the terminal.

I steeled myself for the meeting with Sarah. It had come sooner than I expected. The children jumped around excitedly and pulled me into the back seat with them.

Sarah said a quiet "Hello; welcome to Seattle" and concentrated on her driving. Her eyes brushed past mine in the rear view mirror once or twice, but it was not as upsetting as I had feared.

We stopped in front of a large, two-story house.

"This is home!" the children yelled. A group of neighborhood children were on the sidewalk staring. "Daddy, we want you to meet our friends," the boys said eagerly.

"Not now!" Sarah spoke firmly. "Daddy is probably tired." She turned to me and there was a faint blush in her cheeks.

"I tried to find better lodgings for you, but I'm afraid all I have to offer is our spare bedroom, if you don't mind."

I felt a slight tightening in my chest, but smiled, "That will be fine, if it's not an imposition?"

"Not at all," Sarah smiled faintly. "The children will enjoy having you here."

The children marched me triumphantly inside. Christine and Andrew clung to my hands while John carried my bag and Leif led the way.

I did not recognize the furniture, and John explained, "We sold most of ours in Florida. This house was furnished." So Sarah had been forced to reduce her belongings as well.

Downstairs in the living room I sat down on the couch. I was glad Sarah had not sold our piano and paintings. They were like old friends.

"Where's your mother?" I asked John.

"In the kitchen. Why do you want to know?"

"I just wondered why she wasn't with us."

John glanced at me. "You never wanted to be around mom before."

His words stung. "I've come to visit all of you this time."

John's face lit up. "I like it better that way, dad." He squeezed my hand.

After half an hour the children went outside to play. Sarah remained in the kitchen—I assumed in order to avoid me. If that was how she felt perhaps I should leave, I thought. I did not want to impose. I glanced around the large, pleasant living room with the fireplace at one end and windows opening on a spectacular view. Sarah seemed to be doing all right on her own. I ought to leave her alone and never come back. The thought was so convincing that I almost got up to get my bag. I had not yet unpacked. On the other hand, I had come for a birthday celebration. It would be thoughtless to leave at once. Perhaps I could stay one night and get an early flight back to Los Angeles tomorrow.

Dusk had fallen and I felt vaguely restless. What would happen next? The light from the fireplace flickered over the familiar pictures on the wall, but I felt like a stranger.

Sarah came to the door and feigned surprise. "Where are the children? I didn't know you were alone. Would you like a cup of coffee before dinner?"

"The children are outside." I did not look directly at her. "Don't bother with the coffee, I'm fine."

"Oh," Sarah was flustered. "Then, if you'll excuse me, I'll get the food on the table. It will only be a few minutes."

She disappeared again, and I felt more than ever that I was a stranger and not a very welcome one. I remembered how cold Sarah had been in Florida. She had hurt me deeply then, and I felt the old hurt again. I leaned my head back against the wall, and the amazing events of the last few months since we had last seen each other in Florida passed through my mind.

I had been to the outskirts of hell itself—at the point of death. I had given up, surrendered, and now I was alive but still a little stunned by it all. I was no longer propelling my own life. It was as if I was carried on the back of a broad river moving steadily along. I could observe the objects along the banks as I encountered them, but the view ahead was obscured. I had trusted myself to the river, and now it had brought me here to Sarah's living room with the Seattle rain against the windows and the steady warmth of the fireplace inside.

I heard my children's voices blending with others outside, and the tinkling of silverware and glasses as my ex-wife prepared the table in the next room. I was acutely aware of the moment, and myself in it, hurting in my loneliness. Everything beyond, ahead, was obscure.

Sarah called the children to supper, and they scampered to the bathroom to wash up. I joined them, enjoying their loud voices and laughter.

"I want to sit next to you," Christine whispered and held onto my hand.

Sarah had lighted candles on the table, and the children took their places. I stood in uncertainty by the door until Sarah said, "Won't you sit at the head of the table, David?"

Christine beamed next to me. Sarah sat on the opposite end, and in the light from the candles between us, her face looked soft.

She apologized for the menu of meatloaf, mashed potatoes with gravy, and tossed salad. "Our food budget is limited, but there is plenty of everything."

Leif said grace: "Bless the food, God; thank You for bringing daddy."

Fortunately the children dominated the conversation, telling about their new friends and school. "I liked it better in Florida," John added. Leif chimed in, "I want to move to California; the waves are better for surfing there."

Sarah interrupted quietly, "We're grateful for the home we have right now. We'll see what comes next."

The children wanted to know about my job and I explained, "I'm not working right now, but I hope to be soon."

"Then why don't you move up here?" Andrew was hopeful. "There are jobs in Seattle, aren't there, mom?"

Sarah's smile was a little forced. "Daddy has to do what is best for him. Jobs are hard to find around here now."

"Oh." Andrew looked disappointed.

"Don't worry about it." John broke the silence that had settled over us. "Let's just enjoy having daddy here right now."

"Thank you, son," I smiled at him. "I hope to come back more often—if you want me to."

"Sure we do," the four children said in chorus. I looked at Sarah who blushed slightly and nodded. "Of course we do," she said quietly. "You are welcome whenever you can come." She stood up quickly and began to gather the dishes.

"You children entertain daddy while I clean the kitchen and get the birthday cake in the oven."

I felt a twinge of disappointment. When she blushed, I thought I saw a softer Sarah than the one I remembered. A Sarah I could t̶ to without being countered with icy remarks and pat answers.

The children were chatting eagerly. The last few years I had seen little of them. Now I studied each one. Leif—fast-talking, quick to smile, eager to make arrangements to visit me in Southern California where he could surf; John—quiet, with steady eyes searching mine. I realized I knew less about him than about the others; Andrew—still young enough to climb on my lap, fascinated with trucks and motors; and Christine—giggling and fighting with Andrew for a space on my knee, pretty and blond, but more like a tomboy than I wanted my daughter to be.

With a surge of sadness I realized that I no longer really knew my children. Nor did they know me. I had been the daddy who gave gifts and took them places—a fast trip in the car or boat, to a movie, a restaurant or a fairground where they went on rides while I enjoyed a beer. Now I found myself wishing for a chance to share their thoughts and dreams before they got old enough to leave home—as I had left home, never really returning to a close relationship with my parents. Would these children do the same? A few more years of closeness while they still needed parental care, then gone, to remain strangers forever? The thought brought a lump to my throat.

Sarah had finished in the kitchen. The cake was in the oven, filling the house with the fragrance of chocolate.

Now she stood in the door carrying a tray with steaming mugs of hot chocolate and a heaping plate of sugar cookies, my favorites. "Time for a snack, and then to bed," she announced.

The children extended their time as long as possible.

"Aren't you going to bed with us, daddy?"

My eyes sought Sarah's. "Do you have time for another cup with me later, alone?"

She bit her lip nervously. "Of course, if you want to."

The children were suddenly tense.

"What are you going to talk about?" Leif demanded.

"Nothing serious," Sarah answered him quickly.

"No fighting!" said John. "This is our birthday visit."

"Of course," I said calmly. "Don't worry. We're just going to talk a little by the fire . . . I promise."

They dragged themselves upstairs reluctantly. Andrew called down, "Mom, don't forget to kiss us good night."

Sarah looked relieved.

"I'll come right now."

I waited by the fire while Sarah brought more chocolate from the kitchen. We sipped our hot drinks and looked into the leaping flames for what seemed a long time.

"How have you been?" I said at last.

"Just fine, thank you," she smiled. "How about you?"

I hesitated. "Things have been a little rough, but they're better now."

"Have you been sick?" her eyes showed concern.

I turned to look at the fire. There was a lump in my throat, and I found it difficult to talk. Impulsively, Sarah put her hand on my knee.

"I'm glad you're better. . . . You look much better than in Florida. In fact, you look different." Her dark brown eyes held a question. "*Are* you different?"

I could see no malice in her face, only an openness and warmth that had never been there before.

"What do you think?" My voice was thick.

Sarah's eyes were moist. "You *are* different . . . but what does it mean?"

I groped for words. "I don't know yet. I can't explain it."

"Don't tell me unless you want to." Sarah held up her hand.

"Someday I will," I promised. "Right now I'm just glad to be alive and to be here."

We were silent again, staring into the fire.

"What are your plans now?" Sarah broke the stillness.

"I'll look for a job in Los Angeles. I'm anxious to provide for my family again."

"We haven't suffered," she said quickly. "Everything we need has been provided for."

"Thank God for that!"

"To hear you say that is really something," Sarah smiled.

"I don't know the vocabulary, but I do know Who's responsible for taking care of you and me. I also know that it's time for me to go back to work."

"I'm sure the right job is waiting. We'll be anxious to hear about it."

"I'll tell you first. You can count on it."

We lapsed into silence again. It was my turn to speak first.

"You've changed too. You're more quiet, feminine, not so forceful." She had let her hair grow long and wore it gathered loosely at the nape of her neck, softly framing her face. It was very becoming, and the light from the fireplace shone in the rich, brown color.

Sarah blushed. "Thank you, David; it was nice of you to say that." She looked at her watch and exclaimed, "It's almost eleven. Breakfast is at eight. We better get some sleep." She stood up quickly, holding the tray between us like a shield. I suddenly realized that she felt awkward about telling me good night. The thought somehow pleased me.

"Good night, Sarah," I said cheerfully as she almost ran to the kitchen. "Thank you for a nice evening."

I walked upstairs to my room, aware of a good, tired feeling. The visit was turning out much better than I had hoped. Sarah and I had actually talked. It had been a dialogue, not a dual monologue as always before.

With a deep sense of gratitude and peace I drifted into a dreamless sleep.

SARAH

Seattle, Washington

I listened to David's footsteps going up the stairs and the door to his room closing. My head was whirling. What had happened? Meeting him at the airport had been strange, as if I was surely dreaming. I did not know what to say or do. He looked different— his eyes and his face. Tired, but—I searched for the right word—was it *open?*

The children did most of the talking. When David smiled I found myself watching. The smile was different. It was . . . real. At home I took my time parking the car and followed slowly into the house. I needed time to collect myself. To escape immediate confrontation, I busied myself in the kitchen, very conscious of the sound of David's voice in the house.

He did not sound like his old self, either. My heart pounded as I tested the meatloaf for doneness and poured the water off the boiled potatoes. I was aware of his presence in the living room only a few feet away, and I was hiding, afraid to find out what this strange newness meant.

It was silent in there. I heard the children's voices outside and finally mustered my courage to go in. He was alone, and I stammered helplessly, "What about a cup of coffee? Dinner will be ready in a minute."

He shook his head, and I fled to the kitchen again. This would never do. I was as flustered as an old maid with a "caller" in the parlor. The comparison struck me as ridiculous, but my feelings were bewildering.

Dinner was equally difficult. I was grateful for the children's constant chatter. Once or twice David's eyes met mine across the flickering candle flame, and I hoped he did not notice that my cheeks were flushed.

I escaped back to the kitchen to the dirty dishes and the birthday cake. When most of the evening was gone, I fixed a bedtime snack and hoped David would retire with the children. When he asked me to stay and talk with him a little longer I felt nearly faint with fright.

The trembling inside persisted while I kissed the children good night and tucked them in. They each prayed that God would be with mom and dad downstairs, and I added my urgent SOS, "Please, God, I'm scared!"

What did David want to talk about? I dared to glance at his face as he sat watching the flames. There were new lines etched deep around his eyes and mouth. He looked like he had suffered or been ill, but there was also a new quietness over his features. He looked handsome, I thought with a quickening of my pulse. We exchanged a few casual remarks and I bit my lip over the thought I had carried since he first arrived. "You look different. . . . Are you?"

His eyes held mine for a long time. He did not have to tell me. It had been there from the moment I first saw him at the airport. A new light deep in his eyes that could only mean one thing.

It was incredible. I stared into the flames leaping over the logs. Of course I had believed it could happen, but I had always thought of it as something far off in the future. Now the moment I had been waiting for was reality. The dark veil was gone from David's eyes. The mask was no longer on his face.

The sparks were dancing upwards into the chimney, and I hugged my knees. So often I had tried to imagine what this moment would be like. Now I was totally unprepared. The full implications of it hovered on the edge of my consciousness and made me dizzy.

It was a miracle. Yet now that it had happened, it seemed so normal and natural that it was hard to realize it had ever been different. Here we were, on a rainy night in October 1970, sitting calmly in front of a fireplace *talking!* For years we had been like two radios operating on different frequencies. Now we were tuned in, hearing each other, communicating, and it seemed like the most natural thing in the world.

I looked at him and thought, "He *looks* like the same David I lived with for years." I felt a sudden twinge of fear. "He's the father of my children, and I don't *know* him."

The thoughts spun in my head. Where would we begin? Would it really last, this open communication, or would there be a wall between us once we got past the surface exchange of words?

It was obvious that David was looking at me with new eyes as well. I felt suddenly flustered and wanted to get away.

It was almost eleven. I was relieved to say a hurried good night and fled to my room. There I sank to my knees by my bed. I felt totally bewildered. "God, help me get through this weekend. I want Your will for my life, but I'm scared."

When I crawled into bed the panic had faded. I thought, "One day at a time. David belongs to God now, and we are having a good visit. I won't think about anything further ahead."

DAVID   *Seattle, Washington*

I woke up to the sounds of children laughing and the smell of coffee and pancakes. Then Sarah's voice, "Breakfast is ready!"

The time was eight o'clock, and I jumped out of bed.

Sarah had always been sluggish in the morning, but I found her bright and cheerful seated at the breakfast table with the children.

I felt more at ease than the day before, and the children were obviously happy to see me. The morning sun shone over the roof tops of Seattle and the snowy peaks across the Sound. It promised to be a beautiful day.

By mid-morning the neighborhood children swarmed in for the birthday party. John and Christine proudly introduced me.

"This is our dad. He came all the way from Los Angeles to surprise us on our birthday!" The boys and girls looked impressed, and I caught Sarah's eyes in a quick smile. Her cheeks flushed and she hurried to the kitchen.

The party was noisy. I was not accustomed to so much commotion and felt the onset of fatigue. Sarah was busy, but whenever I caught her eyes the faint blush crept into her cheeks. There was no cold distance between us.

When the guests had gone the children piled into the car, and Sarah handed me the keys. "Would you like to drive?" It was a gesture of confidence and I appreciated it.

The plan for the day called for a trip to the Seattle World's Fair grounds and dinner at the slowly-revolving restaurant atop the Space Needle. The children were ecstatic, but Sarah looked at me with concern. "Are you tired?"

I bravely shook my head. "I wouldn't miss this for anything!"

Back at the house I excused myself and took a nap. When I awoke the house was dark and silent. I had slept through the entire evening and felt oddly disappointed. I had hoped for another fireside talk with Sarah.

Over oatmeal and hot muffins Sunday morning she said, "We won't go to church unless you want to."

"Oh, but I do!"

She smiled gratefully. They attended an Episcopal church nearby, and I enjoyed the music and the sermon. The children sat between us in the pew and I glanced across their heads at Sarah. An overwhelming sense of gratitude forced moisture into my eyes.

After church it was already time to go to the airport. Again I drove the car with Sarah in the front seat with me.

"It's like in the old days, isn't it, daddy?" Christine beamed at us.

"It's better!" John said. "Mom and dad aren't fighting all the time."

Sarah and I had not had a chance to talk privately since that first evening. I wondered if she, too, wished we could have talked more.

The children hugged me goodbye at the gate. Sarah held out her hand and I felt it warm in mine. "It's been good seeing you, David. God bless you, and good luck with your job."

"It's been good seeing you. God bless you." There was a lump in my throat, and I walked quickly towards the plane. From my window seat I could see the five of them in a clump by the door waving until the plane turned and taxied down the runway.

The stewardess handed me a drink, and I sipped it absentmindedly. I wondered what lay ahead for us all. First a job, then regular support to Sarah and the children. Correspondence and more visits, getting to know them all again.

Closing my eyes I leaned back against the seat. I could not think ahead. The present was enough.

I had seen my children and my ex-wife. We had talked. It was more than I had ever thought would happen.

SARAH   *Seattle, Washington*

We watched the plane take off and walked slowly back to the car. I still fe t half dazed by the happenings of the last forty-eight hours.

I had watched David carefully with the children. He still seemed rigid around them, as if he did not quite know how to behave, and he tired easily. But the light was unmistakable in his eyes and the old frozen mask was no longer on his face.

In church I was aware of the people watching us. Aunt Adah smiled and nodded from her pew. Others knew, I was sure, that the man sitting with us was my ex-husband. I did not hear much of the sermon. I could only think of the fact that we were all together for the first time, in church. The future was in a haze, but there was lightness, like a song within me.

On the way to the airport I kept looking at him, the man my children resembled so much, the man I had lived with for so many years. Back then there had been a distance between us, wider than the front seat that separated us now. I wanted to pinch myself to be certain that this was no dream. The Bible said that when a man comes to Christ old things pass away; he becomes a new creature. Was David a new man?

I was both sad and relieved to see him get on the plane. There were so many unanswered questions. I dared not guess at the answers.

In the car going home the children wanted to know, "Is dad a Christian now?"

I nodded, "It sure looks that way!"

"So when are you getting married?" Andrew's eyes were shining.

"We didn't discuss it." I bit my lip.

"Didn't he ask you?" Christine looked aghast.

"Marriage is serious business. Just because two people are Christians doesn't mean they automatically get married."

"What a gyp!" John snorted with disgust. "We've been praying for dad to become a Christian so we could have a real family . . . and now nothing happens."

"First things first," I wanted to change the subject, "Let's just be glad dad is in God's family now."

"I want him to marry you," Andrew was firm. "I'm sure that's what God wants too."

Leif was quiet in his corner and I said, "Aren't you happy for daddy?"

"I guess it's neat," he stared ahead. "I just hope he won't be a Jesus freak like you, not letting us do anything fun." His face was a closed mask and I felt a stab of fear. "I can't reach him," I thought. "God help us."

Christine put her arms around me. "I'm glad daddy loves Jesus." She pressed her cheek against mine. "He's a lot nicer when he doesn't smell of beer and cigarettes."

The house seemed different with the memories of David's visit. That evening I sat alone by the fire after the children had gone to bed.

"Show me what it all means," I whispered. In the silence I felt anticipation, tinged with fear.

Chapter 15

Back in Los Angeles I made a serious effort to find a job, but nothing definite turned up. A couple of prospective employers told me to wait and try later.

Always before, waiting had made me restless. Now I was glad for the time to think and study my Bible. My first concern was to learn more about the possibility of a two-way communication with God. That would be essential for a personal relationship between God and man.

That morning, at the kitchen table, I had cried out, and something very real had happened in response to my plea. Now I dared to address myself specifically to God again: "Put me where You want me. Take charge of the circumstances in my life. Give me the job You want me to have. I want Your will, not mine."

I wrote Sarah a thank you note and borrowed the words of the apostle Paul.

Dear Sarah:

How great is the joy I have in my life in the Lord! After so long a time, you once more had the chance of showing that you care for me. I don't mean that you had quit caring for me—you did not have a chance to show it. And I am not saying this because I feel neglected; for I have learned to be satisfied with what I have. I know what it is to be in need, and what it is to have more than enough. I have learned this secret, so that anywhere, at any time, I am content, whether I am full or hungry, whether I have too much or too little. I have the strength to face all conditions by the power that Christ gives me. [1]

I await God's decision and plan for a job. It concerns all six of us. Praise God from whom all blessings flow!

Love, David.

It was not the kind of letter I would have written before, but then I no longer seemed to be the man I had once been. More and more as I read, I felt I could identify with something the Bible called a "new life."

Since returning from Seattle I had not touched a drink. For the first time in more than twenty years I felt no desire for one.

One morning the phone rang and it was Chuck, the fellow from AA. "How are you doing?" The memories of the losing battle I had fought only a few weeks ago brushed past me.

"Just great, Chuck. Couldn't be better."

"Are you drinking?"

"No. Don't seem to want any."

Chuck's voice was curious. "What happened?"

"It's hard to explain." I struggled to find the right words. "I guess I finally gave up, and turned myself over to God. Since then things have been different."

Chuck was silent for a moment. "So you took the third step we talk about in AA. That's great, Dave!"

"I guess I didn't understand it before."

"It's hard for most people. Pride is the big hurdle, you know. We want to do it all ourselves."

After we had hung up I dug out the card Cliff had given me with the twelve steps of the AA program. There it was, step 3:

"Make a decision to turn our will and our lives over to the care of God as we understand Him." I shook my head. It had been there all the time and I just had not seen it.

God had rescued me and, although I still did not quite understand *how* and *why*, I felt the abiding peace inside that the Bible discussed at length. It was more than an absence of worry. I was jobless, broke, and separated from my family, but I still had an abiding confidence that all was well.

In spite of the fact that the Bible accurately described, and offered a plausible explanation, for my experience, I hesitated to make a commitment to accept the whole book as true. Such a conclusion would have far-reaching consequences, and I dared not come to it lightly.

There was the problem of identifying myself with official Christianity. I had seen it full of inconsistencies, contradictions, hypocrisy, and phoniness. Dead churches had led me to conclude that God was dead as well.

If I could become convinced of the absolute truth of the Bible, I would commit myself unhesitatingly to the God and the Christianity of the Book—not to historical Christendom in the shape of the organized church. I had long despised the label "Christian," yet I would wear it and, in the eyes of the world, be identified with the "group."

I was ready to accept the real thing, if I could be sufficiently convinced that I had found it. I would be a fool to turn it down. Mel had said in one of our discussions years ago: "Don't let the folly of the church and the errors of official Christianity keep you from God."

Total commitment was an extreme position, but I could see no middle ground. God's proposition to man was either true or false. If true, then total commitment in every area of my life was the only response worth considering.

Each day I felt physically and emotionally stronger. I still had no urge to drink and the peace stayed with me. I noticed another change. Since my days as a drill sergeant in the Marine Corps I had used barracks-style profanity in my daily vocabulary. Now, without any conscious effort on my part, those words no longer popped out of my mouth.

I still had no firm job prospects, but now a new thought was pressing on my mind—a strong urge to move to Seattle. The *Wall Street Journal* reported the job market there as the bleakest in the nation with swelling bread lines and welfare rolls. Still I wanted to go.

The urge could be explained by the fact that I wanted to be near my family, but it could also be that God wanted me to go. I had stated that I wanted God's will for my life, and I meant it. If my relationship with God was real I could expect Him to guide me where He wanted me.

I did not expect the guidance to be spectacular. My earlier reluctance to accept the reality of a supernatural half of the universe stemmed from an aversion to the weird and the mystical. But the more I studied the Bible, the more it became apparent that

God's dealings with men most often appeared like perfectly "normal" circumstances. Only in retrospect might they seem miraculous or unusual.

A revolutionary change had begun in my life that morning at the kitchen table, yet I had not been aware of it then. It was more as if I had been suffering from an acute headache that suddenly went away. It took me a while to realize that the pain was gone, and at times I wondered if it had even been there.

I was coming to believe that God, when He chose to, could act in our circumstances in a way that would change things, but it would appear "normal," not "abnormal" to our senses.

If God wanted me in Seattle, He would arrange the circumstances to make it possible. I was practically broke and money would have to be provided. I did not expect a check in the mail from an anonymous donor, or dollar bills growing on the spindly trees in Jane's garden, but I still had the ski boat I had hauled behind my car across the country. During the summer boating season I had tried to sell it, but without luck. If God wanted it sold now, I would find a buyer for it.

On an impulse I called a friend who bought and sold cars. "I've got a 17-foot Glasspar with a hundred-horse motor. Would you like to buy it?"

"Sure, it's just what I've been looking for," Willy answered without a moment's hesitation. "How much?"

"Six hundred." I would settle for that.

"Sold!" Willy chuckled. "I'll bring my check tomorrow."

Feeling strangely elated I called Sarah. "I know Seattle has the highest unemployment rate in the country, but I think God wants me there."

After a moment's silence she answered, with only a hint of tremor in her voice, "If God wants you here, so do we."

SARAH   *Seattle, Washington*

David's call came as no surprise. The three weeks since he left had been a time of reckoning for me. At first I was frantic and cried often on Aunt Adah's shoulder. She patted my cheek and said, "David is a fine man, Sarah. You have much to be grateful for."

"I am grateful," I mumbled. "But I'm frightened. What if he decides to come here and wants to marry me? I'm not ready for that. We lived through twelve years of misery together. I'm afraid to try again. What if we start destroying each other once more?"

"Stop it!" Aunt Adah's voice was firm. "You're being ridiculous. Get your perspective back. David is a brand new Christian. God has begun to work in his life. But he may not come here for a long time. Even if he does, I don't think he'll be in a hurry to get married again."

I drew a deep breath. "I'm sorry. Forget what I said. I'm just all shook up."

"Did David mention marriage?"

"No, not a word," I shook my head.

"I didn't think so. He struck me as a sensible fellow. But that doesn't mean marriage is out of the picture. I think you need to face that."

"All these years I've said that the perfect solution would be for David to find a relationship with God and take his place as the head of our family. He's the father of my children, and they need him. Now that it looks as if it may happen, I'm petrified."

Aunt Adah's blue eyes twinkled. "The hurts in the past were real enough, but the changes in both you and David are significant. If God brings you together in marriage again, you can be sure it will be good."

"Intellectually, I accept that." It was difficult to keep my voice under control. "But, emotionally, I'm a little behind."

"Do you love David?" The question caught me by surprise and I blushed.

"I . . . I don't know . . . as far as feelings go, I don't *feel* love for him. I'm not *in* love, if that's what you mean. But I've learned something about feelings and about love these last couple of years. God doesn't command us to *feel* love, but to *be* loving. If I can only be sure that God wants me to be David's wife again, then I know I *will* love him, and the feelings will follow the fact."

Aunt Adah smiled. "I'm glad you're honest. After the years of hurt it is only to be expected that your feelings are gone." She reached out to pat my cheek. "You're right. Love is first of all a commitment. The question then is, are you willing to commit yourself?"

It was the question I wrestled with through sleepless nights. If I could be sure it was God's plan, then I was willing. The lack of feelings didn't disturb me. I had been fooled by beautiful feelings before. I was sure that a commitment to God's will, would in the end lead to feelings far more solid than the counterfeit I almost fell for.

Nearing despair, I wrote Audrey and Catherine: "Please pray for me. David is a Christian. Pray that I won't chicken out on God's will."

Almost in a daze I went through the regular routine of housework and writing, taking one day at a time. The children talked constantly about daddy, and almost daily the mailman brought a letter for one of us, postmarked Los Angeles.

The November evenings were dark, and we usually sat by the fireplace before bedtime. I looked around at my children's faces and thought, "Our family circle is still broken. When and how will it be made whole again?"

Deep down I already knew what God wanted of me. It would be in line with what the Bible had to say on the subject and I knew it only too well: ". . . If she [a wife] is separated from him [her husband], let her remain single or else go back to him." [2]

David was a Christian now. *If* he should come to Seattle and ask me to marry him, then the choice was mine.

Months ago I had committed myself to the idea of submission as a wife if God should bring me a husband. I had known then that David might be the one, but I had frankly hoped it would be someone else.

Marriage to David would be difficult. Both of us would do and say things to trigger old memories, hurts, and habit reactions. Theoretically, I knew that God could wipe the slate clean, but in practice, that meant living over the rough spots, facing them one by one.

A mediocre marriage was the last thing I wanted. I sat in the big chair by the fireplace where David had once sat. The children were in bed, and I wrestled with my thoughts while the rain hammered against the window panes.

"Lord, I don't want to settle for second-best when I know You always want the very best for me," I whispered into the darkened living room. So far God had always brought the best. If he brought David, could I not trust Him?

There was a churning inside. The solid peace I usually felt had been upset since David left. I was sure it was caused by my reluctance to say wholeheartedly, "Your will, not mine, God."

The choice was still mine. I did not *have* to marry David. I could simply say "no" and continue the life I was living now, waiting for another man, perhaps, in the future. I had a comfortable home and was self-sufficient financially. The children needed the discipline of a father, but we would manage on our own as we had so far.

I was aware of a small voice in the back of my head insisting, "You're a fool if you marry David. He's still the same and your marriage will only be a tolerable compromise. With the accumulated hurts of the last fourteen years to build on, how can it be anything different?"

A calmer, more peaceful voice was countering, "If God does it, it will be better than anything you've ever known. Trust Him."

I felt myself suspended in timelessness as I stared into the glowing embers of the fire. There could be no serious doubt about what I must do. I had come too far to turn back. I had seen too much evidence of the reality of God's love to reject Him now.

Still I felt as if I was taking a plunge.

"I'll do it," I spoke out loud. "If David asks me, I'll marry him. I'll submit to him the way You say I should, and trust You to make our marriage as good as Your promise. Make me into the wife David needs."

The supper dishes had been left in the sink. I suddenly remembered and went out in the kitchen to wash them before going to bed. My hands were in the sudsy water when it hit me. Waves of pure joy, mounting to ecstasy, swept through me. Tears sprang into my eyes. I thought I would burst with happiness.

"I *feel* it," I laughed. "I can feel Your love for David and for me and for the children. How could I ever have doubted that it would be beautiful?"

With hands dripping wet I waltzed around the kitchen floor. I simply could not stand still. I wanted to laugh and cry and sing and shout all at once.

When the calm returned, joy still bubbled inside. I went to sleep with a song running through my head:

> I know the secret of the night—coming down like a bride,
> One day its dress will be white, and every tear will be dried.
> Sorrow and heartache will linger no more,
> We'll know the newness that we've waited for, when all our
> winters have died. . . .*

The happiness almost hurt within me.

In the middle of the night I woke up again. The rain had stopped and the full moon touched the snow on the Olympic Mountains with silver. The melody was still ringing inside.

"I didn't know You could do it like this," I whispered. Warm tears trickled down my face. "I'm so happy . . . thank You. . . . bless David and strengthen him and lead him."

For three days the bubbling joy stayed with me, then it settled into a solid, unshakeable peace.

Audrey wrote: "I'm praising God for what He's doing in your life. It is beautiful."

Catherine wrote: "It's too bad this sort of thing doesn't happen more often. We know God can do it, but most of us are afraid to trust Him. Don't be a chicken . . . the good end is in sight!"

It looked as if the years of waiting were over, but Aunt Adah cautioned me, "Don't rush ahead of God. You have a glimpse of what is happening, but let it come in its own time. Just be sure you are prepared."

In one sense I did not want to rush things. I knew the final outcome, but the practical outworkings might be painful and take months or years. What about my old attitudes? I would have to step aside from the position of leadership in the household and submit

* Words from "I know the Secret" by Sister Miriam Therese Winter © MCMLXVI by Medical Mission Sisters, Phil., Pa.

Sole selling agent Vanguard Music Corp., 250 W. 57th St., N.Y., N.Y. 10019. All rights reserved. Reprinted by permission.

"I know the Secret" was recorded by the Medical Mission Sisters and is available on album AVS 105 from Avant Garde Records, 250 W. 57th St., N.Y., N.Y. 10019.

to David's authority. Adapting myself to him in a way I had never done before. It would not be easy.

The next morning David called to say he was coming. Trembling, I replaced the receiver and sank down on my chair. God help me, I was both eager and afraid to face David again, but I had hoped God would unfold His plan for us in slower motion. My hands shook as I folded them in my lap. "Lord, make me ready," I could barely whisper.

DAVID   *Seattle, Washington*

Driving north, I allowed myself the luxury of feeling a sense of expectation. Things were so much better now that hope came naturally. Not the kind of hope I had clung to in the old days, hoping that things would get better simply because they were so bad that I could no longer bear them. This was a different hope, because things *were* better. So good, that if they never got any better I would be satisfied.

Instead of driving straight to Sarah's house, I searched the neighborhood and soon found what I was looking for, a sign in the window of an older house saying: "Room for Rent."

It was just the room I wanted. Clean and neat, for forty-five dollars a month. It took only a few minutes to unpack the car. Then I walked down the block and a half to Sarah's house. It was midafternoon and I hoped she was home. The children were playing ball in the street and Andrew saw me first.

"Daddy, daddy!" he yelled at the top of his lungs.

"Where's your car?" Leif asked.

"Up the street, where I live."

"Really?" John's eyes widened.

Sarah had seen us through the window and came to the door. This time her welcoming smile held no reticence.

"Come in, you're in time for supper!"

We soon worked out a daily routine. I came to the house for breakfast, and stayed for a second cup of coffee with Sarah after the children left for school. Then I went on my rounds of employment offices, or back to my room to study the Bible and books on Christian doctrine and theology, borrowed from a reference library. An hour or so before dinner, I returned to the house to talk to the children and help with their homework. We spent the evenings together, and Sarah and I talked by the fireplace before I walked back up the street.

Neither of us mentioned remarriage.

The children had asked me when I was going to "marry mom again," and I told them truthfully that I had no idea. "I want to do what God wants me to do."

Leif shook his head. "Gosh, you sound just like mom."

"Has she said something about marrying me?" My heart beat stronger at the thought.

"Naw, we asked her, but she says she wants to do what God wants her to do."

John grinned. "If you can just figure out what God wants you'll be all right!"

"That's right, son," I smiled. "I'm working on it."

A couple of months ago I would have thought seriously of marrying Sarah again, simply because I was tired of being lonely, and I missed the children. Now the picture was entirely different. Under no circumstances did I want to trade the peace I felt for another miserable marriage.

There were several reasons to proceed with caution. Sarah had always been strong and forceful. After two years on her own, and succeeding admirably in making a career for herself as a writer, I was afraid that her independence would be even more pronounced.

Then I had never known a remarriage to be very successful. At best they had been patched up compromises.

Also, I was in the process of becoming a convert to the Christian way of life where Sarah was an "expert." After all, she wrote Christian books, taught Sunday school, and could quote appropriate Bible passages for any occasion. She was a spiritual giant while I was barely a midget who had trouble looking up the books in the Bible when somebody referred to them. If we were to be married I was afraid she would constantly tell me what to do, say, and think as a Christian, as well as interpret God's Word for me. In short, it would be an impossible situation.

The best solution for the moment was to put the thoughts of

marriage aside and enjoy each day as it came. That was not difficult. I found myself laughing with the children and joking with Sarah in a way we had never been able to do before.

For the first time in our years of knowing each other, Sarah and I could simply talk for hours. We walked up and down the Seattle hills, oblivious of the cold, wet drizzle, stopping for a cup of hot chocolate in the Norwegian bakery or a bowl of fish soup in the cafeteria by the fishing wharf. It reminded me of Norway. The people wore Norwegian sweaters and read Norwegian newspapers while they ate their open-faced sandwiches or steaming plates of boiled cod. The recorded music was Norwegian and so were the snatches of conversations drifting our way from the neighboring tables. Oddly enough, I felt quite at home.

Saturdays and Sunday afternoons we took the car ferry across the Sound and drove over backroads on the rugged Olympic peninsula. The children roamed the woods or explored the beach while Sarah and I rested on a fallen log or a moss-covered rock and talked some more. Sarah listened more than she talked. In the past I had often accused her of rambling aimlessly, always interrupting or contradicting me when I tried to make a point. Now her voice was softer, and the look in her eyes warm and open. I found it easy to tell her things we had never shared before. Memories of my childhood and youth, dreams and ambitions, disillusionments, and now my search for new understanding and meaning in the Bible.

Obviously Sarah had changed, as I knew myself to be changing. The big question was: Were we being changed enough? I knew that God's power to change things was real. But could He heal the old wounds and bring us together in a workable marriage? Not just a compromise, but a real relationship in love?

I read again the words in the Bible I had heard so often:

". . . a man should leave his father and mother, and be forever united to his wife. The two shall become one—no longer two, but one! And no man may divorce what God has joined together." [3]

Now I saw what I had never seen before—that *God would make two become one.* A successful marriage was not two people adjusting to each other, but being willing to let God make them one. Before I had always thought of marriage as a contract that could be terminated if it did not work out. Now I was faced with a permanent, lifetime commitment. If Sarah and I should marry we would start out with serious handicaps, among them tight finances and a backlog of bad memories. What if we slipped into the old habit patterns of negative reactions as the daily grind caught us in its web?

There was no chance of our succeeding if we relied on our own resources. Only a supernatural intervention of God could save us from a marital hell.

The basic issue was: to trust, or not to trust, completely in God as I had come to know Him through the Bible. Was I ready to commit myself, not only to Sarah, but to God in a total commitment of my life and future? Did I have enough evidence to dare to accept the entire Bible as truth?

I had tangible evidence that two of the major propositions in the Bible were true. The first concerned my relationship to Sarah. We had once been bitter enemies; now we were closer than friends. Only in the Bible had I found a workable formula for a reconciliation between people. Nowhere else had I found the promise of restoration of broken relationships—between God and man—and between individuals.

The other evidence was my release from alcoholism. Only in the Bible had I found the promise of total release from bondage or addiction. Everything I had read or experienced before had convinced me that "once an alcoholic, always an alcoholic." In AA men who had been sober for five years introduced themselves as alcoholics and told of fighting constantly the desire to drink again. Yet since my initial capitulation to God at Jane's kitchen table, the compulsion to drink had left me. I had taken perhaps a dozen drinks over the following two months, and none in the last month. After one beer, there had been no desire for another one. The Bible was the only literature I had ever read that offered an explanation, and an accurate description, of what I had experienced as fact.

The conclusive proof presented itself one evening as I walked home from Sarah's house. On the corner of my block was a small neighborhood tavern, the kind of place where I had spent literally thousands of evenings. The lighted beer sign in the window shone through the light drizzle and I thought: "I sure don't want to go in there!"

I stopped dead in my tracks. Never in the old days had I passed a bar without wanting to go in, and in the back of my mind a small voice prodded, "Why don't you want to go in and have a couple of beers?"

"I just don't want to."

"Oh, come on. It's been over a month. It'll be fun!"

Quickly I turned the door handle and went in. A few customers were sitting at the bar watching television. I stepped up and ordered a beer.

Always when I had managed to stay dry for an extended period of time the first drink tasted like the nectar of the gods, every drop a pleasure. Now I looked at the amber liquid in my glass, blew the foam off the top, and sipped slowly. The taste was flat, not at all what I had expected. Perhaps if I tried another it would be better, I thought. Instead, the second glass was worse. It actually made me a little nauseous. I tried lighting up a cigar—I had always liked to drink and smoke cigars. After a few puffs I was dizzy and sick. The experience came as a shock. I had always enjoyed drinking. Now I definitely did not.

Walking down the street with the rain in my face the full impact hit me. My body no longer craved the stimulant of alcohol. In fact, I felt much better without it. Once I had been trapped; now I was free. I could scarcely fathom the full meaning of the word. It was not just for now; with a surge of joy I realized that it encompassed the future as well. Never again did I have to be in bondage.

I had been powerless to free myself, but the Bible explained it. My unconditional surrender to God had enabled Him to free me from my miserable condition. No longer was my helplessness a cause for despair, but for hope. The old idea that God helps those who help themselves was a myth, the most cruel myth of all. It was precisely in my weakness that God would demonstrate His strength.

There was no longer any need to hesitate. I did not know all the answers, but I knew enough to make an intellectually honest commitment. Back in my little room I knelt by my chair. The moment called for an outward demonstration of surrender as well. This time I *knew* to Whom I addressed myself: "Lord, I believe Your Word is true. I commit myself and my life to You and to Your Son, Jesus Christ, my Savior. I promise to obey Your will as You make it clear to me through Your Word." I felt a thickening in my throat.

"Lord, without You I am nothing. Thank You for saving me out of the hell I was in. Thank You for giving me life and freedom."

Peace, mingled with joy, grew within me, more intensely real than anything I had ever known before. This single moment seemed the culmination of my entire life. The love of God engulfed me, and I heard my own voice repeat over and over again, "Thank You, Lord, Thank You!"

Committing myself to marriage was next. God would make us one—I believed it was possible—and I would submit to His will. I was ready to propose to Sarah, and I knew that her response would be honest. Marriage would be difficult for her. It was even possible that she would say no.

It drizzled again the following morning as I walked towards Sarah's house. Peace and happiness filled me. God was in charge of our future, and I was certain that it was good!

Sarah

Seattle, Washington

The tension was gone when David returned from Los Angeles. He was more relaxed and we could talk and even laugh together.

"I'm glad to be here," he said the first evening. "I think we need to get to know each other, don't you?"

He didn't mention marriage, and I was relieved. That would come in its own time. I discovered that I enjoyed David's presence in the house and missed him when he was gone. He spent much time plowing through Bible commentaries and volumes on theology. There was nothing haphazard about his approach to Christianity. If I had ever feared that his encounter with God was a surface thing or an expedient device to get back in touch with his family, I could put those fears away.

"I know something significant has happened to me and to us," David's face wore a determined look. "Now I must fit everything else in with it."

We were standing on a bluff overlooking the small boat harbor not far from our house. David held my hand in his, and I enjoyed the feeling of warmth it gave me.

"You know I've always been an extremist," his brown eyes were smiling, but his tone was serious. "I was extremely wrong—and I have to be absolutely certain of what I experience now."

"I like that kind of extremist."

"Then you understand why I can't take your word, or anybody else's, for what the Bible has to say to me. I have to dig into it myself. When I'm convinced of its truth, then I must do what it directs, regardless of what anyone else might say." The determined look in his eyes was unlike the old rigidity I had both feared and despised. There was a light and a quiet strength that somehow made me feel very secure standing next to him.

We jogged home and arrived breathless. John shook his head when he saw us, but smiled. "You are just like kids!"

"Your mother and I used to take life entirely too seriously," David grinned and winked at him. "Don't you think it is about time we get smart?"

Day by day I became more conscious of a rush of happy anticipation as soon as I heard David's car turn in the driveway or his voice and steps at the door. He often brought me little gifts. A rosebud, a pretty cup, a special card, something he had never done in the years before. But he said nothing about marriage, and I wondered about it.

Then one evening we were alone by the fireplace. The children were asleep, and silence had fallen between us. I watched the sparks fly up the chimney. It was wonderful to just sit quietly together, surrounded by peace.

"Sarah," David brought a small box from his pocket. Slowly he opened the lid. There, on blue satin, rested a small white, enameled silver cross. "I think you know what I am going to ask." I caught my breath and held it. "Will you marry me?"

"I belong to God now. . . ." I felt suddenly flustered.

David smiled. "I already asked Him. He says it's O.K."

My heart was beating furiously and I knew my cheeks were burning. "In that case . . . yes!"

"I love you, Sarah." It was a statement of fact. David's eyes held mine for a long moment. Then his arms closed around me, and I could scarcely contain the joy bubbling up inside.

The next morning at the breakfast table David struck his fork against the glass. "I have an important announcement."

The children grew suddenly silent. All looked at him.

"Your mother has consented to marry me."

The silence lasted for several seconds, then all four children cheered. Andrew and Christine looked as if they were going to cry.

"Let us thank God." David looked around the table and we all joined hands. David's hand closed around mine and the touch made me tremble.

"Thank You, Lord, for bringing us back together," David prayed. "Thank You for keeping my family safe while I was gone. Now bless our union and teach us to love You and to love each other. In Jesus' name we pray, Amen."

"Amen," said the rest of us together, the children all but shouting it.

Chapter 16

DAVID   *Seattle, Washington*

We were married at Thanksgiving—it seemed an appropriate date. The problems began to surface almost immediately. One cold and rainy afternoon I returned home after another unsuccessful attempt to find a job—any job. My small cash supply was dwindling. Sarah's income provided our daily necessities, but I did not like the idea of being supported by my wife. For too long I had been unable to provide for my family. The feeling was frustrating and depressing.

Sarah was in the kitchen, and I tried to sound cheerful. "Hi honey, what's for supper?"

Her reaction was like a replay of an old, unpleasant memory. Instead of answering she ran to the bedroom. There I found her face down in the pillow. "It's no use," her voice was muffled by sobs. "We've only been married five days and you're already acting the way you used to before."

"What did I do?" I tried to take her in my arms, but she pushed me away. Her face was red with anger. "The first thing you say when you come in the door is 'What's for supper?' Couldn't you see I hadn't started anything yet? I don't *know* what's for supper."

It was a scene we had played countless times before. Sarah, aroused by frustration and guilt for not having planned her day better, would lash out at me. This time I stifled my impatience. "You know how much I look forward to our evening meal together. I asked only because I was interested in what you were doing."

Her guilt apparently increased, Sarah's eyes flashed in dark anger. "If you want to know the truth—I was busy writing and forgot all about dinner."

My patience was running out. "You should plan your dinner before you start writing in the morning." The look on Sarah's face warned of an impending explosion, and I walked quickly from the room. Irritation was growing inside. Sarah ought to order her time better. After all these years she should have the basic functions of our household under control.

The rain was pouring down to match my mood. "I'm going for a walk!" I slammed the door behind me without waiting for an answer and walked briskly up the street past the little tavern on the corner where the beer sign beckoned in the window. The disappointment nearly made me sick. Sarah was behaving as erratically as she had done years ago.

A sudden thought made me stop: "*Who* is behaving in the same old way?" I stared at the rivulets of rainwater running down the gutter carrying old brown leaves along. "We are *both* acting in the old self-centered way," I muttered aloud and felt instant regret. "Please forgive me, and change these old negative attitudes of mine."

Only ten minutes had passed since I left the house. Now I hurried home with a new buoyancy to my steps.

Sarah was in the kitchen frying hamburgers, her face tear-stained, but smiling. "I'm sorry I acted so silly."

"Don't be sorry." I swung her around. "Be thankful. I think we can learn something from this little incident."

"What's that?" The light was back in Sarah's eyes.

"We fell into the trap of reacting to each other instead of to Jesus Christ. We forgot Who's in charge now."

Sarah nodded. "It's true. I've been reacting to you. I lost the perspective of faith."

Drawing her close I prayed aloud, "Dear God. Thank You for letting the old hurts come to the surface, if that's the only way they can be healed. Help us to turn them over to You as we become aware of them. Thank You for healing our memories and old attitudes, and for giving us a new love for each other."

The time was only fifteen till six. "We'll have dinner on time yet!" I took off my coat. "I'll set the table."

After the children had gone to bed we sat by the fireplace.

"I know how important it is to be on time with the meals. I'm honestly trying." Sarah's smile was still a little defensive.

"I know you are." I took her hands in mine. "For years I was angry because I thought you didn't care. Now I understand that you do, and I don't want you to be anxious if you're a little late." I smiled, and the frown of worry had left Sarah's face. "We've both been at fault. You for being disorganized, and I for demanding perfection."

My demands had always been hard on others as well as myself. For years I had used alcohol to soothe the frustrations I was forced to live with when reality did not match my expectations. Now I was free from the bonds of alcohol, and as a fledgling Christian I was beginning to understand that God loves imperfect people. But that did not mean I was automatically patient and understanding with myself and others. There would be many incidents to trigger the old reactions, and only as I learned to rely on my new relationship to Jesus Christ would the old attitudes slowly change.

For several weeks we seemed to balance precariously on a thin line. A harsh tone of voice, a certain look on Sarah's face, would awaken an old memory or rub a sensitive wound. Instantly I would be tempted to think that nothing had changed. We were heading for the same dead-end street we had been in before.

Always it required a distinct effort of my will to recognize the moment as a crisis point, and to turn myself and the situation over to God. Things were *not* the same. Something was significantly different. Sarah and I had access to God who could turn each painful encounter into a growing experience. Once we surrendered our hurt pride to God, we were brought a step closer to Him and to each other.

In contrast, if I refused to admit my fault, refused to let go of the old hurt, an ice front settled over our house, effectively blocking all communication between us and upsetting the peace within. My old reaction to a tense situation at home had always been to clam up and hope the trouble would go away. Now I suffered when the lines of communication closed between Sarah and myself, and knew that the trouble would not cease until I surrendered the old attitude of rigidity and asked forgiveness and healing.

Both Sarah and I knew that our only hope for survival in

marriage was to submit wholeheartedly to God's pattern as we found it in the Bible. In theory we both agreed that I should be the head of the house. In practice that meant both of us had to learn new roles.

My role as head of the household under God was vastly different from the old domineering attitude I had often assumed in the old days. Now I was to have responsibility and authority, coupled with love and understanding flowing through me from my head, Christ.

In our old marriage I had gladly delegated the daily disciplining of the children to Sarah. She had also made the decisions concerning our social activities, household purchases, and scheduling. Now I discovered that being the head of the household meant a much closer participation in the daily lives of my wife and children. As I began in a fumbling sort of way to take on my responsibilities, I encountered almost automatic opposition from Sarah. It was not deliberate resistance as much as habit reaction, but it caused painful tension.

I said, "Let's drive to the mountains this weekend."

"We can't; I've invited Aunt Adah for dinner."

"I thought we agreed that you would consult me before committing our time."

"I'm sorry," Sarah immediately looked guilty. "I just forgot."

Or, "I want Leif to get a haircut this afternoon."

"Oh, but he doesn't want one," Sarah answered mechanically.

"I didn't ask if he *wanted* one." My anger was near the boiling point. "How can these children learn to respect the authority of their father if you always contradict my decisions?"

Sarah looked crestfallen, and I warmed to my subject. "Perhaps you don't realize how much you make the decisions around here."

"I don't mean to. Please overlook it when I do."

"Overlook it!" My voice had risen. "Wouldn't it be a lot simpler if you just controlled your tongue in the first place?"

Andrew's football had been left in the middle of the living room. Now I gave it a vicious kick that sent it thundering against the wall, missing one of my favorite pictures by a narrow inch. Sarah looked suddenly frightened, and I fought to control myself. "Good grief," I shook my head in disgust. "God, take this temper of mine before I blow the whole thing. I'm a poor example of Christ-like authority."

My anger evaporated instantly, and Sarah dared to smile. I began to chuckle, and suddenly we were both laughing. I pulled her close, and she giggled against my shoulder. "Do you think we're a hopeless case?"

"Not as long as we remember that God loves us no matter how imperfect we are."

"I'm sure glad His patience outlasts yours." Sarah sighed with contentment, and I hugged her closer. We had never been able to laugh together at our mistakes before. The process of becoming the family God promised we could be, would be a long one. But it had begun.

SARAH   *Seattle, Washington*

Jack and Lydia drove all the way from Los Angeles to attend our wedding. "We wouldn't miss it for anything!" Jack embraced us all, and Lydia showered us with kisses. They had remembered to bring small gifts for the children, and Jack slipped away from the house to buy a carnation for David's lapel and a bouquet of miniature daisies for me.

Sunlight flooded the little chapel through stained glass windows. The pastor asked, "Who gives the bride away?"

John stuck his head between us and spoke loudly, "We do!" The four children were beaming proudly behind us, eagerly taking in each word of the ceremony.

"Sarah, do you promise to love, honor, and obey your husband?" I nodded, trembling. It was the commitment I had already made to God months before.

". . . till death do us part," I repeated the words and knew that our vows were irrevocable. Time was suspended. David and I were alone before God, trusting our lives to Him. There was no way back.

Afterwards we had Norwegian wedding cake at home, and the children toasted us solemnly with red Kool-Aid in our finest crystal glasses. They stood with Jack and Lydia on our frozen lawn and waved us off on our honeymoon, a weekend in Vancouver, Canada.

It was our first, and now I was glad we had not bothered with such "romantic nonsense" after our first wedding.

It began to snow while we were there. Beautiful white flakes dancing down from above, making the world look new and pure.

Back home I floated on a cloud of happiness for several days before I realized that the "living happily ever after" was not going to happen instantly or automatically. David did and said things triggering my old reactions, and the nagging little thought was quick to jump up in my mind, "David hasn't really changed and neither have you. Now you're stuck in misery for the rest of your lives."

During the time of our divorce I had learned to manage my household much better than before, yet now I seemed to slip back into the old pattern of carelessness about meals and order. Predictably David was upset, and just as predictably I reacted with guilt, self-condemnation, and anger. The rerun of old scenes usually started with a complaint from David: "I'm out of socks. Why can't you keep up with your washing?"

"I'm sorry, I was busy writing."

"I thought you said you had learned about priorities. Don't you think the needs of your family come first?"

"The bills need to be paid!" I could not resist the reminder of *who* provided the money for the bills. It was a sore point, and David grew pale with rage. "*Your* job is to care for the family here at home. *Mine* is to make the money." We glared at each other for a horrible length of time, and usually David was the first to say, "Honey, I'm sorry. We're forgetting Who is in charge."

Always I was torn between a desire to hold on to my hurt pride and the will to give in to what I knew was God's plan. Sometimes I resisted for hours, and the atmosphere in the house became a dreadful reminder of the hell we had once lived in. My stubborn attitude was foolish, but I hated to admit I had been wrong. When I finally could make myself say I was sorry, David usually had the decency not to rub it in, but took me in his arms to say he loved me. "Even if you *never* learn."

The scenes that started in a familiar pattern ended in an entirely new way. We were weathering small storms together, and with each bout we discovered that our vessel was as seaworthy as she had been promised to be.

I had thought that I had forgiven and forgotten all the hard places, but now it was evident that I had let some things stay in the back of my consciousness like cobwebs and old dirt in corners. Under pressure they were exposed. Then we could talk about them, admitting our true feelings and surrender them to God. The old pain became a source of new understanding and closeness. Once I had looked at our past from my own narrow perspective. Now, for the first time, I began to see myself from David's point of view.

"I didn't know I caused you to feel like that."

"And I didn't know *you* felt like that." David had been as unaware of my suffering. Now at last we could be assured of each other's and God's forgiveness and laugh about the whole thing. The laughter was the biggest miracle. When it came we knew that the healing had been complete.

My adjustment to the new order seemed to come more slowly than David's. We were still living in "my house," following the schedule I had established when the children and I were alone. From habit the children considered me the authority. David had moved in, but I had a difficult time adapting to the fact that he was in charge. Always I took the initiative and offered "helpful" suggestions. When David made a statement I usually responded with a modification or a contradiction. It was such an ingrained habit that I wondered if I would ever break it. Yet my attitude constituted direct disobedience to the Biblical pattern for wives. If our marriage was ever to succeed I would have to change.

"You'll have to change me," I whispered into the night after David had gone to sleep. "God, You know I can't change myself."

DAVID   *Pacific View, California*

The construction industry in the Seattle area was at a near standstill. There were no job prospects in sight, and I was beginning to feel that we ought to move. But where to? The awesome responsibility for my family weighed on me. God had a right place for us, and that was where I wanted to be. But how to find it?

I still felt like a novice in this matter of a two-way communication with God, but I knew that He had directed me to Seattle, and He would direct me again.

In some ways I was better prepared to judge the signals this time. For one thing I was more familiar with the Bible, and I was sure that whatever God wanted me to do would be in agreement with the guidelines I found there.

The solid sense of peace inside me also constituted a very sensitive warning system. It was noticeably upset whenever I stubbornly insisted on my own way.

Looking towards our future, I asked God to guide me and was prepared to move as the circumstances seemed to direct—as long as I felt that peace. If the peace was disturbed, I would stop and take another look.

My thoughts were turning increasingly towards Southern California. At first I shrugged them off. After all, that was where I had gravitated for years in search of better fortune. When the thoughts persisted I began to wonder if God had prompted them after all.

"Where in Southern California?" I mused and almost immediately the name of a small town in San Diego County popped into my mind. Pacific View was nothing like the throbbing megalopolis of the Los Angeles area that I had always been drawn to before. Years ago, when I was stationed at Camp Pendleton, I had often driven through the quiet little community. Once I had taken Sarah and the children there on our way to the mountains.

"Do you remember a little town called Pacific View?" I asked Sarah one evening.

She wrinkled her forehead in concentration. "I think so . . . we drove through there once, didn't we?" Then her face brightened. "I have a friend there."

"You never told me. Who?" I felt a prickling sensation along my spine.

"A girl named Jennifer Carlton. We met at a writers' conference and have exchanged Christmas cards since then. I don't know her very well."

"I've been thinking of going someplace else to look for a job," I said lightly. "For some reason the town of Pacific View interests me."

Sarah's face registered immediate alarm. "Did you pray about it?"

"Are you telling me how to be the head of this family?"

Sarah hung her head, and I ignored a twinge of irritation.

"Why don't you call Jennifer and tell her we're thinking of moving to the area? Find out her reaction. . . ."

"Aren't you a little hasty?" Sarah was hedging.

"Don't fight me every inch of the way." I struggled to keep my temper in check.

Sarah got her friend on the line. They talked for a while, then Sarah covered the mouthpiece with her hand and turned to me. She looked a little amazed. "Jennifer says Pacific View has just started into a building boom. We may have trouble finding a house for rent, but she says you won't have any difficulties in finding a job in construction."

"Tell her to look for us after Christmas," I was suddenly elated.

Sarah hung up and shook her head. "You certainly were on the right track!"

"Maybe next time you'll obey your husband without argument." I could not resist rubbing it in.

Sarah looked remorseful. "It's a habit. Believe me, I want to change."

I did believe her, but her habitual resistance made it hard to stick with my original commitment to God that I would learn to be the head of my house. In the old days I had always cringed from confrontations with Sarah, and now I found it even harder to oppose her. The "new" Sarah was more endearing than the "old," her arguments more reasonable, and therefore harder to resist. When tears came and I knew she was hurt, I wanted most of all to drop the issue, take her in my arms and say, "O.K. honey, whatever you want."

We rented a truck, packed our few belongings, and headed south with a real sense of adventure. In our years of married life Sarah and I had moved often, yet this move was different. I had no preconceived notion of what lay ahead. I was not looking for a dream. Inside was a solid conviction that God was leading us, and that He already had prepared our future, the house, the job, the circumstances.

Jennifer and her husband, Bill, were expecting us. Bill Carlton was a large man with a friendly grin. "I've got friends in the construction business," he shook my hand in a firm greeting. "I'll introduce you later, but first you better look for a house."

The local paper had only three listings in the for rent section, and Jennifer took us straight to see the first one.

"It's usually a matter of first come, first grab," she explained. "You can't be too choosy."

The small green house stood on the edge of an open field only a few minutes from the center of town. Fruit trees grew in back and a neglected rose garden in front. I felt an immediate urge to start digging around the roses.

Sarah walked tight-lipped through the tiny rooms; three bedrooms, undersized bath and kitchen, and a living room that would just barely accommodate our baby grand piano.

"Do you expect me to live in this little cracker box?" She was about to cry.

"We don't have much furniture."

"But I *know* God has something better."

Jennifer was looking at us, and I shrugged with a sinking feeling.

"O.K. honey, I want you to be happy. Let's look some more."

The next listing was a larger house in a tract, and Sarah looked a little more hopeful. I did not like the neighborhood, but I spoke to the owner. When he heard I was unemployed he shook his head, "Sorry, I can't take a chance."

The third house was already rented. I looked at Sarah; her face showed fatigue after our long trip, and a wave of compassion swept over me.

"We'll look some more tomorrow," I put my arm around her. "Right now you need rest."

She smiled with gratitude. "I was afraid you'd insist on going back to that horrible little house. Let's believe God has something better for us."

Personally, I wondered if that first house wasn't best for us after all, but for the next four days I went with Sarah to check on every new house listed for rent. They were all either unsuitable or too expensive. I felt as if we were up against a stone wall. I was restless and ill at ease. The peace I had felt when we first drove into town was gone. Somewhere along the line I had stepped out of God's will.

It was not necessary to ask—I knew what I had done wrong and what I needed to do next. "Honey, do you still have the ad for the first house we looked at?" Sarah's face was a picture of utter dejection, but without a word she reached under the front seat of the car. There it was, the crumpled ad section of the four-day-old newspaper.

At the first gas station I stopped and got out, "I'm going to call the owner, and if the place isn't rented we'll take it."

Before Sarah could speak I walked off and stepped into the phone booth. With a sinking feeling I remembered Jennifer's words, "First come, first grab." The house would be taken. The owner answered the phone, and I explained who I was and what I wanted. For some reason he remembered me. "No, it isn't rented yet." My heart jumped. "I took it off the market after you saw it. I needed to do some more painting. I was gonna put the ad back in the paper tomorrow."

We agreed to meet at the house, and I went back to the car to face Sarah. "I'm sorry, honey," I steeled myself against the look of hurt in her eyes. "I felt that it was the right house for us, but I let myself be influenced by your tears. I was wrong. Thank God the house is still there."

Sarah bit her lip. "If I could be sure God wanted us there, I wouldn't mind it."

I had an impulse to yell at her but took a deep breath instead. "You always want to make sure I'm doing the right thing in *your* opinion before you'll go along. Is that what the word submission means?" The air was charged between us, and Sarah met my gaze for a long time, then shook her head slowly.

"We're going back to rent that house," I spoke firmly. "As your husband and the head of this household I'm telling you that it is the right house for us—the *very* best house we could possibly be in—because it is the house God led us to. Can you accept that?"

Sarah's eyes were moist, but she nodded. "I'll try," she whispered. She was quiet while we drove back to the house where the owner was waiting for us. He did not mind that I was unemployed, and only asked for one month's rent in advance. I felt much better once the rental agreement was signed. The inward peace had returned.

SARAH   *Pacific View, California*

At first sight I hated the little green house. It was a plain little cracker box without any charm as far as I could see. There was very little storage space, and the kitchen had only one cupboard and one small counter. It was the kind of house where my poor housekeeping practices would create chaos.

We had no refrigerator, no kitchen table, no beds, or chests of drawers. Since we were nearly broke, our few purchases were made at the Goodwill and Salvation Army stores and a couple of garage sales. We could afford one set of bunk-beds for Leif and John. Andrew and Christine slept on camping cots. Our "bed" was a folded rubber carpet pad with sleeping bags stacked on top. It was surprisingly comfortable, and David was very pleased with the arrangement.

"Everything is wonderful," he repeated several times daily. "Our first home together. Aren't you grateful?" He dug around the rosebushes in the front yard and proudly brought me the first bud. "Someone had a prize garden here once. I'll soon have it back in shape." He placed the bud in a vase on my desk and went back outside, humming to himself.

Grateful was not exactly the word to describe how I felt. Yet to be thankful for all things was the proper Christian attitude.[1]

Everything would work together for good; how well I knew that. Yet every time I looked at the tiny, six-cubic-foot, twenty-year-old refrigerator Jennifer and Bill had lent us, despair welled up inside me. That refrigerator was the last straw. Maybe I was spoiled, but while I was alone, God had provided for our physical comfort much better than He seemed to be doing now. My thoughts went back to the rambling house on the beach in Florida and the roomy two-story in Seattle. I even had more money then—and we had never been reduced to sleeping on the floor or keeping our clothes in cardboard boxes.

"Why, Lord, why?" I swallowed a big lump in my throat as I prepared for my weekly chore of defrosting the little refrigerator. The food was piled on the kitchen table and counter, and I put a pot of boiling water on one of the two small shelves to melt the ice faster. My big, modern frost-free refrigerators had never required this much work. My time was really too valuable to waste on such menial chores.

David had laughed heartily when he first saw the refrigerator. "You must admit it fits the size of our kitchen. God knows what we need, honey." He held me so hard I couldn't pull away. "And there's no room for leftovers to spoil!"

It was true, I had always kept small containers of food till they molded in the refrigerator. Guilt over the waste had finally brought me to ask God to teach me to be more careful. That had been just before leaving Seattle. My washrag poised in midair, I sat back on my heels as the thought struck home. Of course, that was it. God Who loved me and wanted the very best for me, would not put me in a tiny cracker box of a house, let me sleep on the floor, and keep my food in a miniature refrigerator unless He had a very good reason.

The lump in my throat had dissolved, and I began to chuckle. The situation was not without humor. God Who knew my weaknesses would not let me get by with a half-hearted lesson in organized housekeeping. In this little house I was forced to keep things in their right place in order to avoid total chaos. The tiny refrigerator was a most ingenious way to stop my habit of wasting food. Already I was more efficient, and it was nice to know precisely what was in the refrigerator and what I intended to use it for.

When David came in from the garden, I was singing as I put the food neatly back on the two small shelves. Closing the door I felt almost fond of the scratched up little box.

"You're right," I smiled at my astonished husband. "God knows exactly what we need." I swallowed my pride and continued, "I'm sorry I didn't accept your word when you said this house was right for us. Please don't pay any attention when I oppose you in the future."

The truth was, I was becoming sick and tired of opposing David every time he made a suggestion. Deep down, I wanted to submit to him, yet something in me refused to do it without at least a token argument. The problem stemmed from the fact that I forgot, in the heat of a crisis, that it was not just David and me involved, but God as well. Submission to David was only one aspect of my submission to God, in a wider, deeper sense.

My reluctance could only be rooted in doubt. Doubt that God was *really* in charge. I had nearly panicked when David first said that we were moving to Southern California. God had moved us to Seattle, and therefore I assumed He wanted us there permanently. Later, when David wanted to rent the little house, I was distraught because I assumed again that he had not bothered to ask God. Since I had been provided with beautiful houses before, I expected the pattern to continue.

Both times I had been proven wrong, but had I dared to trust God in spite of what I thought was my husband's disobedience or neglect, we would have avoided much strain and conflict. The heart of the issue was not if I trusted David to be always right—but if I trusted God to control our circumstances even when David made the wrong decision.

The tea kettle was steaming when a brand new thought hit me: "Submission to your husband is one of God's practical tools to remold you into His image for you."

Why hadn't I seen it before? It made beautiful sense. I had asked God to remold me years ago, when I first came to Him. Back then I had not known who I was or what it meant to be a woman. One passage had struck me as I first read it in my Bible: "Don't let the world around you squeeze you into its own mold, but let God re-mold your minds from within, so that you may prove in practice that the plan of God for you is good, meets all His demands and moves towards the goal of true maturity." [2]

It was exciting to think about it. Submission served beautifully to strip off the old attitudes, forcing me to give up *my* way for someone else.

Sipping my hot tea I looked across the fields bordered by tall eucalyptus trees. Leif was there, walking our neighbor's new stallion around the corral. Leif's old love of horses had been re-kindled, and he had already found a steady job cleaning stables and riding the boarding horses each afternoon.

"God," joy was expanding inside me. "I'm so glad You brought us here. I'm so glad I'm married to David. I yield myself to You, through my husband. Empty me of my stubborn self and fill me with your love, joy, and peace."

Inside was a solid assurance that all was well.

Chapter 17

DAVID   *Pacific View, California*

The first week in Pacific View I helped Sarah get our little house in order and dug in the rich, dark soil of our garden. Never had I felt such peace and contentment. All my life I had thought that prosperity was a requirement for happiness, yet now I owned less worldly goods than in my entire adult life, and had never been happier.

Bill Carlton introduced me to Ray McGillis, a wiry man in his mid-forties with graying, thin hair. Ray was the superintendent on a large construction project and nodded approvingly as I told him my qualifications. "Sounds good, Dave," he rubbed his chin. "Several projects are starting up in April. I can almost guarantee there'll be a spot for you."

April was two months off. How would I feed my family in the meantime? I checked at the employment office who told me the same story. Wonderful outlook for April—nothing now. I felt a twinge of disappointment. I had been so certain that everything would unfold smoothly once we arrived in the spot where God wanted us.

Later, digging in the rich soil near the apricot tree where I planned our vegetable garden, my mind went over once more what I had read earlier: "My God will supply all that you need from His glorious resources in Christ Jesus." [1]

"That's great," I muttered. "So why aren't You providing?" There was a vague uneasiness in the pit of my stomach. Was I ignoring something important? Putting away the shovel I went inside to look up the passage. My eyes scanned the page, and I felt myself grow hot under the collar. The verse immediately above the one I had quoted read: "Your generosity is like a lovely fragrance, a sacrifice that pleases the very heart of God." So generosity had preceded the assurance of God's provisions.

The question of giving money to God was a touchy one since money had always been important to me. However, I felt I had reached a workable conclusion. In committing my life to God, I had also committed all I owned. I could not consider "my" money *mine* anymore than I could consider "my" life *mine*. I belonged to God, and my belongings were also technically His. So to take a portion of my earnings and return it to Him was only a small token of my trust in our relationship.

Of course, I would have nothing to give until a job provided me with a pay check. And first there were bills to be paid and urgent needs to be met for Sarah and the children. My unease had grown while my mind worked. "What's wrong?" I posed the question silently. The instant response made me apprehensive; I was suddenly reminded of the sale of my boat.

"Don't be a fool," I thought quickly. "You only have a little over a hundred dollars to your name."

"To *Who's* name?" The question was pointed.

"To God's name," I conceded reluctantly. But I was a reasonable man, careful in business. It made little sense to give away sixty dollars—ten percent of the sales sum—when my family would need groceries. It would not be a responsible act, and God wanted me to be responsible, did He not?

Even as the argument raged in my mind, I knew it was futile. This was a testing point from which I could not run. Now was the time, while I was poor and jobless, to prove with a definite act whether or not I believed that God was capable of providing for our material needs.

I looked up to see Sarah coming into the bedroom, and knew what I was required to do. "What's the address of that ex-heroin addict in Los Angeles you wrote the book for?" There was a question in her eyes, and this was one time I almost wished she would talk me out of something.

"I've come to the conclusion that I must trust God with our finances in a tangible way," I said slowly. "I am going to send Sonny ten percent of what I sold my boat for."

Sarah's response was a bright smile. "That's wonderful, David. Now I know God will take care of our needs."

Driving to the post office with a roll of ten dollar bills in my pocket, the internal struggle continued. My hand was curiously reluctant to fill in the sum on the money order, and I felt almost physical pain as the clerk counted my money and put it away. It was as if she was tearing part of my flesh. Not till I walked away did a wave of tremendous relief sweep over me. I had not realized till then how much I had considered that money "mine." Letting go when I thought I really needed it for myself, had been hard.

My car swung down a side street in front of a lumberyard. Almost without thinking I stopped and went in.

The manager showed the telltale signs of the heavy drinker—red veins on the nose and cheeks, and puffed, watery eyes. Less than a year ago I had stared at the same signs in my own mirror.

"Do you know anything about lumber?" he asked when I told him I was looking for work.

"Yes."

He pointed towards the lumber stacks in the back. "Let's go see."

As we walked he quizzed me thoroughly. I named the sorts and sizes and he nodded his approval. "You sound like you know enough. We need a clerk. When can you start?"

The pay was $97.50 a week. Five days a week and every second Saturday. Clerks were not allowed to sit down during their working hours. By the end of the first week my feet were hurting so badly that Sarah had to massage them for half an hour each night before I could go to sleep. Yet I was satisfied. I was the breadwinner for my family again.

At first I worked hard to impress the other clerks. I wanted them to realize that I really knew the business. The poor fellows were stuck in a minor job like that while I was on my way to better things. My co-workers did not seem to appreciate my greater abilities; in fact a couple of them showed resentment. They were probably envious, I thought, but their attitude made me uneasy.

"What's wrong?" I asked inwardly one morning. As usual I was sipping my coffee in solitude while two other clerks were chatting amiably in another corner.

"Acting the big shot, aren't you?" The thought was piercing.

"That's your old trick—judging and labeling others, thinking you're better than they."

It was undeniably true. I cringed as I looked over at the two men finishing up their coffee. "I'm sorry, Lord," I muttered. "Help me to see others the way I should see them. Help me be a clerk among clerks."

Things changed after that. The fellows I worked with were nice guys, family men like myself, and we had much in common. The job went easier too, and I would have come close to enjoying it, if it had not been for the manager.

Mr. Guiness was a hard man to work for, insisting on petty details that made extra and tedious work for his employees. He was usually grumpy in the mornings and unpredictable in the afternoons after a lunch of several martinis. It was as if a dark cloud moved ahead of him and at any moment we could expect an outburst of thunder.

Day after day the manager was after me, it seemed. In the old days I would have used alcohol to soften the impact, but that kind of cop-out was out of the question now. I had to face the real issue, my bruised ego. It might have been easier in another kind of job, but in a lumberyard, where I had once been the hard boss yelling at my employees whenever I suffered a hangover, it was almost more than I could bear.

One afternoon I wrote up a big order, several hundred dollars worth. I was pleased with myself and thought that Mr. Guiness would at last show a sign of approval. Instead, he squinted at the order form and barked, "Your handwriting is sloppy. Write it over again and stay on the lines!"

I wanted to tear up the form and throw the bits in his face. Instead I swallowed and forced a smile, "Yes, sir!"

But the anger simmered inside. I had reached my limit. This was it. No one, not even God, could expect me to take any more. I drove home in a cloud of gloom and pulled in at the liquor store on the corner. If ever a man needed a drink, this was the time for it.

After supper, when the children had gone to bed I brought out the bottle of Pernod. "Have a drink with me, honey."

Sarah stared but managed a thin smile. "I'll just have a cup of tea and keep you company."

I poured a glass and drank it down. Alcohol was not all that bad.

Besides, I had been made practically immune. A little relaxer after a hard day could do no harm, and I deserved it.

After the fourth glass I noticed a gray feeling inside, like a clammy fog. My mind was fuzzy. Tension was building, and I waited for Sarah to say something so that I could get release in an argument. She sat quietly sipping her tea, nodding sympathetically now and then while I repeated the sad tale of persecutions and trials at work. When I could stand the tension no longer, I got up and went to the bathroom. With a terrible sense of letdown I leaned against the lavatory and glanced into the mirror. My own face, gray and drawn, with dark circles around the eyes, stared back at me.

"My God," I let out a groan. "What am I doing?" The memories came rushing back: The hotel room in Missouri with the gun in my drawer . . . vomit all over the floor . . . the pain . . . the horror at dawn in Florida. Jane's kitchen table. How could I forget the reality of the hell I had escaped? I had been healed. I was no longer a slave of compulsive drinking, but I was not immune. The addictive power of alcohol was as much a threat to me as to everybody else. And I could get sucked right down the tube again if I wanted to.

I straightened myself and walked back into the kitchen. There I resolutely put the cork in the bottle and handed it to Sarah. "Don't throw it out—because I don't want to forget again—but put it up high."

In the bedroom I lay down on the bed. A jasmine bush was blooming just outside the open window. I drew a deep breath. "Thank You for the job in the lumberyard and for Mr. Guiness." It was no longer difficult to say it. "Help me to rely on You instead of reacting to the circumstances."

Sarah brought the ointment and began to rub my tired feet. "Did you notice the apricot tree in bloom?" she asked brightly.

"It's the first time we ever had an apricot tree," I smiled. "It's my favorite fruit."

Sarah looked down at my feet. "Isn't it great how God has an eye for detail? Rubbing your feet makes submission very tangible." She chuckled. The bottle in the kitchen cupboard was not mentioned, and I felt a sudden rush of emotion.

"I love you, wife." My voice was suddenly hoarse. "I hope I'm not as hard on you as Mr. Guiness is on me."

Sarah laughed. "I'm sure God sees to it that each of us gets exactly what we need."

SARAH   *Pacific View, California*

Apparently the process of becoming one with David involved my submission to him in a number of ways I had not even considered when I first committed myself to it. Part of our old life style had been my busy goings and comings alone or with the children, while David stayed home. Now David announced, "These separate activities aren't good for our family unity. From now on we'll either go together or stay home together. The six of us need a chance to get to know one another."

It sounded like a great idea at first, but soon it became apparent that when I wanted to go someplace, David usually didn't. Since I was supposed to do the submitting, we stayed home. I tried manipulating in devious ways, such as dropping remarks I thought would sway David's opinion, "That fellow you wanted to meet is going to be there."

Or I would fix David's favorite food to "soften" him, then ask casually, "There's a special speaker in town tonight, how about going?"

When David said "No!" my false mask of sweetness exploded. "You wouldn't go if God commanded you from a burning bush!"

David looked pained. "Believe me, honey, if I thought we ought to go, we would, no matter how tired I feel. But we *need* to have quiet evenings at home. We have years to catch up with."

By now I had reached the boiling point. "We need the fellowship in the church meeting more. How do you expect to grow as a Christian just sitting here at home?"

David gritted his teeth in an effort to stay calm. "You've already heard everything the speaker is going to talk about. Now it is time to stay home and practice some of it with your family."

My temper usually left as quickly as it came and I was ashamed of myself. The hard part was having to admit it to David. When I skipped that part, and slammed the door behind me to the bedroom, David came after me, and in his arms I managed to say, "You're right. I'm just so used to going to all the meetings. I'm afraid I'll miss something if I stay home."

My last holdout was the monthly writers' meeting I attended with Jennifer. The children jokingly referred to it as "mom's night out," but I had a sneaking suspicion that I would soon be denied even that small privilege. One morning at breakfast David buttered his toast and said in an offhand way, "Tonight is the writers' get-together, isn't it? I wish you would stay home."

Immediately, I flared up. "Are you forcing me to stay?"

"Of course not," David talked patiently, as if to an errant child, and his tone made me even more furious. "We miss you when you're gone. Why don't you make a special dessert after supper and we'll play some games with the kids?"

Suddenly it was imperative that I go to that meeting. "If I go, will you pray for me?" My heart was beating furiously.

David smiled. "I always pray for you. I just hope you'll decide to stay home."

In the end I went, and David kissed me goodbye. He and the children had already pulled out the monopoly game and Christine was fixing hot chocolate, while Andrew was making popcorn. Something tugged at me to stay. Instead, I waved cheerfully and breezed out the door.

The meeting was at Jennifer's house, and we usually had a good time, but that evening a new writer showed up. He had written a story slanted for *Playboy* magazine, a poorly-done and boring account of a homosexual love triangle. Listening, I felt increasingly miserable. I should never have come.

Driving home I was still depressed. "Why did You let me go?" I said aloud. "Why didn't You stop me, Lord?"

The answer rang through my mind. "Obedience can't be forced. I want you to submit to your husband, but the choice is yours."

There it was again. The freedom to choose between right and wrong, and I had chosen the wrong. All evening I had felt chilled, exposed, vulnerable—as if I had stepped out from under a secure, protective covering.

The light was still on in our bedroom when I pulled into the driveway. "Don't ever let me go when you think I ought to stay home!" I snuggled close to David.

He shook his head. "I'm afraid I can't make it that easy for you. I can only tell you what I think you should do, but the choice is yours."

The evening's lesson had been an impressive one. Still, I balked when David asked to be informed of my whereabouts during the day while the children were in school. "And I want you home before they get here. They need you."

"You mean I can't go *anyplace* without consulting you? I'm not a child anymore." His demand sounded almost like a joke, but I knew better.

David pulled me close. "You and the children are in my thoughts all day long. If I think you're out running errands wearing yourself down while the children are home unattended, I worry about you."

The enclosure of his arms seemed suddenly very comforting. My anger melted. "You really *do* feel responsible for me every minute of the day, don't you?"

David nodded and kissed me lightly. "That's the general idea."

"Then I don't mind. And please don't be too upset if I complain a little. You know it's old habit."

Reporting to David on my daily activities had unexpected benefits. We rose at dawn, an hour before the children, for a leisurely cup of coffee and talk. David read to me from his Bible while the first rays of the morning sun glittered in the dew on the pyracantha bush outside our window. His voice was deep and resonant. Sometimes I closed my eyes as I listened, and the words came alive. At such times I felt an almost overwhelming sense of wonder over the events of the last months. Only a year ago David and I had been separated by an invisible chasm that seemed unbridgeable. Yet now I felt myself grow closer to him daily. Our little kitchen seemed a snug haven, filled with light and love and my well-planned day stretched before me, uncluttered and unhurried.

There were moments of tension when David vetoed something I had set my heart on doing, but as I bent my will to his, I discovered that the end result was better than if I had insisted on my own way. Frequently someone called to ask a favor or to get me to "volunteer" for a task. I had always found it difficult to say no, and in the past my schedule had been crowded with things I really did not have time for. Now the matter was settled quickly. I asked

David, and if he said yes, the timing always worked out perfectly. If he said no, I only had to tell the caller, "My husband prefers that I stay home." There was never any objection or hurt feelings.

Jennifer called one day to ask me for lunch. When I said I would ask David first, she howled with laughter. "Do you ask his permission to go to the bathroom?"

"Don't be silly. We're just following the Biblical pattern, and it really is a practical arrangement."

"I've been a Christian much longer than you. I tell you you're going too far. You do have a right to a life of your own." Jennifer sounded concerned.

"I thought Jesus said it was better to give up our rights than to insist on them." I could not resist the argument.

"Of course," Jennifer answered lightly. "That's elementary, my dear, but it does not apply to marriage. You give a little and he gives a little. Fifty-fifty."

"It's more like a hundred-hundred with us," I giggled. "I give a hundred percent, and so does David, when it is required. Any other way we have problems."

"You two are extreme," Jennifer sounded a little impatient. "Your marriage was a total wreck. It takes radical means to put it back together again. Bill and I have been Christians for years. We do fine as a team. He knows he can't push me too far, and I know I can't push him. We balance each other perfectly."

I suddenly realized that I would not want to trade Jennifer's balancing game with my own position for anything in the world.

"See if your husband will let you go out for lunch," Jennifer laughed. "You need to be liberated!"

David thought lunch with Jennifer sounded like a good idea, and we agreed to meet at a sandwich shop near Jennifer's office.

She brought up the question again. "Do you really think every wife should ask her husband about every little thing she wants to do?" She looked as if she was only half serious.

I bit into my french dip sandwich. Jennifer's clear blue eyes looked straight at me through dark-rimmed glasses. She was an efficient legal secretary, and I knew that her marriage to Bill was basically good. "I'll grant you that David and I are extremists," I began, and Jennifer looked relieved. "I was too independent, too radical the other way. Maybe some other couple doesn't need to be as concerned with outward submission in every detail. It's the attitude of submission that counts." I drew lines on my napkin with my fork. "If a husband wants to delegate a certain responsibility to his wife, that's a matter between the two of them and God." I looked straight into Jennifer's pensive eyes. "Nevertheless, the principle is valid. I'm convinced of it. God requires an attitude of total submission from a wife—regardless of the practical outworking in each individual case."

Jennifer nodded thoughtfully. "I think you're right. Although I don't take it as seriously as I should. There doesn't seem to be the need for it in our case. It is so totally contrary to the ideas of women's liberation and equality between the sexes, or don't you believe in that?"

In a flash I remembered how I had felt in Arizona when Pastor Borror brought up the subject of submission for the first time. Then I had been annoyed and upset. Now I smiled. "You used the very words I once threw at my pastor. Yes, I do believe in the liberation of women. In fact, I've never felt more liberated in my life."

Jennifer's face registered astonishment.

"Don't you remember what Jesus said?" I asked. ". . . If ye continue in my word . . . ye shall know the truth, and the truth shall make you free." [2] Jennifer nodded slowly and I went on. "I don't mean to give you double-talk, but now that I am submitting to the true role of a woman as I see it in God's Word, I really am experiencing a freedom—a liberation—I never even came close to finding before. As for equality between the sexes, I believe in that too, but I've discovered that equality does not mean alikeness."

Jennifer's face broke into a slow smile. "You mean, there's a real difference between men and women?"

"Right." I held my coffee cup poised and smiled broadly. "I did not feel this way before, but now I say wholeheartedly, thank God for the difference!"

Back home I found David in the garden, weeding his lettuce bed. "I've just discovered I'm a liberated woman," I laughed. David stood up and rinsed the soil off his hands with the watering hose while I continued talking. "I'm more me, more in love, and glad to depend on you. Not because I have to, but because I want to." I felt so light inside I wanted to run across the field.

"Are you sure you don't mind being dependent on me?" David looked serious, his eyes searching mine.

"At first I was afraid. I thought it would make me more vulnerable and helpless if something should ever happen to you." I put my arms around his waist. "Now I know that I am really dependent on God who put you in charge of me. If anything should happen to you, He will take care of me."

"I'm glad you feel that way." David's arms tightened around me. "Because what I have to tell you next may be hard to take."

Apprehension shot through me. "Surely by now I've adapted every area of my life to the new system," I tried to sound cheerful. "What's on your mind?"

The inward struggle showed on David's face, and I felt a tightening of my stomach muscles. "It's your writing," he said slowly.

"But I only write what you approve of," I spoke rapidly. I was convinced that I had submitted the professional area of my life completely to my husband's direction.

"Your first priorities are here at home. The children need your full attention. I need you and want you to spend more time doing things with me."

My mouth felt dry. "I thought we had already agreed on that," my voice shook.

"Honey, I think you know what I mean," David's eyes were pleading. "I want you to stop writing altogether."

Something within me reacted instantly. I pulled away from him. "You know I signed a contract before we married to write another book." I spoke harshly, defensively. "I can't break the contract. The publisher would not understand."

David frowned. "I've thought and prayed about that, and I think this is the answer." With long steps he went to the picnic table where his Bible was open. "Why don't you read it for yourself?"

My hands trembled; anger nearly choked me. The words were fuzzy before my eyes, but their meaning was unmistakable: "If a woman promises the Lord to do or not to do something—while she is still at home in her father's house—and if the father refuses to let her do it, then the promise becomes automatically invalid. If she takes a vow, and later marries—and if her husband refuses to accept her vow, his disagreement makes it void, and Jehovah will forgive her. If she is married and living in her husband's home when she makes the vow—and her husband hears of it and says nothing, then the vow shall stand; but if he refuses to allow it—it is void. So her husband may either confirm or nullify her vow." [3]

Streaks of red flashed before my eyes, and I threw the book down. "So you're forcing me to quit writing," I spoke through clenched teeth.

"No, honey," David flatly denied the charge. "I won't force you. The choice is yours, as always."

"You hypocrite!" I hurled the words at him. "You might as well be forcing me; shoving a Bible under my nose when you know I can't ignore what it says." I stopped to catch my breath. David's face was a blank. "You've always been jealous of my writing. Why don't you admit that you've been looking for an excuse to stop me?"

"Please, honey. . . ."

"Don't say please to me! You're forcing me to quit doing something I think is important, something I think God wants me to do. Well—I'll quit! I won't write another word—and I hope you'll regret what you've done!"

With the last salvo ringing in the air, I ran inside and flung myself on the bed. "God, you know I've been writing for You," I sobbed convulsively. "Don't let David stop me."

All my life writing had been part of me. And it had been part of the "new" me I had just begun to discover over the last few years. Without writing, my days would be meaningless and empty. I pounded David's pillow with my fists and looked at my desk where my typewriter was surrounded by reference books, paper and pencils, and my copy of the manuscript I had just finished and put in the mail the day before. For so long my days had been ordered around my regular writing hours, and whatever assignment I worked on had filled my mind, even when I was away from my desk.

The fury inside had settled into a hard little knot in my stomach. Resolutely I got up and put the typewriter in its case under the desk. With lips pressed tightly together I put the books and papers in a cardboard box to go under the desk as well. I would do my part and submit to David's demand. Obviously he still felt insecure and threatened by my career. Only God could take care of his problem, and I hoped it would be soon.

The next days I forced myself to keep house and cook. It was suddenly boring, and I did not know what to do with myself once the work was done. For years I had complained about a lack of time; now the hours dragged, empty and gray. Over my head hung a storm cloud, and the children and David walked on tiptoe to avoid an outburst. Not since leaving Georgia had I experienced such a mental depression and chill inside. Occasionally I caught sight of my own sour face in the mirror. It was perhaps childish to be so demonstrative about my feelings, but David had started it all, and I was waiting for him to admit his mistake.

"You want me to write, don't you, Lord?" I had withdrawn to the quietness of the backyard where a large pepper tree provided a shady spot. I had brought my Bible—not because I wanted to read it, the last few days I had avoided that as much as possible—but I wanted to look occupied if David should happen to look my way. He was spending his Saturday afternoon rummaging among his tools in the garage, and I knew he could see me through the window. Absentmindedly I leafed through the pages, careful not to read the words. Suddenly a thought pierced through my defensive shield: "Aren't you forgetting that if God wanted you to write, He could have kept David from doing what he did?"

A bird was singing directly above me, and the sun filtered through the leafy branches to make a cheerful pattern of light and shadow over the open book in my lap. I felt suddenly foolish. The truth was so simple, and I had so stubbornly refused to see it. Some words on the page had been circled in red. Now they seemed to burn into my consciousness: ". . . you are to respect, honor, adore, be devoted to . . . and deeply love and enjoy your husband." [4]

It was the words, "enjoy your husband," that brought the sudden rush of helpless tears to my eyes. For the last few days I had tried, with clenched teeth and bitterness heavy inside me, to respect and obey him. But enjoy him? Never!

"Lord, I can't!" My attitude was wrong and I knew it. "Lord, You want me to enjoy my husband. I can't force it, or fake it. My feelings are against it. Please help me. Change me. I *want* to do Your will."

The birdsong seemed happier and the sunshine brighter. A

beautiful calm had replaced the tight knot inside me. Now I wondered why I had made such an issue over David's request. If God didn't want me to write, it was because He had something better for me to do. Why should I fuss over that? I ought to be grateful.

A large butterfly flittered among David's tomato plants. Suddenly I realized how much I wanted to work with him in the garden, planting, weeding, and watering. Maybe I could try planting some flowers. Nasturtiums and sweet peas would look beautiful climbing over the fence.

David was in the kitchen, fixing himself a cup of coffee. His face lit up when he saw me. I swallowed my silly pride and put my arms around him. "I'm sorry for everything; can you forgive me?" With my face hid against his neck I mumbled, "I'm glad you didn't give in to my foolish demonstration."

David's hand stroked my hair. "You don't know how close I came to telling you to get back to the typewriter and forget what I said. I hated to see you suffer." His voice was warm with compassion. I had been silly to think he acted out of jealousy of my career. "Now I want you to relax." He held me at arm's length, and happiness showed in his eyes. "Your next assignment is to have some fun with your husband and children. You've been hard at work at that typewriter for years."

A tremendous burden had lifted. Ever since I was a teen-ager, the urge to write had been compulsive, driving me. Now the pressure was gone, and I felt a new freedom. I did not *have* to write again.

That afternoon I called the publisher and explained why I could not fulfill the contract I had signed, and when I mentioned the quotation from Numbers, he said, "I'm familiar with that Scripture . . . and I certainly respect your husband's decision. In fact," he chuckled over the phone, "I think he has the right idea. You need to concentrate on your family. You need a rest from writing."

His reaction hurt my professional pride a little; I thought he would have asked me to reconsider. Then I shrugged off the disappointment. After all, others could write books. But who else could be a wife to David and a mother to our children? A rush of gratitude welled up within me. I was fortunate to have a husband and children who *wanted* to be with me constantly.

Chapter 18

DAVID   *Pacific View, California*

In April, Ray McGillis, the superintendent of construction I had met when we first came to Pacific View, called me. He had left his job and wanted to do some building on his own. "I've got some land and money, you have a contractor's license and experience. The market is booming, and I think we can do well. How about it?"

Ray had a solid reputation in the business community, I had discovered through the lumberyard grapevine. Also I had come to know him in church as a sincere Christian. This looked like the opportunity I had been waiting for.

"Sounds good. Let's get together and talk."

We reached an agreement and soon got underway building custom homes. In a seller's market, they were bought as quickly as we could put them up. My income was now considerably increased, and the children were demanding that we move to a bigger house.

"I'm ashamed to have my friends come here," Leif looked embarrassed. "It looks like we're poor." The other children all agreed, "Me too!"

I looked at Sarah across the kitchen table. She was frowning. The children's reaction had brought up a point we were both aware of. Now that our relationship as husband and wife was taking form according to the Biblical formula, it was time for a reconstruction of the family relationships involving the children.

Their attitude towards our "poverty" had surprised me at first, but I realized they were only reflecting the philosophy I had expounded to them over the years—that prosperity and happiness were linked together. Now that I had discovered a different and more reliable set of values, the responsibility rested with me to teach my children as well.

"Don't you know real happiness does not depend on the size of our house?" I looked at the four faces around the table.

They nodded, but the answer was slow, "Yeah, but. . . ."

My words would have little effect unless our daily lives demonstrated what we believed. My eyes met Sarah's. She smiled encouragingly, and I took a deep breath. The task before us would take a great deal of time and patience.

"Mom and I are sorry we didn't know how a family should function," I said slowly. "We have all suffered in the past. But now that we've discovered a better way, we want to follow it."

"That's O.K. dad, we understand," John looked embarrassed.

"Thank you, son," I smiled. "But I think it's time to explain a few facts to you."

The children were eyeing me with some skepticism. I realized that our talk sessions would have to be short.

"Why don't you read us the basic rules for the family?" I handed my open Bible to Leif and pointed to an underlined passage. His tanned face showed apprehension, but he read emphatically, stopping now and then to glance at his attentive audience.

"You wives, submit yourselves to your husbands, for that is what the Lord has planned for you. And you husbands must be loving and kind to your wives and not bitter against them, nor harsh. You children must always obey your fathers and mothers, for that pleases the Lord. Fathers, don't scold your children so much that they become discouraged and quit trying." [1]

John whistled between his teeth. "Boy, I'm glad that last part is in there."

Andrew looked thoughtful, "Does it mean that we *have* to obey you, even when we don't want to?"

Leif wore a resigned look, "Since God made the rules I guess we disobey Him when we don't obey our parents." He grimaced. "I don't like it, but maybe it will make self-discipline a little easier when we're older."

I marveled at the children's quick grasp of the basic idea. Now it remained to be seen how well it would work in practice. Many of their ideas of Christianity came from Sunday school and church. I didn't want my fate to be theirs; I had gone to Sunday school for years as a child without grasping the meaning in terms of my personal relationship with God and others. Our children had a tendency to do what I had done; separate what they had learned about God from what they called "real life." I wanted them to experience firsthand the reality of God's love and concern for them. We often talked about the two-way communication with God, and the importance of surrendering our own will to Him because His will is always better for us.

"I know, daddy," Andrew's blue eyes were solemn. "I just hate to do it because I know sometimes I won't like what's better for me."

"In the end you'll *know* and be glad." I put my arm around him. "God brought some hard things my way that I now am very grateful for."

"Like the job at the lumberyard when your feet hurt?"

"Exactly," I chuckled. "Your dad thought he was a big shot and needed to learn to be a little nicer."

"You still need it," Leif's comment was terse. "You've got a hot temper!"

"That's a point I'm talking to God about daily. God isn't through teaching me yet."

"That's O.K., daddy." Christine patted my cheek. "We asked God to bring you back, and it took a long, long time. But now I don't even remember what it was like before."

There was a lump in my throat. "The important thing is that God *always* answers prayers. Not always as soon as we want it, and not always the way we think is best, but He always hears us and responds." I had a sudden inspiration. "Let's be specific and ask Him for something each of us really wants. If He wants us to have it, we'll get it."

Everyone agreed, and I began, "Dear God, You've given us everything we need, and we thank You for it. Now I have a personal request. I would like to have a four-wheel-drive truck and camper."

It was a desire I had not mentioned to anyone, not even Sarah. Andrew whistled softly between his teeth beside me.

"I was going to ask You for a ten-speed bike, but if You can get us the truck, that's all I need."

John's voice was wistful, "Can You get us a little ranch outside town so we can have animals and I can take my dog hunting?"

It was Leif's turn. "Just get me a job so I can buy a surfboard again."

Christine hesitated, then spoke boldly, "I would like a little dog for my very own."

John snorted, "We don't need another dog!"

"Please, son, leave that decision to God," I broke in.

Sarah had been silent for some time. I turned to her. "How about you, honey?"

She blushed slightly. "I would like our own house with a frost-free refrigerator."

There was general enthusiasm around the table until John turned suddenly gloomy, "I bet we'll never get a ranch."

"Faith means you believe something before you see it. Can you do that?" I asked.

"It's hard." John stared at the table top.

He had voiced my own struggle. "I know what you mean, son. But as we see God's answers, it becomes easier to trust Him."

Weekends and evenings were family-centered. We usually attended church Sunday morning, but seldom included other activities during the week. So many of the church arrangements seemed to separate the family into different groups. We needed to be together, to bridge the gap that had formed during our years apart.

As our immediate family relationships solidified, other relationships were coming into new focus. One weekend, Mel Goodson, who had last seen me as an alcoholic, and whose generosity had rescued me from the slums of Miami, flew to Pacific View on a visit.

"I came to see for myself," his gray eyes appraised me carefully. "In Florida I was afraid I'd come to your funeral next." Mel had gained weight and looked unhappy. I knew that his divorce had been painful, and the thin net of purple blood lines on his cheeks told me that he was drinking more. His tone was as jovial as ever, but underneath I caught a note of quiet despair.

"You might say I experienced a form of death," I said slowly. "I'd like to tell you about it."

Mel had never shared my antagonism toward Christianity, but he was a skeptic. Now, he listened in silence as I told what had transpired since he last saw me in Miami.

"I'll never forget those frogs, and the mark of death on your face," he shook his head almost in disbelief. "The change is incredible. If I had not seen it for myself. . . . You're a new man, cousin. Whatever happened to you *must* be real." A shadow of pain crossed his face. "Pray that I'll find the answer for myself."

When he left I felt a wave of compassion for my old friend. The intensity of the emotion surprised me. Never before had I felt so involved—concerned for the life of another. "Only You can save him, Lord," my prayer was fervent. "Make Yourself real to Mel."

Less than a month later I received a cryptic note:

Dear cousin:
    Last night at Miller's Creek Chapel, yours truly heard an evangelist from Tennessee tell about the living Jesus Christ. It dawned on me that he was right, and I went forward to the altar to surrender myself into the keeping of my Savior. Today at noon the evangelist baptized me in the creek. Hallelujah!
                                        Your brother in Christ, Mel.

A mist had formed in my eyes, obscuring the words. Mel Goodson, the intellectual skeptic, with a Ph.D. in political science, had found the answer in a little white chapel in the woods near Miller's Creek where I had gone fishing as a boy. Remarkable! Wonderful!

We had been married for a year when my parents came for their first visit, in time for Christmas. Sarah was a little nervous. "I hope they'll understand that this isn't just a convenient arrangement for the sake of the children."

"What we say won't mean anything," I pulled her near me. "They will judge by what they see." Our relationship with my parents had not been close for several years. The blame for that rested squarely on me. Now I sincerely prayed for an opportunity to be a better son.

The week of their visit went by only too rapidly. The first couple of days we felt their watchful eyes and restrained manner. They had suffered much during our difficult years. Could they dare to believe that the change was significant and lasting? Slowly they relaxed, my mother first. Now I felt I could say what had been on my mind for some time.

"Now that you are retired, we would like for you to consider spending the winters with us. The California climate is good for you."

Dad grinned, "Never mind the climate, son. We'd like to be near you in any weather." He cleared his throat. "You don't know what it means for your mother and me to see you happy together as a family again."

Mother's eyes were brimming. "You told us in your letters—but seeing it for ourselves. . . ." Her voice failed, and my heart ached as I looked at them. They had aged in the past few years, and mother still did not look well. If only they could experience for themselves the newness we had found.

My sister Jane drove down frequently from Los Angeles. She was an attractive girl, carefully groomed and always dressed in the latest fashion. Men usually turned their heads to stare as she walked by. At twenty-five she seemed to have not a care in the world as a well-paid secretary in a large oil firm. But she smoked too much, and tension was chiseling fine lines around her expressive eyes.

"I know you were an alcoholic when you stayed with me," she allowed in a rare moment of quiet conversation. "And I can tell that things are different now." She wrinkled her pretty nose. "You say God had something to do with it, and I am not going to argue with you. I just don't think He can do anything for me."

It was not the time to press the issue. I remembered how disgusted I had been with well-meaning people who tried to tell me about their faith when it made absolutely no sense to me. Jane was one of the people I had grieved in my pre-Christian experience. She had needed the support of her older brother, and I had been totally oblivious to her need. Now I only wanted to convey to her that I loved her, and cared about her, and that I would like to help her if she ever needed it.

"We're not going to preach to anyone," I told Sarah after one of Jane's visits. "Let's just concentrate on accepting them and loving them where they are in their search for reality."

The principle was harder to apply with our own children. Leif, who was fifteen, was voicing his doubts about the validity of Christianity. Many of his arguments mirrored my own ideas of the past, and my reaction was spurred by a mixture of guilt and fear for his future.

"I'll probably get around to accepting Christianity all the way," his slender fingers ran quickly through his brown hair. "But I'd like to try some other things first—like you and mom did."

"I don't want you to be hurt like we were." I was tense.

"I won't be. I just want to do my thing." He looked cocksure.

"Some of those things can trap you before you know it." I felt the urge to shake my oldest son to make him see. The tension was heavy between us. There was a distance now, between Leif and the rest of the family. He was pulling away, and whenever he showed a reluctance to join us in a project, my anger—fed by fear—was on the verge of exploding. The rebellion I saw in him could well be the foreshadow of friction with the other children as they grew older. More than ever I sensed that it was essential to establish a solid relationship between us before the children would embark on lives of their own.

Although material success no longer held the fascination it once had, still I sometimes longed to be more prosperous. It would be nice to be able to afford a comfortable new house and a good education for the children.

A letter postmarked Los Angeles came to my desk one day, and I opened it with a curious foreboding. It was from Frank Lavarte, the man who had almost hired me a year and a half ago. Now his company was planning an elaborate community in a picturesque rural part of San Diego County not far from Pacific View. Would I be interested in the job as operations manager?

It was the opportunity I had hoped for. Now I had come full circle from poverty back to a top management position for a large, national corporation. It was the route I had gone before in my own strength, and failed.

This time the challenge was to recognize my own insufficiency and lean on God for wisdom and strength. In my new position I was faced with decisions involving millions of dollars. By the trial-and-error method, I quickly learned that whenever I turned each decision over to God, the operations came together smoother, and with less waste of time and material than is common on a project of that size. The interoffice politics were no less intricate than what I had experienced when working in Arizona, but as I confessed my helplessness to God, the tensions eased and conflicts seemed to melt away.

The vice president in charge of construction was pleased and told me there would be bigger challenges ahead when this project was finished. He mentioned a substantial salary increase. "It pays more and it requires more." His direct eyes measured me. "Are you prepared to sacrifice your time with the family? Put the job first? Then I'll promise you greater success than you've ever known."

It was the goal I had always striven towards. Security, a large home, travel, a new car and boat, all the things we had ever wanted. But it would come in exchange for more of my time spent away from home. A few years ago the choice would have been easy. Now I was aware of a battle inside me—almost as fierce as when I wrote out the money order to Sonny with most of my last hundred dollars.

"Where do *You* want me," I said inwardly. The answer was only too clear as the faces of my family flashed before me. They needed *me* more than wealth.

I had come to respect my employer in the months we had worked together. He was a competent man, fair, and as demanding of himself as of others. I was genuinely sorry to leave, but there could be no other choice. "When this project is over, I'll leave," I told him, and he nodded.

"The choice is yours, Dave," his handshake was firm. "I'll miss you, but I think I understand. You have a fine family." A wistful look crossed his face. "Had my children been as young as yours, and had I been given the choice once more, I might have taken your course."

Driving home that day I had another talk with God. "I commit my future once more to You," I said aloud. "I recognize my responsibility to Sarah and the children. Provide the way for us to grow together in Your love." The future was unknown, but I had a sense of happy anticipation as I drove up in front of our little house.

SARAH   *Pacific View, California*

When David established his authority in disciplinary matters, the effect in our household was dramatic. It took only a week of a consistent, united front from David and me, to make the children realize that the new order was here to stay.

The transformation was evident when Andrew answered the phone one afternoon, then turned to me, "Mom, it's Bob. May I go to his slumber party tomorrow night? It's his birthday, and we can take the bus from his house to school the next morning." Andrew knew that our rules did not allow any of the children to spend the night away from home when a school day followed. His request was the kind that had always started a lengthy pleading for permission.

Now I looked up from my sewing and said calmly, "Did you discuss it with dad this morning?"

Andrew hesitated only a split second, then turned to the phone once more. "My dad makes all the decisions around here. I'll call you when he gets home." He hung up and ran out whistling.

Warmth and light seemed to permeate the kitchen. I put aside my sewing and prepared a tray of lemonade and cookies for the children. We had reason to celebrate. Had the phone call come for Andrew a couple of weeks ago, the atmosphere in our house would now be wrought with loud arguments, to be continued when David came home from work. Instead we had peace, and I marveled at the difference. The ugly quarrels of the past had torn the whole family apart. The children often took sides against one another or tried to manipulate David and myself into disagreement as well.

With a shudder I remembered my own losing battle with discipline while the children and I were alone. Sometimes I had resorted to what we called a "family council," to settle an argument. We had operated on the democratic principle of majority rule— with my vote carrying veto power. Yet it had never been very successful. Most of our disputes deteriorated into quarrels, and the losers pouted for hours, sometimes days.

Now we had "family court." Whenever a difficult question arose between two of the children—or between them and us—the court convened around the kitchen table with David presiding as judge.

All final decisions were based on the highest authority, the Bible. The court was a smashing success. The children unanimously agreed that the system was fair.

"I can argue a point with dad because he sometimes makes a mistake," John allowed. "But I can't argue with the Bible."

The greatest advantage was the consistency. "It sure is nice to know where we stand," the children admitted. "Before, when things were flexible, you and dad used to change your minds a lot. Now you say something and stick with it."

We had never before realized how time-consuming and destructive the arguments over discipline had been. Now, with rules firmly established and the order of authority functioning, we all could relax more. The children began to show more consideration for one another as well. We could listen to one another, and share our true feelings without threat of ridicule or conflict.

Christine as the youngest—and the only girl—often ended up on the losing end in contests with her brothers. John had acted as her protector in the past, but now at twelve, he had decided that all girls were stupid. His nine-year-old sister received the brunt of his contempt. The situation became so tense that David called the court together. "Jesus commands that we love one another," he stated. ". . . Anyone who . . . calls his brother [or sister] a fool must face the supreme court. . . ." [2]

"But I don't like girls," John protested.

"I understand your feelings, son," David responded carefully. "Nevertheless we're commanded to love even our enemies."

"That's impossible!" John looked scornfully at Christine, who cringed.

"I agree, as long as we try to do it alone," David nodded. "But when we admit to God that we don't know how to love and ask Him to help us, He'll do something about it."

"I don't know." John stuck out his lower lip. "I sure don't feel like loving my sister."

David hid a smile. "Maybe it helps to realize that love isn't something you have to feel. It is something you do. If you act kindly towards Christine, no matter how you feel, that's love. You remember when mom and I didn't love each other. Only God could change our feelings."

A few days later Christine burst into the kitchen, her face radiant and grimy with dirt and perspiration. "Mom, may I have a glass jar? John and I found an ant colony, and he is going to help me capture it."

Later, I found John alone in his room. "How come you decided to help Christine?" I asked.

"Gosh, mom," John's face turned red. "If you have to know, I asked Jesus to help me tolerate the little brat. She doesn't bother me so much anymore."

Things were changing, and one of the biggest changes was in me. Now I had time to cook and to care more for our little house. The flowers I had planted grew in the garden and I kept fresh ones in vases indoors. Our home took on a cheerful, well-cared-for look, and my old frustrations over housework were replaced by a steady contentment.

The change within me was even reflected in the way I dressed. One day David mentioned casually, "I'm tired of looking at you in jeans. I saw a cute dress in a shop window. Just right for wearing around the house."

The dress was unlike any I had ever worn or thought of buying for myself. I stared at my own image in the floor-length mirror and color crept into my cheeks. The pastel colors and soft lines were flattering, and my heart beat faster as I stepped from the dressing room to meet David's look of approval.

At home I put away the old jeans and brought out my sewing machine. Little by little I replaced the dresses in my closet I had never felt "quite right" in. At last I was beginning to look on the outside the way I felt on the inside.

The children showed their appreciation for the new me. Every so often one of them came to give me a quick hug. "It's so nice when you're not working, mom. Aren't you glad you can spend more time with us?" The boys brought their friends home more frequently, and raided the cooky jar right before my eyes. "You don't mind, do you, mom, now that you have time to make more?"

They no longer asked to move to a larger house. No one complained about the lack of privacy. "I don't want a room of my own," John declared. "It's more fun to be together."

Even my old dream of a large house had dwindled now that our small house was well-organized and allowed me time for other projects.

Christine was my enthusiastic helper and showed a real talent for homemaking. She did not seem to have any of the negative attitudes towards housework that had been my curse in the past. Neither did she show signs of the role confusion I had struggled with.

She declared herself fortunate to be a girl, and spoke of becoming a veterinarian or a forestry-worker. Whatever her choice for the future, I was grateful that she seemed to have her priorities straight. She was learning to cook and care for a house as easily and naturally as she had once learned to wash herself and brush her teeth. When the day would come for her to have a home of her own, she would not be handicapped by helplessness as I had been.

Then, two days before her birthday in October, a small gray and white, long-haired dog came to our door. He had no tags and no owner showed up when we advertised in the "found" column of the newspaper. After two weeks "Skipper" was registered in Christine's name. She was overjoyed. "It is exactly the kind of dog I asked God for."

Leif's jobs as a student salesman and stable boy soon earned him enough to buy the surfboard of his choice. Andrew's ten-speed bike was a birthday gift, and not long afterwards David made a surprise announcement at the Saturday breakfast table.

"Finish eating and we'll go look at our new truck and camper!" A dealer friend in church had offered us a good buy. That weekend we took our first of many exploring trips in the back country. Andrew's eyes were shining as he rode with David in the cab up a steep trail only a four-wheel-drive truck could climb.

"Now I believe God can do *anything*," he said exuberantly.

Only John was not completely satisfied. "I figured I asked for the wrong thing," he muttered pessimistically.

"I'm not so sure," I tried to cheer him up. "Hang in there believing a little longer. God may have a ranch with a frost-free refrigerator waiting for us. You have to admit that everything else has worked out beautifully."

"I guess so," John brightened a little. "I won't complain, even if we don't get that ranch. At least we can take the camper on a hunting trip!"

Chapter 19

DAVID   *Rancho Cielo Azul, California*

The idea of getting a small ranch had been in the back of my mind for some time. Working with the soil and with animals would be the perfect family project.

Gathering the family around the kitchen table, I told them what I was thinking. "You boys are old enough to help me on construction projects. We will work as a team, on the ranch and outside, as God provides the opportunities."

My words sparked instant enthusiasm. Everyone had something to say.

"We'll have a horse!" Leif was more excited than I had seen him for months.

"Or a mule," piped Christine.

"A tractor!" Andrew rubbed his hands together.

"Cattle!" announced John. "I want to raise beef."

"Let's pray about it," I broke into the pandemonium. "And let's be willing to do it God's way."

The following weekend and each weekend after that we climbed into the truck and camper and scouted the mountains of Southern California. I felt certain that "our" ranch was waiting for us there.

Spring had blossomed into summer when we came to a pleasant valley at about three thousand feet elevation, way above any smog. Small ranches bordered the narrow blacktop road. I spied a realtor's sign at a crossroads and stopped.

The friendly gray-haired man smiled and shook his head at our request. "Everybody is looking for small family ranches nowadays."

He glanced at the eager faces of our children. "Fine looking youngsters you've got."

"Good workers too," I put my hand on Andrew's shoulder. "We want to work the land, have a few animals."

The realtor scanned his slim notebook. "Wait a minute. There's a new listing. A widower going to the old folks' home. He wants a family to take over."

The ranch house was nestled in a grove of ancient live oak trees, and was newer and larger than I had hoped for. The widower was selling his furniture and equipment as well, and Sarah stopped in the middle of the kitchen floor. "Look!" She laughed and pointed. There was a large, frost-free refrigerator standing next to an equally large, frost-free upright freezer.

The outbuildings held a workshop and fully stocked toolroom. Andrew's eyes popped wide open when he saw it. Near the main house was a small, two-bedroom cottage—perfect as a winter home for my parents.

The land had not been worked for several years, but the soil was rich and dark. Two wells provided plenty of water in an otherwise dry area.

The widower was stooped, with sparse white hair and a crippled leg. He moved slowly, showing us around, but his blue eyes were quick and observed each of us carefully. He smiled at the expression on the children's faces. They had been instructed to keep their comments until later and were obviously bursting to enter the conversation between the old man, the realtor and myself.

"So what do you think?" The blue eyes looked at me expectantly.

I nodded, "We like it."

"Good!" His face wrinkled in a wide smile. "I've been waiting for the right folks to come along." He paused and surveyed us all once more. "I hold the deed to this place, but the wife and I gave it to the Lord many years ago. He has blessed us here." His eyes seemed to hold mine with an unspoken question, and the realtor removed his hat and fingered it nervously.

Reaching out to shake the old man's hand, I spoke carefully. "We asked God to lead us to the right place. We would not be here otherwise."

The rough, work-worn hand clasped mine. The blue eyes shone

with an inner light. "I thought so when I first laid eyes on you folks. God bless you!"

The first thing we did after moving in was to join hands in the living room, all six of us. "It's Your ranch, Lord," I said. "Bless it and teach us to care for it."

We named it Rancho Cielo Azul—Spanish for Blue Sky Ranch. All my life I had talked about "blue skies ahead." Now the skies above us were clear and brilliantly blue almost every day of the year.

The quality of life I had always hoped to find is here. Not because of geography or outward circumstances—but an inward peace and contentment dependent only upon God's nearness.

Our daily life is quiet, even simple, compared to the city. Each day starts and ends with animal chores, feeding, and milking. We have a few of each: cows and pigs, sheep and lambs, goats, rabbits, chickens and ducks, a horse and a mule.

Andrew has become a good tractor and truck driver. John works with the cattle, breeding for improved beef stock. Leif left for the army when he turned seventeen, but spends his leaves on the ranch and appreciates having something solid to come back to.

Christine helps care for the animals and does her share with Sarah in the house. The produce from a large garden fills the freezer and rows of cans in the pantry. The boys and I butcher our meat, cure and smoke the hams and bacons. Most of the food we put on our table is either grown or produced on the ranch. Sarah bakes the bread, churns butter, makes cheese and various kinds of sausage.

Unanimously we agree that ours is a good kind of life. We work long hours, but we have fun together, and we have found a small church in the valley where we all feel at home.

The small upsets and crises that come to us seem minor compared to our past. There is a consistent quality of peace in our lives now that I never thought possible. The oneness between Sarah and myself becomes more solid with each passing day.

A few lines from a psalm describes the vivid contrast of my life before and after I surrendered into God's hands.

> He gives families to the lonely,
> and releases prisoners from jail, singing with joy!
> But for rebels there is famine and distress.[1]

SARAH   *Rancho Cielo Azul, California*

We had been at the ranch for three months when David came to me in the garden one morning. I was digging in the flower bed around the goldfish pond, and our honeybees were buzzing among the roses behind me.

David pulled me to my feet and led the way to the lawn chairs in the shade of the big oak. "Are you happy?" His light-filled brown eyes looked deep into mine.

"You know I am!" It was true that I had never been happier. It was an abiding contentment, deep and with an undercurrent of joy. Sometimes I felt like pinching myself, wondering if it could last, then I chased the doubt away. It was what God had promised—an abiding peace and joy in Him. Somehow I knew it would last, regardless of outward circumstances, as long as I trusted in Him.

"Do you ever think of writing again?" David smiled, and I shook my head slowly.

"Not really. Maybe someday, but right now there is so much else to do."

David took my hand; it was grimy with dirt and black soil caked under my fingernails. "I've thought about it—and prayed about it," his voice was even. "Frankly, I would prefer having you work with me on our projects here all day long, but," he paused, and I felt a curious tingling in my stomach, "I think the priorities are well established in your life now. You are wife, mother, homemaker—and writer."

The rush of joy was unexpected. "What do I write about?"

He smiled at my eagerness. "Maybe you should start by telling what God has done for us."

The bees were hovering over the water lilies in the pond. Birds sang joyously in the tree over our heads. It seemed at last I had really come home. There were no loose ends. God was fitting everything I had ever done, everything that had ever happened, into His good pattern for my life.

Gratitude flowed through me. It was wonderful to feel so alive, with life so full of meaning. The greatest wonder of all was the solidity of my relationship with David. The words of Christ were real now. "The two shall become one—no longer two, but one! And no man may divorce what God has joined together." [2]

It was an ongoing process, and could still be temporarily upset if either one of us refused to yield ourselves to God's will as we knew it. But the solid foundation was there. Far more reliable and permanent than mere human feelings.

Never again could the false idea of "falling in or out of love" threaten our relationship. I loved my husband, not just because I felt a certain way about him. We had learned there was more to love and marriage—Thank God!

Notes

Unless otherwise indicated, all Scriptures are taken from the J. B. Phillips translation of the Bible.

Chapter 2

1. *The Feminine Mystique*, by Betty Friedan (New York: Norton, 1963).

Chapter 3

1. Luke 2:11,14 (KJV)
2. Eph. 3:17–19 (KJV)
3. John Conlan was elected to the U.S. Congress in 1972 from the State of Arizona.
4. "Just As I am, Without One Plea," Charlotte Elliott, 1836
5. Rom. 12:2

Chapter 4

1. 1 John 5:14,15 (author's paraphrase)
2. 1 Cor. 6:19 (KJV)
3. 1 John 4:16,18
4. 1 John 1:9 (KJV)
5. Rom. 8:28
6. Eph. 5:22,23
7. 1 Pet. 3:1

Chapter 5

1. *Calvary Road*, by Roy Hession (Fort Washington, Pa.: Christian Literature Crusade, 1964)
2. Matt. 7:5 (author's paraphrase)
3. 1 Cor. 7:10

Chapter 6

1. Phil. 4:6,7

CHAPTER 7

1. *The World of Formerly Marrieds,* by Morton M. Hunt (New York, McGraw, 1966)
2. Isa. 42:16 (KJV)
3. Isa. 43:19 (KJV)

CHAPTER 8

1. Jer. 29:11–13 (*Living Bible*)
2. 1 Cor. 14:33 (KJV)
3. Gal. 5:13,14 (*Living Bible*)
4. Col. 2:14 (*Living Bible*)
5. 1 Tim. 3:1–12; Titus 1:5–8 (author's paraphrase)
6. Matt. 5:17,27
7. Matt. 19:8,9
8. 1 John 1:8,9
9. John 8:7 (author's paraphrase)

CHAPTER 9

1. 1 Cor. 13 (author's paraphrase)

CHAPTER 10

1. 1 Pet. 3:1,2 (*Amplified Bible*)

CHAPTER 12

1. 1 Tim. 2:10,11 (*Living Bible*)

CHAPTER 15

1. Phil. 4:10–13 (*Good News for Modern Man*)
2. 1 Cor. 7:11 (*Living Bible*)
3. Matt. 19:5,6 (*Living Bible*)

CHAPTER 16

1. 1 Thess. 5:18
2. Rom. 12:2

CHAPTER 17

1. Phil. 4:19
2. John 8:31,32 (KJV)
3. Num. 30:3–13 (author's paraphrase)
4. 1 Pet. 3:2 (author's paraphrase)

Chapter 18

1. Col. 3:18–21 (*Living Bible*)
2. Matt. 5:22

Chapter 19

1. Ps. 68:6 (*Living Bible*)
2. Matt. 19:6 (*Living Bible*)